Early Learning and Child Well-being in Estonia

Please cite this publication as:
OECD (2020), *Early Learning and Child Well-being in Estonia*, OECD Publishing, Paris, *https://doi.org/10.1787/15009dbe-en*.

ISBN 978-92-64-38460-6 (print)
ISBN 978-92-64-38840-6 (pdf)

Photo credits: Cover © Rawpixel.com/Shutterstock; © Cherry-Merry/Shutterstock; © Anurak Pongpatimet/Shutterstock; © Motortion Films/Shutterstock.

Corrigenda to publications may be found on line at: *www.oecd.org/about/publishing/corrigenda.htm*.

Foreword

Estonia is an international education leader, achieving high levels of performance and equity among students. The Estonian education system is striking in its openness to learning and improving. Education leaders and practitioners in Estonia embrace data and other evidence as a means for continual improvement. Systems like Estonia that can learn, can adapt and can continue to learn will inevitably serve their students well. They will also postion themselves well for the opportunities and the challenges of the future.

Estonia places great priority on children's early years, in addition to students' later education. The early childhood education and care system in Estonia is coherent and holistic, emphasizing children's social-emotional development and well-being. At the same time, early years provision is firmly part of the Estonian education system as a whole, rather than separate and unrelated. To better understand children's trajectories through the education system, Estonia has supported OECD efforts to collect comparative data on children's early learning.

Estonia was one of three OECD countries that participated in the International Early Learning and Child Well-being Study. The study provides policy makers, education leaders, parents and the wider community with insights on how well five-year-old children in Estonia are faring. The study moves beyond speculation and beliefs, and enables children to show us how they are doing. The findings are enriched by comparisons with children in England (United Kingdom) and children in the United States.

The study investigated how well five-year-old children were developing across the range of skills they need to be well-positioned to succeed in education and grow up into happy, healthy and responsible citizens. These skills include both early cognitive development and social-emotional development. Children without this balance of skills will struggle to do well in school and in other areas of their lives.

The study highlights early differences between groups of children, such as between boys and girls and between children from advantaged and disadvantaged families. This helps us to see how we can better support children and their families, both in the earliest years and in the first years of schooling. Education systems that orient their priorities from an institutional lens to children's actual needs will have greater success overall and will be better able to achieve improved equity.

Children love to learn and supportive, caring environments help them to do so. Our job is to ensure we are providing such environments.

Andreas Schleicher

Andreas Schleicher

Director for the Directorate for Education and Skills

Special Advisor on Education Policy to the Secretary General

Acknowledgements

The International Early Learning and Child Well-being Study (IELS) was a collaborative effort between participating countries and the OECD secretariat.

The development of this report was guided by Andreas Schleicher and Yuri Belfali and managed by Rowena Phair. The lead author of the report was Javier Suarez-Alvarez, with chapters contributed by Lauren Kavanagh (Chapter 3) and Malek Abu-Jawdeh (Chapter 4). The publication was edited by Elizabeth Zachary and designed by Fung Kwan Tam. Administrative support was provided by Valentine Bekka and Matthew Gill. Communications support was provided by Rachel Linden.

To support the technical implementation of IELS, the OECD contracted an international consortium of institutions, led by Maurice Walker at the Australian Council for Educational Research (ACER). The consortium also included the International Association for the Evaluation of Educational Achievement (IEA), led by Anja Waschk, and cApStAn, under the lead of Roberta Lizzi.

To help to ensure that the study was rigorous and valid, IELS was guided and supported in its work by a Technical Advisory Group (TAG) and a Measurement Advisory Group (MAG). The members of the TAG were Iram Siraj (Chair), Rosemary Cahill, and Szilvia Papp. The members of the MAG were Ray Adams, Alla Berezner, Dan Cloney, Wolfram Schulz, Maurice Walker, and Nathan Zoanetti.

This report was prepared in close collaboration with the Estonia IELS team, of which Tiina Peterson from the Estonian Ministry of Education and Research was project lead. Anne-Mai Meesak and Lauri Veski, from Innove, provided feedback on earlier chapter drafts; their help in improving this volume is gratefully acknowledged.

Table of contents

BOXES

FIGURES

TABLES

Executive summary

The first five years of a child's life can be a period of great opportunity, and great vulnerability. Children learn at a faster rate than at any other time in their lives, building the foundations for their future cognitive and social-emotional skills development. Building advanced cognitive and social-emotional skills is far more difficult and less effective at later ages without a strong early foundation. Education systems that wish to achieve a step-change in student outcomes are well advised to increase their focus on the quality, responsiveness and effectiveness of their early years policies for children.

The International Early Learning and Child Well-being study (IELS) puts a spotlight on how children are faring at five years of age. The study directly measures key indicators of children's learning, as well as collecting a broad range of developmental and contextual information from children's parents and teachers. The study does not attempt to measure everything. Instead, it focuses on those aspects of development and learning that are predictive of children's later education outcomes and wider well-being. These are: emergent literacy and numeracy, self-regulation, and social-emotional skills. Across these four early learning domains, a total of ten dimensions of children's development and learning were included in the study.

Estonia participated in this study with two other OECD countries: England (United Kingdom) and the United States. Each of these countries recognises children's early years as critical to children's later learning and well-being. Each country participated in this study to enhance the body of international evidence available to policy makers, education leaders and practitioners, and parents to improve children's early learning outcomes. The information from the study provides each country with insights to inform their approaches to children's early years and their approaches in the early years of schooling. This report presents the findings of the study for Estonia.

MAIN FINDINGS

Children in Estonia have particularly strong self-regulation and social-emotional skills in addition to sound levels of literacy and numeracy

Children in Estonia showed comparatively stronger early self-regulation and social-emotional skills than children in England and the United States. At the same time, children in Estonia were at or close to the overall averages for emergent literacy and numeracy skills. Children in Estonia scored significantly higher than children in England and the United States in identifying others' emotions and prosocial behaviour. They also scored significantly higher than children in the United States in emergent literacy, numeracy, working memory and mental flexibility, and significantly higher than children in England on their capacity to inhibit impulse responses. However, children in Estonia scored significantly lower than children in the United States and England in non-disruptive behaviour, and lower than children in England in emergent numeracy.

Differences between children based on socio-economic background are smaller in Estonia than in England or the United States

The combination of household income and parental and education levels – which together create the socio-economic index applied in this study – were associated with higher emergent literacy, numeracy, working memory, mental flexibility, emotion identification, prosocial behaviour and trust. However, relationships between early learning skills and socio-economic background were comparatively smaller in Estonia than in England or the United States. Additionally, the association between socio-economic background and early learning skills was not significant in inhibition, emotion attribution and disruptive behaviour in Estonia.

Early learning among Russian-speaking children, especially girls, is stronger than among Estonian-speaking children, despite coming from lower socio-economic backgrounds

Russian-speaking children had significantly higher outcomes than Estonian-speaking children in emergent literacy, numeracy, working memory, emotion identification, emotion attribution, prosocial behaviour and trust, after controlling for socio-economic status. These differences were more prominent after accounting for socio-economic status than before. In Estonia, there was an overall gender gap in favour of girls in emergent literacy, self-regulation skills and social-emotional skills, but there was no equivalent gender gap for emergent numeracy skills. This result is in line with the patterns observed in England and the United States. However, in Estonia, Russian-speaking children showed more prominent gender differences than Estonian-speaking children.

Children's early learning relies on the interrelated development of cognitive and social-emotional skills

While the positive association between socio-economic status and early learning outcomes varied across countries, the positive association of social-emotional skills with other early learning outcomes was relatively stable. In Estonia, the percentage of variation in emergent literacy explained by social-emotional scores was between 5% and 27% (compared to 13-33% in England and the United States), between 6% and 26% for numeracy scores (compared to 12-28% in England and 7-22% in the United States), and between 4% and 11% for working memory scores (compared to 7-18% in England and 5-22% in the United States), after controlling for socio-economic status.

A variety of activities within and outside the home best support children's early learning, and moderation is sometimes best.

Regardless of socio-economic background, the number of children's book at home and the frequency with which children were read to by their parents were significantly related to cognitive and social-emotional outcomes. Similarly, regularly taking children to special activities outside of the home (such as sports, dance lessons, scouts) was positively associated with both children's cognitive and social-emotional skills. Some activities were more strongly associated with particular skills than others. For example, regular role-playing with parents was positively associated with less disruptive behaviour but less so with children's emergent literacy, numeracy or self-regulation skills.

Nevertheless, more is not always better. There were positive associations between the use of digital devices and self-regulation outcomes, but negative associations with levels of trust. At the same time, children who used devices weekly rather than daily had higher scores in some early learning domains, pointing towards moderate rather than frequent use of digital devices.

Reader's guide

WHAT IS IELS?

The International Early Learning and Child Well-being Study (IELS) puts a spotlight on how children are faring at five years of age. IELS directly measures key indicators of children's learning, as well as collecting a broad range of development and contextual information from children's parents and teachers.

WHAT ASPECTS OF LEARNING AND DEVELOPMENT WERE OF FOCUS IN IELS?

IELS conceptualises early learning as holistic, involving cognitive and socio-emotional skills whose development are interrelated and mutually reinforcing. The study does not measure everything. Instead, it focuses on those aspects of development and learning that are predictive of children's later education outcomes and wider well-being. These are: emergent literacy and emergent numeracy, self-regulation, and social-emotional skills. Across these main early learning domains, 10 dimensions of children's development and learning were assessed in the study.

WHO PARTICIPATED IN IELS?

Three OECD countries participated in the study: England (United Kingdom), Estonia and the United States. This report uses "England" as shorthand for England (United Kingdom). IELS covered children who were aged between five and six years of age during the study administration period of October to December 2018 and who were enrolled in a registered school or early childhood education centre. Samples were drawn and weighted to be representative of the target populations in each of the three participating countries. This report uses "five-year-olds" as shorthand for the IELS target population.

Educators and parents also participated in IELS by providing contextual information about children's learning and lives. "Educators" is the term used to describe the teachers or early childhood education and care (ECEC) staff members who responded to staff questionnaires in IELS. The report uses "parents" as shorthand for the parents, guardians or others who completed the IELS parent questionnaire with respect to participating children.

WHAT DOES THIS VOLUME CONTAIN?

The results from IELS are presented in four reports: an international report and an in-depth report on each of the three participating countries. This volume focuses on the findings for Estonia.

A GUIDE TO INTERPRETING FINDINGS IN THIS REPORT

Data underlying the report

IELS results are based on direct and indirect assessment of children's skills in a range of learning domains. The metric for all learning scales in IELS is the same and the metric used for the scales does not have a substantive meaning (unlike physical units of measure, such as ounces or yards). There is theoretically no minimum or maximum score in IELS; rather, the data are scaled to have approximately normal distributions, with the means around 500 and standard deviations (see below) around 100. Results are presented for a subgroup of children only when estimates are based on at least 30 children from at least five ECEC centres or schools. Important contextual information about children's lives and learning was collected from their parents and educators. Some information was collected only from educators, some only from parents, and in some cases, parents and educators both provided perspectives on the same issue (e.g. how well a child is developing in a particular domain). When parent and educator reports are compared in tables, figures or text in this report, those analyses are based on the subsample of children for whom both parents and educators provided information.

Estonian and Russian-speaking children

Estonian-speaking children in this report correspond to children who took the assessment in Estonian while Russian-speaking children correspond to children who took the assessment in Russian.

This report also provides results by home language, where children lived in homes where at least one parent mostly spoke a language other than the assessment language.

Overall IELS averages

Where cross-country averages are provided in any of the IELS volumes, these averages correspond to the arithmetic mean of the three country estimates.

Statistically significant differences

Unless otherwise stated, a difference reported as statistically significant is significant at the .05 level. This means there is a less than 5% probability that the reported difference occurred by chance; a statistical test has been carried out to establish this. Statistically significant differences in this report are denoted by darker tones in figures and by bold font in tables.

Interpreting correlations

A correlation coefficient is a measure of the degree to which two variables tend to move together. The coefficient has a value between plus and minus 1, which indicates the strength and direction of association. If a correlation is positive, it means that as one variable increases, so does the other. If a correlation is negative, it means that as one variable increases, the other decreases. In this report, a correlation coefficient with an absolute value between 0 and 0.19 is interpreted as weak, between 0.20 and 0.49 as moderate, between .50 and 0.79 as strong, and between 0.80 and .99 as very strong.

Standard deviation

The standard deviation is a measure of the dispersion of a set of data from its mean. The more spread apart the data, the higher the deviation. In a normal distribution, 68% of the scores are within one standard deviation of the mean, 95% within two standard deviations, and 99% within three. As mentioned above, IELS learning scales all have an approximate standard deviation of 100.

Standard Error

Scores reported in this volume are population estimates, based on the sample of children selected. However, it is unlikely that the 'true' or population mean is exactly the same as the sample. Some variation or error around estimates is to be expected. Thus, each mean has a standard error, which allows us to estimate how accurately the mean found in our sample reflects the 'true' mean in the population. The 'true' mean score can be found in an interval that is 1.96 standard errors on either side of the obtained mean, 95% of the time.

Rounding figures

As a result of rounding, some figures in tables may not add up exactly to the totals. Totals, averages and differences are calculated on the basis of exact numbers and are rounded only after calculation. Percentages and mean scores are rounded to whole numbers, and standard errors are rounded to two decimal places.

ADDITIONAL TECHNICAL INFORMATION

Readers interested in additional technical detail regarding IELS are directed towards the short technical note at the end of this volume and to the IELS Technical Report (OECD, 2020).

This report uses the OECD StatLinks service, meaning that all tables and figures are assigned a URL leading to an Excel workbook containing the underlying data. These URLs are stable and will remain unchanged over time. In addition, readers of the e-books will be able to click directly on these links, and the workbook will open in a separate window if their Internet browser is open and running.

Abbreviations and acronyms

ASBI	Adaptive Social Behaviour Inventory
ECEC	Early childhood education and care
EEIS	Estonian Education Information System
ERDF	European Regional Development Fund
ESF	European Social Fund
EU	European Union
GDP	gross domestic product
IELS	International Early Learning and Child Well-being Study
MoER	Ministry of Education and Research
NATO	North Atlantic Treaty Organisation
PIAAC	Programme for the International Assessment of Adult Competencies
PIRLS	Progress in International Reading Literacy Study
PISA	Programme for International Student Assessment
TIMMS	Trends in International Mathematics and Science Study
SES	Socio-economic status
SEN	Special educational needs

Early learning matters: The International Early Learning and Child Well-being Study

The International Early Learning and Child Well-Being Study (IELS) puts a spotlight on how children are faring at age five. This chapter presents the rationale for focusing on children's learning and development in the earliest years, and outlines the importance of having evidence on early learning that is comparable across countries. The chapter also provides information on the overall design of the study.

THE EARLY YEARS: A WINDOW OF OPPORTUNITY ... AND RISK

The first few years of a child's life is a period of great opportunity, but also one of great risk. The cognitive and social-emotional skills that children develop in these early years have long-lasting impacts on their later success throughout schooling and adulthood. Although the quality of later schooling is important, strong early learning accelerates later development whereas a poor start can inhibit it (Bartik, 2014[1]; Heckman, 2006[2]; Schoon et al., 2015[3]; Sylva et al., 2008[4])

Early learning and child well-being are interrelated and mutually reinforcing. Children thrive in caring families, where they feel safe and happy, and where they are supported to learn about themselves and their social, cultural and physical environments. The day-to-day interactions and activities between young children and their parents and other family members foster children's well-being and their emerging cognitive and social-emotional skills (Melhuish et al., 2008[5]).

Children also learn in settings outside of their homes, including in their wider family networks, their neighbourhood communities, in early childhood education and care (ECEC) settings, and in school. Children from even the most socially deprived homes can thrive when they have sustained access to high-quality and responsive learning environments. A positive early platform of learning enables children to develop the skills they need to succeed in school and later life (Figure 1.1).

Figure 1.1 **Children's early learning and later life outcomes**

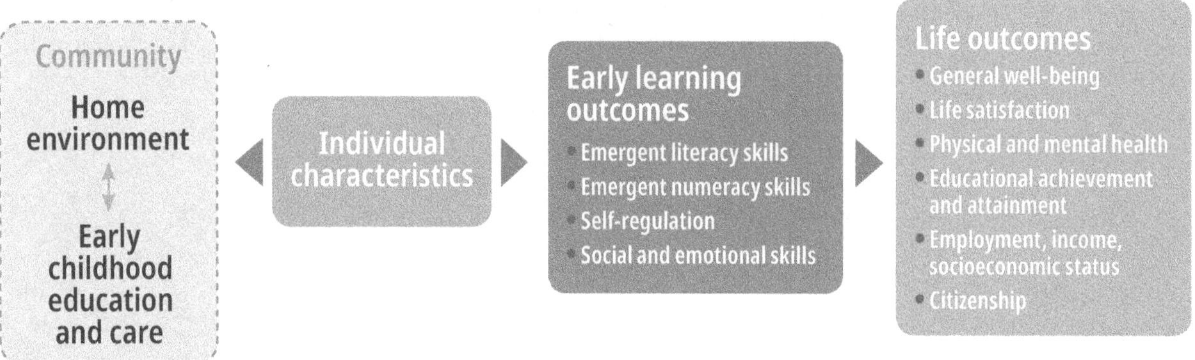

Source: Shuey and Kankaraš (2018[6]), The Power and Promise of Early Learning, https://doi.org/10.1787/f9b2e53f-en.

The window of positive early learning starts to close when children are around seven years old, due to a sharp decrease in brain malleability at this point (World Bank, 2018[7]). Investment in children's early learning enables normal, timely development, and shapes children's long-term ability to learn (Figure 1.2). If children have not developed core foundation skills by this point, they will struggle to progress well at school, and may also have social and behavioural difficulties in adolescence and in adulthood. Seeking to ameliorate a poor start at older ages is complex, challenging and costly, and yields low success rates (Heckman, 2006[2]). At a system level, the proportion of children with poor early development constrains the extent to which any education system can achieve success for these children and perform well as a whole.

Figure 1.2 **Risk and protective factors affect development trajectories**

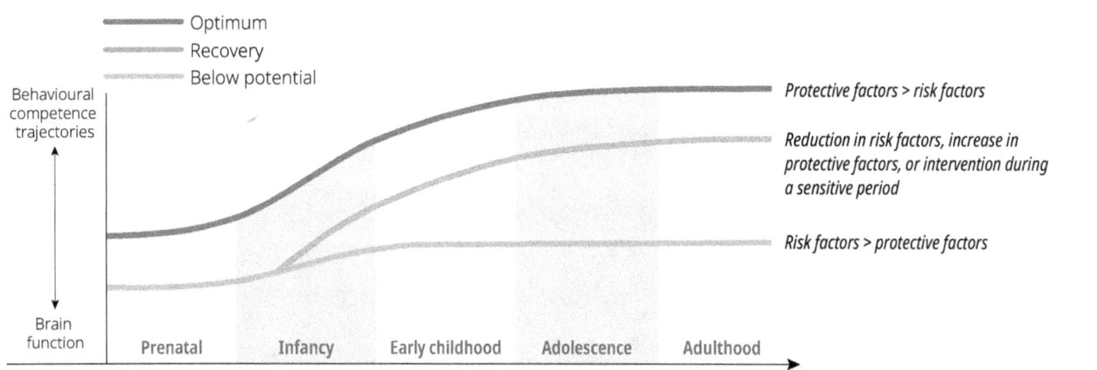

Source: Adapted from Walker et al. (2011[8]), Early Childhood Stimulation Benefits Adult Competence and Reduces Violent Behavior, https://doi.org/10.1542/peds.2010-2231.

Countries are increasingly focusing on early years policies as a means to lift overall educational performance and mitigate disadvantage. Many countries have increased ECEC participation rates and their overall investments in early years policies (Figure 1.3). Yet early learning remains a relatively neglected areas of international education research. As a consequence, there is little internationally-based evidence on how to improve early years policies and achieve better results for children.

Figure 1.3 **Change in enrolment rates of children aged 3 to 5 years (2005, 2010 and 2017)**

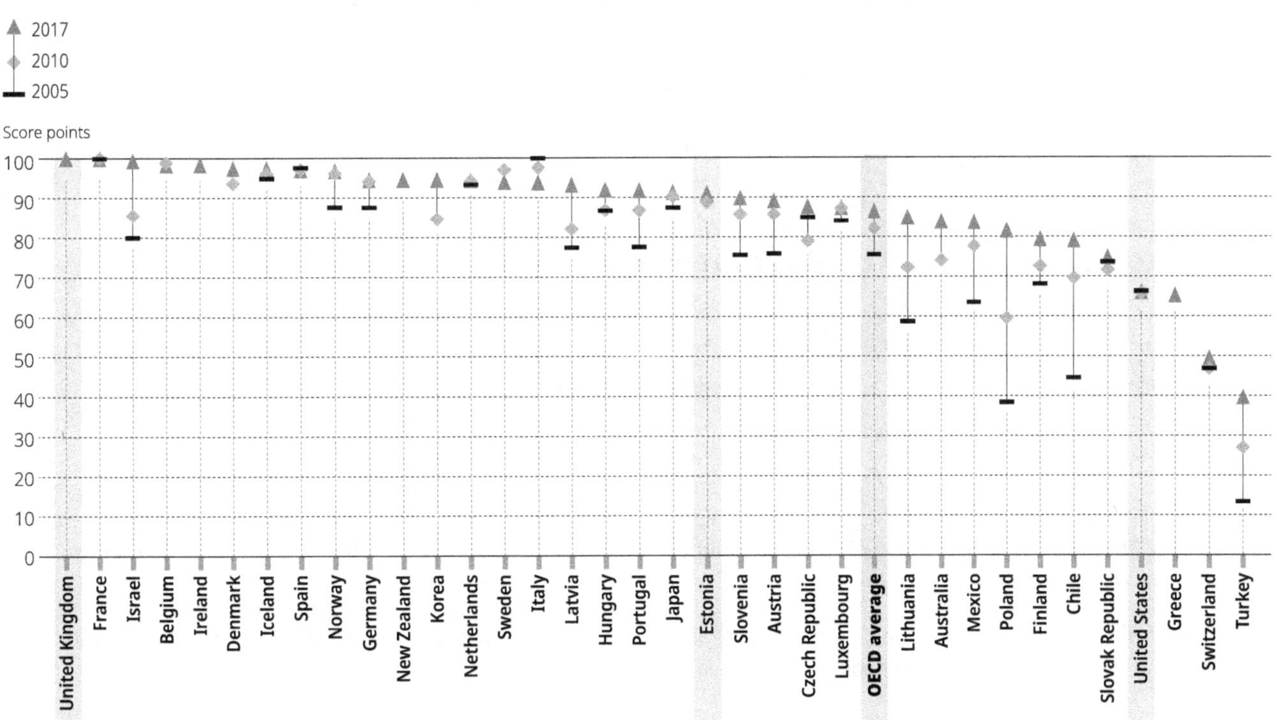

Source: OECD (2019[9]), *Education at a Glance 2019: OECD Indicators*, https://dx.doi.org/10.1787/f8d7880d-en.
StatLink https://doi.org/10.1787/888933977866

The promise of early childhood education may not always deliver for some children. This may be due to, for example, the quality and responsiveness of provision, the extent to which provision focuses on the types of skill development children need most in the early years, and the timeliness and continuity of provision. At a system level, countries could learn a great deal from each other on how to enhance early learning outcomes for all children, by using a common framework for doing so.

COUNTRIES CAN LEARN FROM EACH OTHER TO IMPROVE CHILDREN'S EARLY LEARNING OUTCOMES

The International Early Learning and Child Well-Being Study (IELS) was designed to help countries assess their children's skills and development and to increase understanding of how these relate to children's early learning experiences and well-being. The study provides countries with comparative data on children's early skills, along with a framework to foster the growing interest in early childhood outcomes. Using this information, countries can better identify factors that promote or hinder children's early learning. The study analyses associations between children's early skills and elements of their individual characteristics, home learning environments and education experiences.

IELS directly assessed the emergent literacy and numeracy, self-regulation and social-emotional skills of a representative sample of five-year-olds enrolled in registered school or preschool settings in each participating country or economy. Three countries participated in IELS in 2018: England (United Kingdom), Estonia and the United States.

Children were assessed through developmentally appropriate interactive stories and games delivered on a tablet device, supported on a one-to-one basis by trained study administrators. The assessment was carried out in the school or ECEC setting the children attended, and participating children were supported on a one-to-one basis by trained study administrators. The assessments did not involve any reading or writing, and prior experience with digital devices was not needed. The parents of participating children and the staff member or teacher who knew each child best were also asked to participate, in order to provide fuller information on each child.

IELS took a holistic approach to understanding a child's early learning development at the age of five (Figure 1.4). It consisted of a play-based direct assessment of children's abilities in the four early learning domains of emergent literacy, emergent numeracy, self-regulation and empathy. In addition, IELS collected information from parents and educators to better understand children's early skills across a wider set of early learning domains, including children's prosocial behaviour and levels of trust.

In addition to the direct assessment of learning domains, IELS collected information from parents and educators to indirectly assess children's emergent skills. Critically, the study also gave children a voice, with their input shaping some of the study's more innovative results.

Figure 1.4 **IELS approach to gathering direct and indirect information**

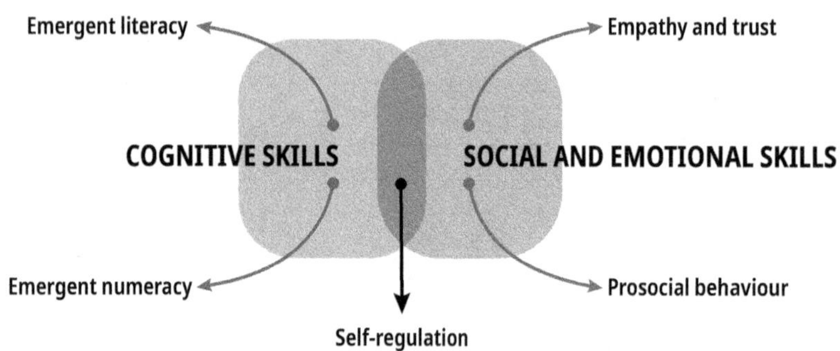

IELS emphasised the well-being of children participating in the study above all else. Tasks were engaging and developmentally appropriate. Participation was voluntary. Trained professionals – who also liaise with staff in the child's school – administered the assessment. The study minimised the level of input required from participating schools, teachers, children and parents, while still collecting the relevant information.

The results from IELS are presented in an international report and in a series of in-depth reports for each of the three participating countries. This volume focuses on the findings for Estonia.

References

Bartik, T. (2014), *From Preschool to Prosperity: The Economic Payoff to Early Childhood Education*, W.E. Upjohn Institute, http://dx.doi.org/10.17848/9780880994835. [1]

Heckman, J. (2006), *Skill formation and the economics of investing in disadvantaged children*, http://dx.doi.org/10.1126/science.1128898. [2]

Melhuish, E. et al. (2008), "Effects of the Home Learning Environment and Preschool Center Experience upon Literacy and Numeracy Development in Early Primary School", *Journal of Social Issues*, Vol. 64/1, pp. 95-114, http://dx.doi.org/10.1111/j.1540-4560.2008.00550.x. [5]

OECD (2019), *Education at a Glance 2019: OECD Indicators*, OECD Publishing, Paris, https://dx.doi.org/10.1787/f8d7880d-en. [9]

OECD (2018), *Early Learning Matters*, https://www.oecd.org/education/school/Early-Learning-Matters-Project-Brochure.pdf (accessed on 4 February 2020). [10]

Schoon, I. et al. (2015), *The Impact of Early Life Skills on Later Outcomes*, http://discovery.ucl.ac.uk/10051902/1/Schoon_2015%20The%20Impact%20of%20Early%20Life%20Skills%20on%20Later%20Outcomes_%20Sept%20fin2015.pdf (accessed on 31 July 2019). [3]

Shuey, E. and **M. Kankaraš** (2018), *The Power and Promise of Early Learning*, http://www.oecd.org/edu/workingpapers (accessed on 14 February 2019). [6]

Sylva, K. et al. (2008), *Final report from the primary phase: Pre-school, school and family influences on children's development during Key Stage 2 (7-11) Publication Details*, http://ro.uow.edu.au/sspapers/1807 (accessed on 4 February 2020). [4]

Walker, S. et al. (2011), "Early childhood stimulation benefits adult competence and reduces violent behavior", *Pediatrics*, Vol. 127/5, pp. 849-857, http://dx.doi.org/10.1542/peds.2010-2231. [8]

World Bank (2018), *World Development Report 2018: Learning to Realize Education's Promise*, https://www.worldbank.org/en/publication/wdr2018 (accessed on 4 February 2020). [7]

The context of early learning in Estonia

This chapter provides contextual information to inform the interpretation of the IELS results in Estonia. It highlights demographic information about children and their families in Estonia; the national early learning policies; an overview of the early childhood and care services available; and discussion of their quality and impact. The chapter concludes with an overview of major issues and debates relating to the early learning sector in Estonia and a statement about what IELS can contribute to a growing body of international evidence on early learning.

PROFILE OF CHILDREN AND FAMILIES

Estonia is recognised worldwide for its high performing and equitable education system. In recent decades, Estonia has been increasingly recognising the importance of early childhood experiences in shaping outcomes throughout later life. Of the approximately 1.3 million inhabitants as of January 2019, Estonia had approximately 65 000 children aged 1 to 7 enrolled in 614 preschool institutions in the academic year 2018-19.

This chapter provides contextual information to inform the interpretation of the International Early Learning and Child Well-being Study (IELS) results for five-year-olds in Estonia. Specifically, it highlights demographic information about children and their families in Estonia; the national early learning policies; an overview of the early childhood and care services available, including levels of participation; and a discussion on their quality and impact. The chapter concludes with an overview of major issues and debates relating to the early learning sector in Estonia and a statement about how IELS can contribute to a growing body of international evidence on early learning.

Estonia's population comprises Estonian-speaking and Russian speaking citizens

Estonian speakers represent around 70% of the population, Russian speakers around 25%, and other groups such as Ukrainian, Finnish and Latvian speakers around 5% combined. The share of Russian-speaking Estonians has remained constant in recent years (Figure 2.1). According to the 2000 census, 74.7% of children attending a preschool institution speak Estonian as their mother tongue, and 24.7% speak Russian as their mother tongue. Income by primary language shows that around 23% of Estonians speakers are among the top 20% of earners in the country, compared to around 13% of those who primarily speak a different language (Statistics Estonia, 2019[1]). In comparison with other OECD countries (OECD, 2019[2]), income inequality in Estonia (Gini[1] = 0.314) is similar to Canada (Gini = 0.307) and Italy (Gini = 0.328), lower than Latvia (Gini = 0.346) and higher than Finland (Gini = 0.259).

Figure 2.1 **Population share by primary language, Estonia**

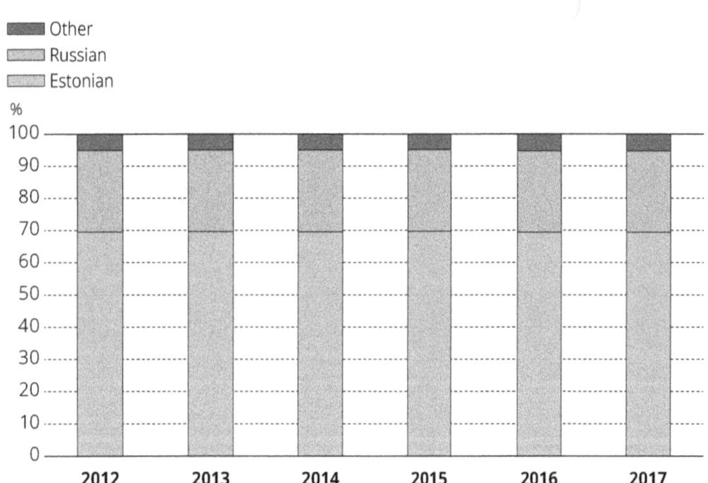

Source: (Statistics Estonia, 2019[1]) http://andmebaas.stat.ee/Index.aspx?lang=en&SubSessionId=da2e6b42-6b36-4f33-87cc-e7e993bae966&themetreeid=6 (accessed on 10 April 2019).

StatLink https://doi.org/10.1787/888934105945

The poverty rate for children is among the lowest across OECD countries

The poverty rate for children aged 17 and under is 0.096[2], which is among the lowest across OECD countries, including the United States, Lithuania and Latvia, although still higher than Finland and Norway (OECD, 2019[3]). By child age group, the relative poverty rate[3] of children aged six and under was 15% in 2017, which is the lowest rate over the last decade for three- to six-year-olds, although not for those aged two and under (Statistics Estonia, 2019[1]). The gross domestic product (GDP) of Estonia in 2016 was USD 30 895 per capita, which is similar to Lithuania and the Slovak Republic, lower than the OECD and the European Union (EU) averages, and higher than Russia and Latvia (OECD, 2019[4]).

Women with higher education are more likely to have children

Among women who gave birth in Estonia in 2017, 13% had basic education, 37% secondary education and 50% higher education. In the International Early Learning and Child Well-being Study (IELS), 53% of mothers with five-year-old children had completed higher education (i.e. bachelor's degree or master's degree, professional degree or doctorate), which was higher than in the other two countries participating in the study (40% in England and 39% in the United States). Since 2011, most women giving birth in Estonia have been tertiary educated, while the share of women with only secondary or lower education giving birth has decreased (Figure 2.2). The average age of women at childbirth rose to 30 in 2017 from 27 in 2000. The average age at childbirth for women with basic education was 28, compared to 32 for mothers with higher education. Children are born more often into families where there is already a young child and where parents are married or in a cohabiting union. They are also usually financially secure and live outside of large cities like Tallinn and Tartu (Raid and Tammur, 2018[5]). After the introduction of parental benefits (i.e. income) to encourage consecutive births, the birth of the next child is often planned to take place before the youngest in the family is 2.5 years old. Families where the first two children are of the same sex are somewhat more likely to have a third child.

Figure 2.2 **Education level of women giving birth, percentage by year, 2000 to 2017, Estonia**

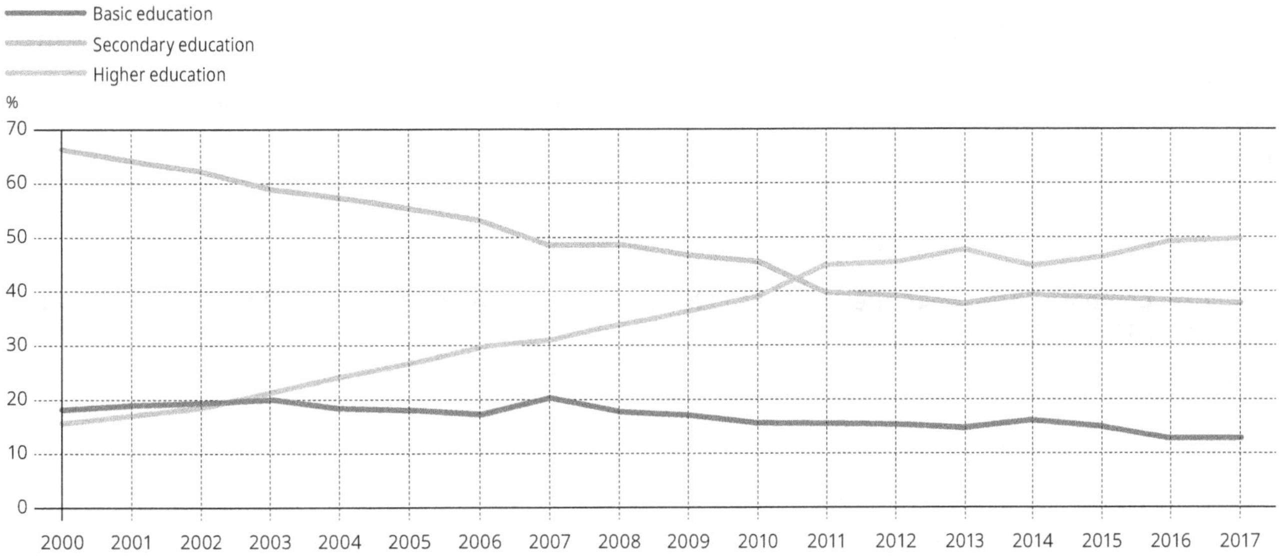

Source: (Statistics Estonia, 2019[11]) http://andmebaas.stat.ee/Index.aspx?lang=en&SubSessionId=da2e6b42-6b36-4f33-87cce7e993bae966&themetreeid=6 (accessed on 10 April 2019).

StatLink https://doi.org/10.1787/888934105964

Most parents take more than one year and up to three years of parental leave

Estonian parents are eligible for three years of parental leave with guaranteed employment in the previous workplace upon returning from leave. The parental leave system also grants 140 days of paid maternity leave and 10 days of paid paternity leave. The system has been redesigned in recent years to motivate fathers to use parental leave (e.g. the introduction of "daddy month", which entitles fathers to take one month of parental leave instead of 10 days). In addition, paid parental leave of 435 days is provided after the initial 140 days of paid maternity leave. Parental leave cannot be taken by both parents at the same time and the benefit is granted until the day the child attains 18 months of age, and it may be taken 30-70 days before the date of birth. Figure 2.3 shows that the vast majority of parents (85.9%) take more than one year and up to three years of parental leave. Approximately 90% of mothers take parental leave, compared to only 5% of fathers. The most common reason reported by men for not taking parental leave is that their partner took maternity leave (76.8%).

To compare Estonia with the other countries participating in IELS, statutory maternity leave in the United Kingdom is 52 weeks, while there is no statutory entitlement to paid maternity, paternity or parental leave in the United States. Most mothers take parental leave in Estonia, and for a longer time than in the other two countries participating in the study.

Estonia's fertility rate is at the EU average, although still lower than other countries in the region

Long-term population trends across OECD countries are characterised by an increase in the elderly population and a decrease in fertility rates, which have reached a plateau of around a 1.7[4] over the last 20 years (OECD, 2019[6]). In 2016 there were 98 million people in the EU aged 65 and over, compared with 80 million children aged 0-14. In Estonia the number of children aged 0-14 has exceeded the number of adults aged 65-79 for more than ten consecutive years (Figure 2.4). Unlike countries such as Spain or Italy, where the fertility rate in 2016 was substantially below the OECD average (1.3 compared to 1.7), the Estonian fertility rate is at the EU average (1.6), although still lower than Sweden (1.9), Russia (1.8) and Latvia (1.7).

Figure 2.3 **Percentage of parents taking parental leave, by duration, Estonia**

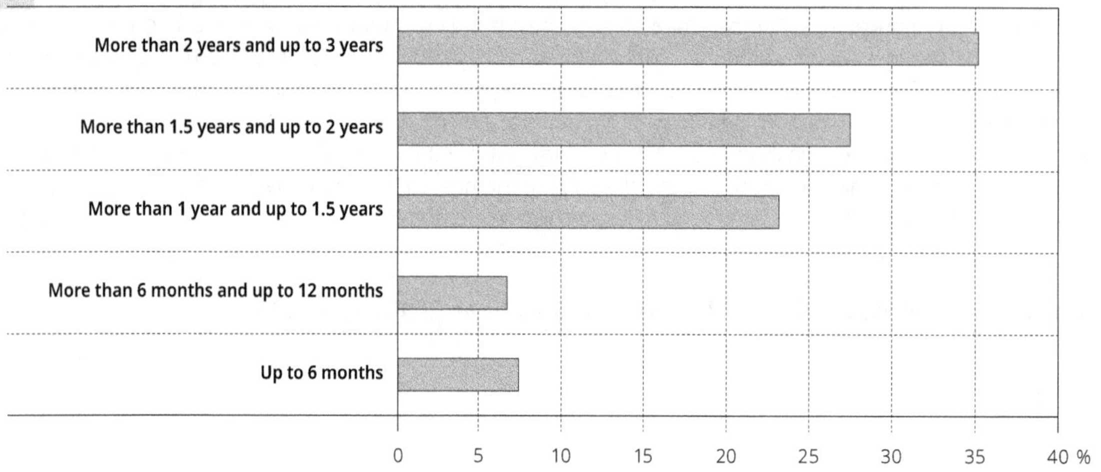

Note: Last data available correspond to 2010.

Source: (Statistics Estonia, 2019[11]) http://andmebaas.stat.ee/Index.aspx?lang=en&SubSessionId=da2e6b42-6b36-4f33-87cc-e7e993bae966&themetreeid=6 (accessed on 10 April 2019).

StatLink https://doi.org/10.1787/888934105983

Figure 2.4 **Comparison between the number of children aged 0-14 and the number of adults aged 65–79 in Estonia, 2000 to 2018**

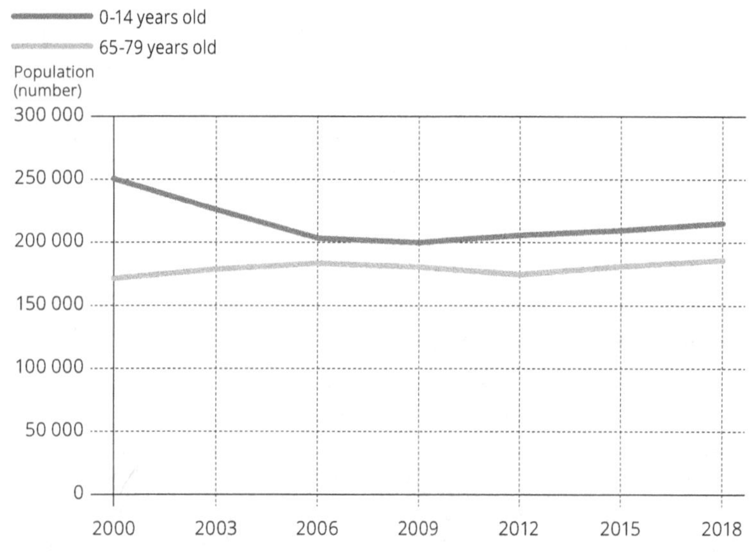

Source: (Statistics Estonia, 2019[11]) http://andmebaas.stat.ee/Index.aspx?lang=en&SubSessionId=da2e6b42-6b36-4f33-87cc-e7e993bae966&themetreeid=6 (accessed on 10 April 2019).

StatLink https://doi.org/10.1787/888934106002

The immigrant population of Estonia has been increasing, while the number of students with an immigrant background seems to be decreasing

Estonia has an increasing immigrant population. In 2017, the immigration ratio in Estonia was 13 per 1 000 inhabitants, which is more than twice the average of other European countries (around 5 per 1 000 inhabitants) (Eurostat, 2019[7]). Furthermore, in 2017 Estonian net migration was positive for the third year in a row (Figure 2.5). Nearly half of immigrants to Estonia were those with Estonian citizenship, followed by Russian, Ukrainian, Finnish and Latvian citizens. Two-thirds of emigrants were Estonian citizens, followed by Russian and Finnish citizens and stateless persons. Most migrants were in their 20s and 30s. Despite the increased immigrant population, the percentage of students with an immigrant background seems to be decreasing. In the Programme for International Student Assessment (PISA) 2018, fewer than 3% of 15-year-old students in Estonia were first-generation immigrants. In PISA 2015, the percentage of students with an immigrant background was 10%, which is around 2% lower than in PISA 2006. In IELS, which follows PISA definitions[5], approximately 2% of five-year-old children had an immigrant background in Estonia.

Figure 2.5 **Comparison between number of immigrants and number of emigrants in Estonia, 2005-2017**

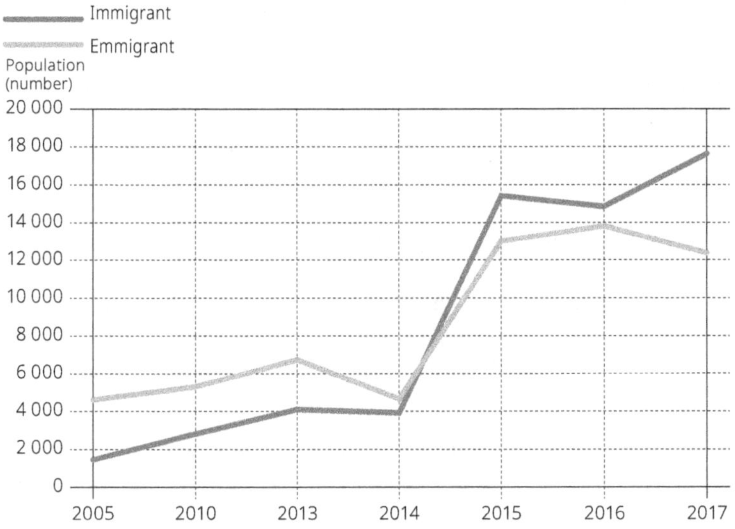

Immigrant
Emmigrant
Population (number)
20 000
18 000
16 000
14 000
12 000
10 000
8 000
6 000
4 000
2 000
0
2005 2010 2013 2014 2015 2016 2017

Source: (Statistics Estonia, 2019[1]) http://andmebaas.stat.ee/Index.aspx?lang=en&SubSessionId=da2e6b42-6b36-4f33-87cc-e7e993bae966&themetreeid=6 (accessed on 10 April 2019).

StatLink https://doi.org/10.1787/888934106021

STRATEGIES TO STRENGTHEN EARLY LEARNING

Roles and responsibilities are clearly defined

The division of responsibilities between state, local government and schools is clearly defined. At the level of legislative and administrative power, the *Riigikogu* (parliament), the government of the Republic of Estonia, and the Ministry of Education and Research (MoER) administer the education system. The Ministry is responsible for developing and adopting national curricula, educational standards, national development plans and state supervision, among other responsibilities. At the local level, municipalities and towns are primarily responsible for ensuring access to general education from preschool to upper secondary education, compulsory school attendance, and maintaining preschool institutions and schools.

The Estonian Lifelong Learning Strategy 2020 sets out the government's intent to provide all people in Estonia with learning opportunities that are tailored to their needs and capabilities throughout their whole lifespan to maximise opportunities within society, work and family life (Ministry of Education and Research, 2014[8]). The Lifelong Learning Strategy outlines five general goals (Box 2.1) and is a reference point for education budget decisions up to 2020. The strategy states that local governments are responsible for ensuring access to quality preschool education, as well as necessary support services. Additional specific strategic measures in the strategy related to early childhood education and care (ECEC) include:

- Developing an in-service education system for teachers to achieve high-quality courses based on the specialised nature of the educational institution.
- Requiring local governments to create an appropriate number of childcare and preschool places, to fulfil the objectives of preschool curricula, and to offer opportunities to all children to participate in preschool education at least one year before starting school.
- Requiring preschool institutions to apply appropriate age-related measures to provide good quality Estonian language learning. Children are offered activities in the Estonian language, and children with other languages are provided with additional support.

In addition to the Lifelong Learning Strategy, the Estonian government has developed the Strategy of Children and Families 2012-2020 to improve the well-being and quality of living of children and families (Ministry of Social Affairs, 2011[9]). This strategy aims to:

- Support the sustainability of society by creating knowledge-based and uniform child and family policies.
- Support positive parenting to improve the quality of living and the future of children.
- Guarantee the rights of children and create a functional child protection system to support the development and well-being of children.

- Provide adequate economic security for families.
- Create equal opportunities for men and women and foster the reconciliation of work, family and private life to promote a quality everyday life that meets the needs of each family member.

The Strategy of Children and Families includes strategic objective indicators to improve the well-being of children and families and their quality of living. Examples of these indicators include the total fertility rate (up to 1.77), the relative poverty rate (down to 16.5%), and the share of children aged two and under (up to 35%) and aged three to six (maintain the level) in informal childcare.

Box 2.1 **Estonian Lifelong Learning Strategy 2020**

The general objective of this strategy is to create learning opportunities for all people in Estonia throughout their life, according to their needs and abilities, to guarantee personal fulfilment in society, work and family life.

The five strategic goals are:

1. **Change the approach to learning**. Implementation of an approach to learning that supports each learner's individual and social development, as well as the acquisition of learning skills, creativity and entrepreneurship at all levels and in all types of education.
2. **Ensure that teachers and school leaders are competent and motivated**. The assessment of teachers and school leaders, including their salaries, should be consistent with the qualification requirements for the job and their work-related performance.
3. **Increase the concordance of lifelong learning opportunities with the needs of the labour market**. Create opportunities for study and career services that are good quality, flexible and diverse, and that take the needs of the labour market into account, in order to increase the number of people with professional education across different age groups and regions.
4. **Apply a digital focus in lifelong learning**. Apply modern digital technology in learning and teaching in a more efficient way, and with better results, to improve the digital skills of the general population and to guarantee access to the new generation of digital infrastructure.
5. **Create equal opportunities and increased participation in lifelong learning**. Create equal opportunities for lifelong learning for every individual.

The Ministry of Education and Research has initiated the preparation of the Estonian Education and Research Strategy for 2020–2035, which aims to develop a realistic long-term vision of how to develop the education system and research in Estonia. It is hoped that the strategy will help the country be a society of healthy and happy people that manages itself based on agreed values, responsible citizens and a successful economy that can compete internationally.

Source: Ministry of Education and Research (2014[8]) *The Estonian Lifelong Learning Strategy 2020*, Ministry of Education and Research, https://www.hm.ee/sites/default/files/estonian_lifelong_strategy.pdf (accessed on 11 April 2019).

Central authorities provide local governments and preschool institutions with the national curriculum and standards for ECEC

Estonian national authorities have developed specific policies on ECEC, which are presented in the Preschool Child Care Institutions Act, the National Curriculum for Preschool Child Care Institutions, and the Private School Act. The parliament of Estonia (i.e. *Riigikogu*) established in the Preschool Child Care Institutions Act (Riigi Teataja, 2018[10]) that the two main functions of a preschool institution are to:

- Create possibilities and conditions for the formation of a healthy personality that is socially and mentally alert, self-confident and considerate of others, and that values the environment.
- Maintain and strengthen the health of the child, and promote his or her emotional, moral, social, mental and physical development.

The Preschool Child Care Institutions Act establishes that learning and teaching should be conducted in Estonian unless the local government council decides it should be conducted in another language. Local government councils are responsible for ensuring that all Estonian-speaking children have the opportunity to attend a preschool institution where learning and teaching are conducted in Estonian in the rural municipality or city where they live. The director of a preschool institution approves its curriculum on the proposal of the teachers' council after hearing the opinion of the board of trustees – a permanent body that, together with the director and the teachers' council, manages the preschool institution. Private preschool institutions are regulated by the Private Schools Act, with curricula approved by the owner of the institution and entered into the Estonian Education Information System.

The Preschool Child Care Institutions Act came into force in February 1999 and was updated in February 2018 (Riigi Teataja, 2018[10]). Changes included policies to support children with special needs, such as their admission to a group with other children without special education needs or a group for children with special needs, and policies to ensure that there is a sufficient number of teachers working in a preschool institution and complying with qualification requirements. Teachers are responsible for observing children's development in preschool institutions and adjusting learning and teaching to the child's special needs when necessary. The evaluation and support of a child's development should be based on the principles provided in the National Curriculum for Preschool Child Care Institutions. The director and manager of the preschool institution are responsible for organising children's support services, such as speech therapists and special education teachers, and ensuring that children receive the support they need.

Over the last decade, Estonia has developed specific policies related to pedagogical and curricular approaches. The National Curriculum for Preschool Child Care Institutions (Riigi Teataja, 2008[11]) aims to support the quality of provision in early education and determines the objectives and principles of teaching and learning, the organisation of teaching and learning, the expected general skills and the expected development of six- to seven-year-old children, as well as principles for assessing the development of children.

The Values Development Programme in Estonian Society 2015-2020, implemented by the University of Tartu with the support of the MoER, aims to support the formation of shared values in Estonia and contribute to the formation of attitudes that become the basis for a happy personal life and the successful functioning of society. The programme aims to support children's values education and systematic values development in educational institutions, including preschool, so that each child can grow up in an environment that facilitates the development of their personality and integration into society. The programme has a strong emphasis on supporting teachers and educational staff, as well as parents, to achieve these objectives, and is connected with other strategies such as the Lifelong Learning Strategy 2020 and the Strategy of Children and Families 2012-2020.

Every preschool institution develops its own curriculum, although it must be based on the national framework

According to the National Curriculum for Preschool Child Care Institutions (Riigi Teataja, 2008[11]), every preschool institution is responsible for developing its curriculum according to local needs, interests and children's abilities. Nevertheless, curricula must be based on a national curriculum, which establishes that teaching and learning should be versatile and consistent with child development. Moreover, the curriculum must be carried out in co-operation with children's families.

Preschool institutions have the autonomy to apply multiple methodologies and pedagogies. According to Eurydice, the most widespread teaching practices are the step-by-step methodology, the Reggio Emilia approach, the Montessori approach and active learning methods such as Bruner's discovery learning. Private preschool institutions, such as Waldorf preschool institutions and Christian preschool institutions, sometimes use alternative pedagogical methods that are more aligned with their overall approach. Alternative pedagogies are also implemented for children with special educational needs based on the effectiveness of the methods and advice from pedagogues.

Local governments and the board of trustees have autonomy in deciding how the time of preschool institutions within their jurisdiction is organised. Institutions may operate throughout the year or seasonally, and opening hours may vary across jurisdictions. Nevertheless, the daily schedule should take health and well-being considerations based on each age group and the child's characteristics. For example, the daily schedule for children aged one to three includes time for sleep at least once a day, while older children should be provided with at least one hour for resting, which can be for sleeping or for other quiet activities. The daily schedule for children with special needs is provided based on the developmental characteristics of the child. The daily schedule for the oldest cohort, aged six to seven, is oriented to facilitate a smooth adaptation and transition to school life, and includes tasks that involve developing memory, imagination and thinking, and study skills.

Teaching and learning in early education aim to foster the physical, mental and social-emotional development of children

According to the National Curriculum for Preschool Child Care Institutions (Riigi Teataja, 2008[11]), teachers in Estonia must support the development of children's skills through play, teaching and learning activities, with play-based activities the primary basis for teaching and learning in preschool institutions. Teaching and learning are oriented to support the child's physical development and the development of healthy habits, mainly through outdoor play. This approach aims to support children in developing a comprehensive and positive self-image, an understanding of the surrounding environment, as well as help them learn ethical behaviour and initiative, improve essential working habits, and participate in physical activity. The Preschool Child Care Institutions Act (Riigi Teataja, 2018[10]) establishes that the two main functions of a preschool institution are to: 1) create possibilities and conditions for the formation of a healthy personality that is socially and mentally alert, self-confident and considerate of others, and that values the environment; and 2) maintain and strengthen the health of the child and promote his or her emotional, moral, social, mental and physical development.

EARLY CHILDHOOD EDUCATION AND CARE PROVISION

Types, prevalence and spread of provision

Although participation is not compulsory, all children are entitled to attend a preschool institution from 1.5 to 7 years old

Since 2014, Estonian national policies have established that local governments – i.e. town and rural municipalities – are obliged to provide all children aged 1.5 to 7 years old who permanently reside in their catchment area the opportunity to attend a local preschool childcare institution. This obligation includes children with special educational needs such as physical, speech or intellectual disabilities. Preschool institutions (*koolieelsed lasteasutused*) are divided into crèche (*lastesõim*) for children up to three years of age, preschool (*lasteaed*) for children up to seven years of age, and preschool for children with special educational needs up to seven years of age (Figure 2.6).

Since 2006, Estonia has had a childcare system, regulated by the Social Welfare Act, with a network of more than 373 providers. Alternative structures of childcare include provision for children 2 to 8 months of age (Beebi koolid). Although, these centres are generally not free, they are becoming increasingly popular among parents interested in being more involved in the learning processes of their children. The focus of these centres is on the development of a child's creativity through music, rhythm and manual activities.

Children who have reached seven years of age by 1 October must attend school that year and remain in school until they acquire basic education or reach 17 years of age. Although attendance at a preschool education institution is not mandatory, the Lifelong Learning Strategy 2020 aims to provide all children with at least one year of preschool education before starting school.

Figure 2.6 **Overview of ECEC provision in Estonia**

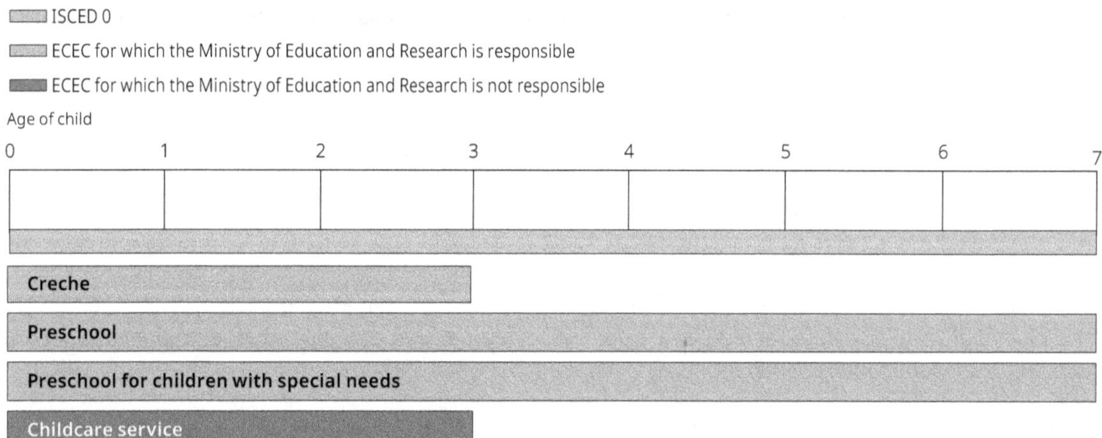

Note: For a full description of the International System of Classification of Education (ISCED) levels, see http://uis.unesco.org/en/topic/international-standard-classification-education-isced.

Source: Adapted from Riigi Teataja (2018[10]), *Preschool Child Care Institution Act (2018)*, www.riigiteataja.ee/en/compare_original/529012018008.

Parents are free to choose the preschool institution or childcare provider they prefer. Local governments allocate places based on the preferences of parents and proximity to their home or work. Therefore, children residing in the catchment area of the preschool institution have priority over children from outside the area, followed by parents working in the catchment area. Children from other areas would only be accepted if vacant places still existed. Children with special educational needs are admitted to integrated groups based on a written application from the child's parents and on the recommendation of an external advisory team.

Estonia's provision of preschool education is predominantly public

Municipal preschool institutions represented 90% of the total number of childcare institutions in the 2018/19 academic year. Local governments are responsible for considering the needs of families in their region, including whether the institution operates throughout the year or seasonally, and the hours of operation, as well as provision. Children from different socio-economic backgrounds have relatively equal access to formal preschool education in Estonia, similar to Denmark and Iceland (Vandenbroeck, Lenaerts and Beblavý, 2018[12]). Such equitable access is not common across all OECD countries. Estonian national policies have a strong emphasis on providing access to early education in rural areas, and this provision heavily relies on local governments to provide quality access to all children within the catchment area. Preschool institutions are divided into Estonian, Russian and mixed centres based on the language of instruction. Most preschool institutions where the language of instruction is Russian are also public institutions.

The high participation of children in preschool institutions creates a smooth transition to school

The Estonian Lifelong Learning Strategy 2020 establishes the need to develop flexible opportunities for all children to participate in preschool education at least one year before starting school. In Estonia, children's participation in preschool institutions is high, which creates a smooth transition to school life (Ministry of Education and Research, 2014[8]). Each parent in Estonia has to submit a "readiness for school" card to the primary school before compulsory attendance with a description of the child's achievements in the development of general skills according to the National Curriculum for Preschool Child Care Institutions. This measure aims to help teachers plan the transition to school life, and the curriculum, according to the child's individual development and characteristics.

ECEC workforce

The share of ECEC teachers with tertiary education in Estonia is increasing, although the share of women remains among the highest in the OECD

The ECEC workforce is divided into three main staff categories – teacher, assistant and childcarer (i.e. childcare worker) – and two categories of leaders – director and headteacher. The minimum qualifications required for teaching assistants and childcarers are compulsory school and one year of studies at a healthcare college. Since 2015, the minimum requirement for ECEC teachers, directors and headteachers has been a three-year bachelor's degree programme. In the 2018/2019 academic year, 19% of teachers had a higher education degree equivalent to a master's degree, 50% had a higher education degree equivalent to bachelor's degree, and 29% had some form of post-secondary education. In addition, 70% of directors and headteachers had a higher education degree equivalent to a master's degree and 29% had a higher education degree equivalent to bachelor's degree. The share of ECEC teachers with higher education was 20.9% in 1995, 25.6% in 2001 and had reached 69% by the 2018/2019 academic year. Some 69% of staff are aged 40 or older, and most teachers are women (Veisson, 2018[13]). The share of women among teaching staff in preschool education in Estonia is one of the largest among OECD and partner countries with available data (99.4%) (OECD, 2018[14]).

Professional development for ECEC staff has been strengthened

There is high demand from applicants for ECEC teacher training (a ratio of seven applicants for every place); however, the proportion of young people, and particularly males, is still low. Following recent policy reforms, preschool teachers attend on average 35 hours of professional development per year, with costs covered by the state and employers. Policy reforms have also aimed to encourage ECEC leadership, for example, the Teacher and Leadership Programme was initiated for the period 2015-2020 to provide a comprehensive professional development system for teachers and heads of preschool institutions.

Financing early childhood education and care

Parental ECEC fees cannot exceed 20% of the minimum wage

Children in Estonia predominantly attend public preschool childcare institutions (96% in the academic year 2018-19). Preschool institutions are financed from the state and local budget, parents and donations (Riigi Teataja, 2018[10]). Parents cover the costs of catering for children, the daily cost of which is decided by the board of trustees and approved by the director. The local government covers other costs such as those related to the management of the institution (e.g. staff remuneration). Local governments may decide that parents need to partially cover the costs of their child's ECEC attendance, depending on the age of the child, the management of the preschool institution or other costs. However, the amount per child cannot exceed 20% of the minimum wage established by the Estonian government. Attendance fees may also differ based on family socio-economic status.

Private preschool institutions also receive support from local government. Representatives of local governments and preschool teachers are responsible for agreeing the minimum salaries of teachers at preschool institutions. Expenses to support the salaries and in-service training of teachers, as well as requested Estonian language training for non-Estonian speaking children, are allocated in the state budget.

Expenditure on ECEC as a share of GDP is one of the highest among OECD countries

Government spending in Estonia on ECEC as a share of GDP was 1.17% in 2015 and 1.16% in 2016, which is above the OECD average of 0.8%. In 2015, annual expenditure on ECEC was USD 6 514 per child (OECD, 2018[14]). The spending on ECEC has led to the salaries of preschool teachers increasing from 67% of the average salary of a full-time full-year similarly educated adult in 2016 to 79% in 2018. In 2016, the average gross salary of a municipal preschool teacher was EUR 819 per month, which is more than the minimum salary of EUR 430 and a quarter less than the country average. Since 2017, additional support has been allocated to municipalities to motivate them to raise preschool teachers' salaries. Local governments that have increased the salaries of tertiary-educated preschool teachers to 80% of a school teacher's salary by 1 September of each year receive the support. The average gross salary of preschool teachers rose from EUR 936 per month in 2017 to EUR 1 038 in 2018 and EUR 1 125 in 2019. Furthermore, in 2020, preschool teachers with a master's degree now receive the full EUR 1 350 minimum salary of primary teachers.

PARTICIPATION IN PRESCHOOL INSTITUTIONS

The share of children participating in preschool institutions is high

In 2016, 71% of two-year-olds were enrolled in an ECEC setting in Estonia, compared to an OECD average of 45% and an EU22[6] average of 42% (OECD, 2018[14]). Enrolment rose to 90% for three-year-olds, compared to an OECD average of 76% and an EU22 average of 82% (Figure 2.7). Nonetheless, enrolment for children under the age of two was substantially lower, presumably reflecting parental leave benefits. In 2016, childcare services were used by 4% of children aged one and under, 16% of children aged two, 5% of children aged three, and approximately 2% of children aged four to six (Statistics Estonia, 2019[1]). As shown in Figure 2.7, participation has remained relatively stable in recent years.

Figure 2.7 **Enrolment in preschool institutions by age, 2014 to 2016, Estonia**

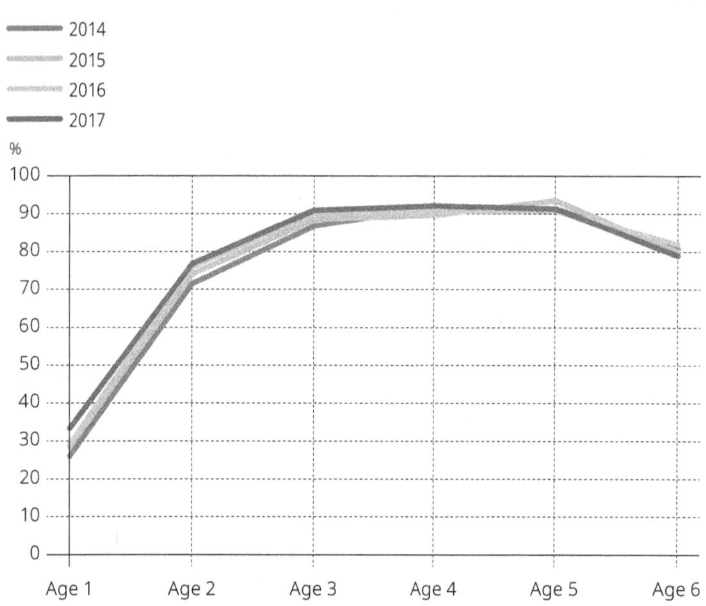

Source: Adapted from Statistics Estonia (2019[1]), *Statistical database*, http://andmebaas.stat.ee/Index.aspx?lang=en&SubSessionId=da2e6b42-6b36-4f33-87cc-e7e993bae966&themetreeid=6, (accessed on 10 April 2019).

StatLink https://doi.org/10.1787/888934106040

Most children attending preschool (96%) attend public institutions

In Tartu, for example, only 7% of six-year-old children in 2017 did not attend a preschool institution, and approximately 34% of those children used a childcare service. According to information provided by local governments, the remaining children not attending preschool institutions were at home with parents or grandparents according to the parents' wish, or had moved abroad with their families without notifying the population register (Ministry of Education and Research, 2018[15]).

Most children attend preschool institutions (up to seven years old), although participation in preschool basic schools, which are those attached to primary schools, has increased in recent years. The share of children attending crèche centres (up to three years old) shifted to preschool institutions after 1999, the year that the Preschool Child Care Institutions Act came into force. As a result, the number of preschool institutions increased to over 500, where it remained relatively stable, although has slightly decreased in recent years. The number of schools providing preschool education – preschool basic schools – has increased by around 40% since 2001. Preschool basic schools are the most common form of provision in rural areas, where the number of children in the region is not large enough to justify the creation of a separate preschool institution (Schreyer and Oberhuemer, 2017[16]).

The number of hours three- to six-year-olds spend in ECEC is higher than the European average

In 2017, children aged two and under in Estonia spent on average 30 hours a week in ECEC (European Commission/EACEA/Eurydice, 2019[17]). More than 80% of children aged three to six spent 30 hours or more in formal ECEC, compared to only around 40-50% of children in the European Union. The number of hours may vary across preschool childcare institutions as they are responsible for defining opening times based on the needs of the families (e.g. office working hours). Therefore, in some cases the number of hours children spend in ECEC might be more than 40 hours a week. The estimated years of attendance at a preschool institute for three- to six-year-olds has been 3.5 over the last five years. The earliest starting age is from birth, although the usual age to enrol in ECEC is three years old (OECD, 2018[14]). The share of boys and girls is very similar, with a slight but consistently longer attendance for boys (Statistics Estonia, 2019[11]).

QUALITY AND IMPACT OF PRESCHOOL INSTITUTIONS

The staff-child ratio is lower than the OECD average for three- to six-year-olds, but higher for those under three

Staff-child ratios can contribute to high-quality learning environments as they increase the potential for frequent and meaningful interactions (OECD, 2019[18]). The staff-child ratio in Estonia is lower than the OECD average for three- to six-year-olds, but higher for those under three (OECD, 2019[18]). The set number of children per staff member is between 7 and 10. The maximum number of special needs children in a group is smaller, ranging from 2 to 6, depending on the special needs of the children.

Preschool institutions are subject to internal and external evaluations

The Ministry of Education and Research regulates the quality provision of early education through the National Curriculum for Preschool Child Care Institutions (Riigi Teataja, 2008[11]) and provides administrative supervision of the teaching and education at preschool institutions, although only in individual cases or through thematic monitoring, if required. The MoER is responsible for administrative supervision over the legal activity of preschool institutions and managers to ensure that preschool education is available and accessible on equal grounds. It also supervises the organisation, quality and performance of teaching and learning. A supervisory agency appoints the persons exercising supervision and involves experts if necessary. Administrative supervision includes visiting an institution to inspect teaching and education and accessing the documents of the institution, as well as preparing statistical and financial reports and verifying data in the Estonian Education Information System (EEIS).

In 2006, the MoER introduced the obligation for preschool childcare institutions to conduct internal evaluation to support the creation of an internal quality assurance system, and to ensure that institutions are supporting the continuous development of children and the institution itself. The head of a preschool is responsible for establishing the procedure for internal evaluation and seeking approval from the board of trustees in advance. Preschool institutions can apply for compensation from the MoER to use external services to provide advice on internal evaluation. Preschool institutions prepare an internal evaluation report at least once every three academic years and are required to list their strengths, areas for improvement and performance indicators, which are available to the public in EEIS. The objective of the performance indicators is to allow preschool institutions to monitor improvement and compare themselves with other preschool institutions of the same type. The results of each institution are published in the educational statistics virtual environment, HaridusSilm, which is available for the public to access.

The MoER also conducts external assessments of learning outcomes to give preschool institutions, their owner and the state objective and comparable feedback on attainment regarding the learning outcomes provided in the national curricula. Evaluation of learning outcomes is intended to: 1) support the development of children, teachers and the institution; 2) collect the evidence necessary for making decisions relating to children and the institution; and 3) submit proposals for decisions on education at the state level and provide institutions with examples of good practice in teaching.

In 2016, the MoER, in collaboration with the University of Tartu (survey developer) and Foundation Innove (survey administration), prepared satisfaction surveys for preschool teachers and parents. The Satisfaction with Education Survey aims to expand feedback on the quality of education and create conditions for the systematic monitoring of the well-being and performance of preschool children and teachers. It focuses on six components that are assessed by both preschool teachers and parents. The data collected from the satisfaction surveys serve to provide feedback to preschool institutions on the quality of the working and study environment, as well as parent satisfaction with the preschool. The survey was piloted in 2017, and the main study was implemented in 2018.

Box 2.2 **Quality of ECEC provision in Estonia against EU structural indicators**

According to the European Union's structural indicators, Estonia meets multiple quality indicators of ECEC from birth to the start of compulsory education:

- Children are legally entitled to an ECEC place from the age of 1.5. Although ECEC is not compulsory, 94.6% of children aged three to six attend preschool institutions.
- At least one staff member per group of children in ECEC is qualified to a minimum of bachelor level in the field of education.
- The ECEC curriculum or educational guidelines cover the entire ECEC phase, not only children aged three and over.
- Language support measures are available in ECEC. For example, measures to improve the language of instruction for children who speak another language(s) at home.
- Home learning guidance to foster the child's learning at home is provided through information and ideas to families about how to help their children with curriculum-related activities, decisions and planning.
- There are parenting programmes for those with children aged three or older, where parents attend formal courses covering a variety of topics related to children's education and development.

Source: (European Commission/EACEA/Eurydice, 2019[17]) *Key Data on Early Childhood Education and Care in Europe – 2019 Edition,* http://dx.doi.org/10.2797/966808.

Estonia was the highest-performing OECD country for reading and science in PISA 2018 and among the strongest across all participating countries and economies

Since Estonia joined PISA in 2006 it has been one of the highest performing countries in science, and its performance in reading and mathematics has significantly improved since PISA 2009, by 22 and 11 points, respectively (Figure 2.8). In PISA 2018, Estonia was the highest-performing country in the OECD in reading and science, third for mathematics, and among the top performers across all participating countries and economies in the study (OECD, 2019[19]). Estonia achieves a high level of performance and equity among PISA 2018 participating countries and economies. Estonia's ECEC programme is much more equitable than those in other OECD countries, with parental educational attainment not affecting children's participation in ECEC, unlike in most OECD countries (OECD, 2018[14]). In most countries, children under three whose mothers did not attain tertiary education are less likely to participate in ECEC; however, in Estonia, they are as likely to participate as those with tertiary-educated mothers (OECD, 2018[14]).

Figure 2.8 **Average performance of Estonia in PISA, 2006 to 2018**

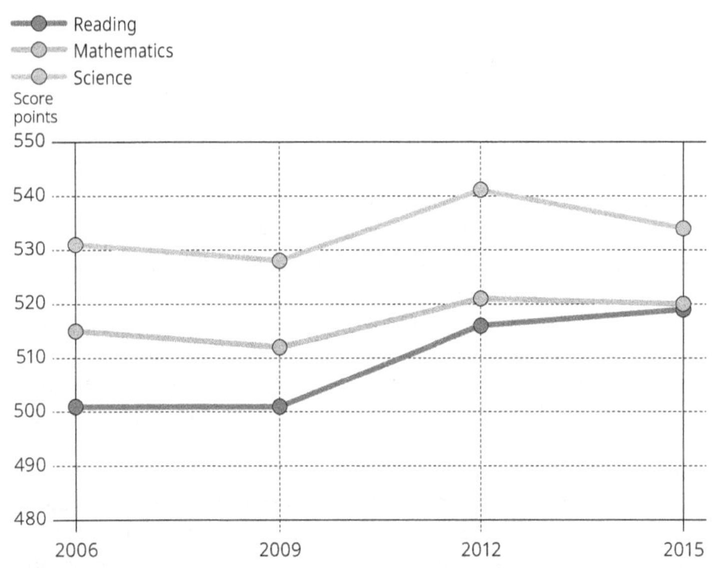

Source: (OECD, 2019[19]), *PISA 2018 Results (Volume I): What Students Know and Can Do,* https://dx.doi.org/10.1787/5f07c754-en.

StatLink https://doi.org/10.1787/888934106059

Estonia also achieved a high level of performance and high student satisfaction in PISA 2018, and had the highest proportion of students with a growth mindset (i.e. with the highest percentage of students who disagreed that their intelligence cannot change very much), which is strongly associated with reading performance. However, the exposure of 15-year-old students to bullying in Estonia was above the OECD average (25.4% versus 22.7%), while their overall life satisfaction was slightly higher than the OECD average (OECD, 2019[20]). According to the International Survey of Children's Well-being, 76% of 8-year-old children in Estonia experience high life satisfaction compared to 68% of 10-year-old children and 50% of 12-year-old children (Kutsar, Raid and Soo, 2018[21]).

POLICY ISSUES AND DEBATES AROUND EARLY LEARNING

Mitigating language barriers for Russian-speaking children is a priority

A recent OECD review of the Estonian education system highlighted the importance of increasing the hours of Estonian language instruction to help Russian-speaking students become proficient in the country's official language, Estonian (Santiago, Levitas and Shewbridge, 2016[22]). The report indicates that language acquisition problems pose barriers to, and raise the costs of, Russian-speaking children advancing through Estonia's education system. Language barriers are likely to distort the choice of Russian-speaking students in favour of vocational programmes at the upper secondary level. On the one hand, the need to form groups for Russian-speaking children in preschool institutions seems to be decreasing as parents increasingly prefer their children to attend groups instructed in Estonian to increase their likelihood of reaching higher education. On the other hand, the share of Russian basic school graduates with at least B1 level[7] of Estonian remains around 57% (Ministry of Education and Research, 2018[15]). Although the share of Russian and other language speakers who also speak Estonian has increased over the last ten years, it has remained stable recently, and achieving a sufficient Estonian language level by the end of basic school remains a challenge for many students.

The Language Immersion Programme, launched in 2015, is currently implemented in 100 institutions, of which 63 are preschools and 37 are primary schools. Results so far are promising, with 86% of basic school graduates using this programme achieving B1 level Estonian. In September 2018, the government launched the Professional Estonian-speaking Teacher to Every Russian-speaking Preschool Group programme, which supports the training of 53 new Estonian teachers for the 53 Russian groups within 21 preschool institutions in Tallinn and Eastern Estonia – which represent around 8% of all Russian groups in the country. The programme aims to support the teaching and learning of the national language for children with other languages, and help them acquire sufficient skills in both languages so that they can successfully participate in Estonian society. The aim is that by 2025 there will be no solely Russian-language groups in preschools, but instead there will be groups of Estonian-Russian children taught in Estonian and Russian in parallel (bilingual teaching).

Estonia has increased spending on the ECEC workforce

Since 2016, Estonia has increased spending on the ECEC workforce, which is reflected in the reduction of the salary gap between preschool and primary teachers. In 2016, teachers' salaries were among the lowest across OECD countries, and the difference between ECEC and primary school teachers' salaries was one of the highest (OECD, 2018[14]). Since 2017, the national government has invested part of the state budget to support local governments in ensuring that the salary and status of preschool teachers are equal to teachers in schools (EUR 61 million during 2017-2021). Preschool teachers' salaries increased to 80%, 85% and 90% of the minimum salary of primary teachers in 2017, 2018 and 2019, respectively. Moreover, preschool teachers with a master's degree now have the same salary as primary teachers.

Attracting younger adults to the teaching profession, especially men, is still a challenge. Various policy initiatives have been implemented to make the teaching profession more attractive and to boost the status of ECEC in society, such as the creation of professional standards and competency models, the re-organisation of continuing professional education, providing feedback on teaching performance, improving the digital competence of learners and teachers, and improving the in-service training system.

Although several policy initiatives have been implemented in recent years to better integrate students with special educational needs (e.g. the Preschool Child Care Institutions Act, 2018), teachers sometimes still lack knowledge of how to deal with these students (Ministry of Education and Research, 2018[15]).

After a shortage in 2014, access to preschool education has improved over the last five years

In 2014, Estonia suffered a shortage of ECEC places (Schreyer and Oberhuemer, 2017[16]), particularly in Tallinn and Tartu, which resulted in long waiting lists (Tavits, 2018[23]) and lower accessibility for low-income families compared to other countries in the region (Schreyer and Oberhuemer, 2017[16]). Since 2014, all children aged between 1.5 and 7 years have been entitled to attend a preschool institution; the Estonian Lifelong Learning Strategy 2020 was also introduced in this year. After the implementation of these initiatives, and with the help of the European Social Fund (ESF) and the European Regional Development Fund (ERDF), EUR 47 million was invested during 2014-2020 to help local governments create around 3 200 new ECEC places. Since 2016, local governments have created around 1 000 of these new preschool and childcare places in the urban areas of Tallinn, Tartu and Pärnu. Local governments co-operate with the private sector to provide childcare for children under three.

The cost of municipal preschool education does not appear to be a barrier for most families to access ECEC in Estonia (Browne et al., 2018[24]). Figure 2.9 shows the typical cost of childcare in different OECD countries for a family with two children aged two and three where the father earns at the median of the full-time earnings distribution and the mother at the 25th percentile. In Estonia, ECEC fees paid by parents in public preschool institutions run by local authorities are low (4% of gross earnings for this family type) compared to the OECD average. However, it is worth noting that the number of years attending preschool education in rural areas is 3.8 compared with 4.3 in cities, which is a higher difference than the OECD average of 0.2 (OECD, 2016[25]).

Figure 2.9 **Comparison of childcare costs across OECD countries**

Percentage of gross earnings for couple with two children aged two and three, 2015

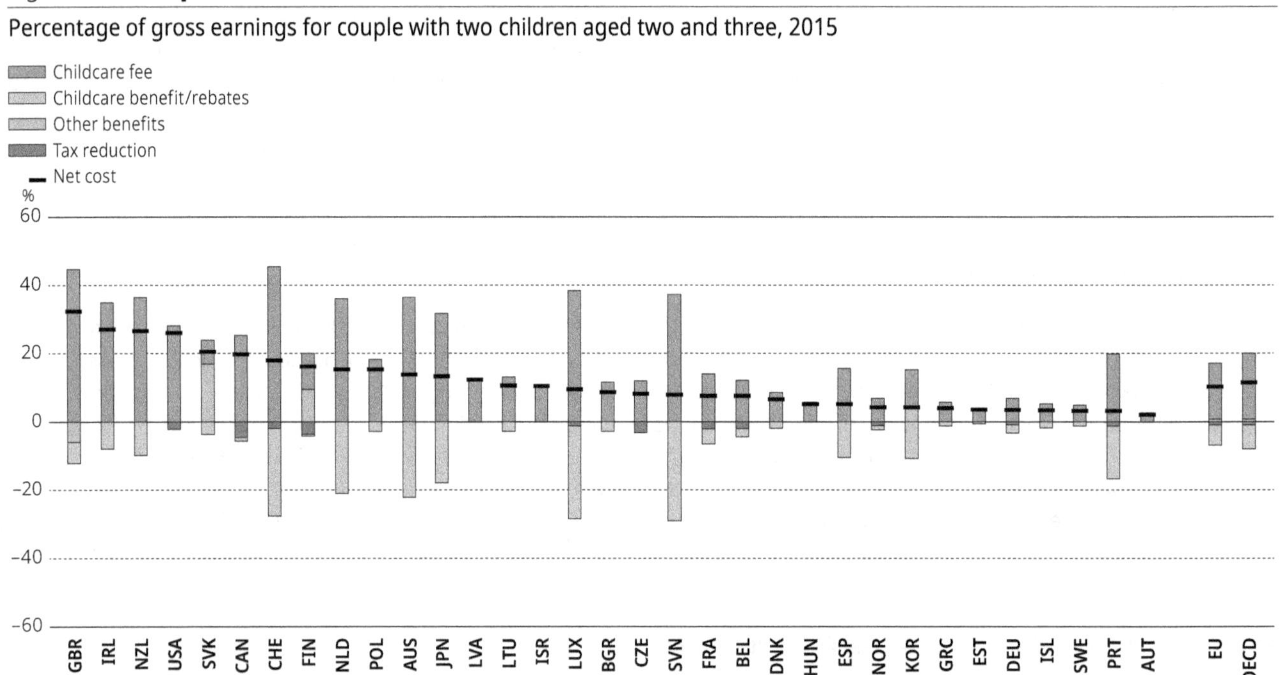

Note: Cost assumes father earns at the median of the full-time earnings distribution and mother at the 25th percentile.

Source: Browne et al. (2018[24]), *Faces of Joblessness in Estonia: A people-centred perspective on employment barriers and policies*, https://dx.doi.org/10.1787/6d9cd656-en.

The number of hours children spend in ECEC between the ages of three and six is high compared to the EU average

The ECEC enrolment of children aged three to six has remained high over the last decade compared to the EU average, and more than 80% of children in this age group in Estonia spend 30 hours or more in formal ECEC, compared to only 40-50% on average across the European Union. Figure 2.10 shows a upward trend in the European Union to increase the number of hours children from the age of three to minimum compulsory school age spend in formal ECEC; however, this target is still far below the number of hours children of this age spend in ECEC in Estonia.

The participation rates of children under three participating in ECEC in Estonia are lower than the EU average, which is possibly related to the generous parental leave benefit system that provides three years of parental leave with guaranteed employment in the previous workplace upon returning from leave. The ECEC enrolment of children under three has increased during the last decade, notably since amendments to the Preschool Child Care Institutions Act adopted in 2014, which allowed local governments to be flexible in providing preschool places for children aged 1.5 to 3. For instance, a local government may, with the parents' consent, change the place of a child under three from a preschool institution to a childcare service. Figure 2.11 shows the impact this amendment and other policy efforts have had on enrolment; however, enrolment is still below the average of the European Union.

Figure 2.10 **Percentage of children aged between three and the minimum compulsory school age in formal ECEC, by hours per week, 2008 to 2017**

Comparison of Estonia with the EU average

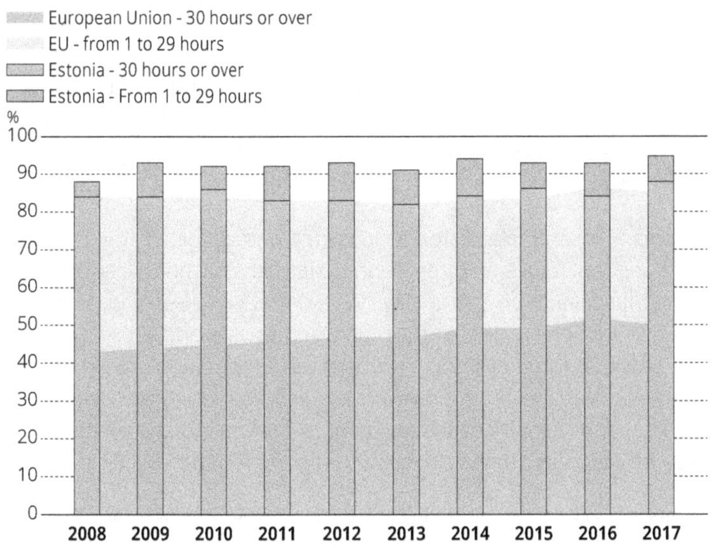

Source: Eurostat (2019), F*ormal Childcare by Age Group and Duration – % Over the Population of Each Age Group*, http://ec.europa.eu/eurostat/product?code=ilc_caindformal&language=en&mode=view (accessed on 11 April 2019[26]).

StatLink https://doi.org/10.1787/888934106078

Figure 2.11 **Percentage of children under three in formal ECEC, by hours per week, 2008 to 2017**

Comparison of Estonia with the EU average

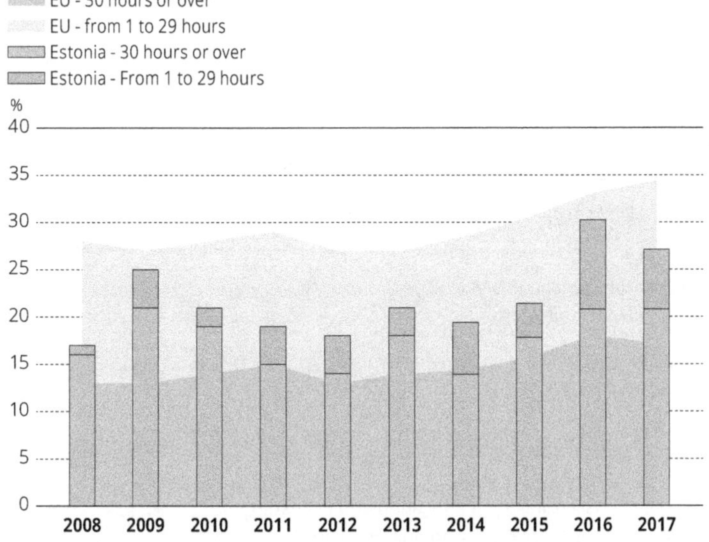

Source: Eurostat (2019), *Formal Childcare by Age Group and Duration – % Over the Population of Each Age Group*, http://ec.europa.eu/eurostat/product?code=ilc_caindformal&language=en&mode=view (accessed on 11 April 2019[27]).

StatLink https://doi.org/10.1787/888934106097

There is little evidence on the quality of early learning internationally

Early learning is a powerful tool for developing children's cognitive and social-emotional skills, and improving the future outcomes of students. However, providing access to ECEC does not guarantee good results for children and their development, and may even negatively impact children's development if quality provision is not ensured. High-quality ECEC not only means ensuring the provision of adequate structural characteristics, such as a qualified workforce and a clear national framework to support local governments, but also ensuring that the children most in need of support have access to ECEC, and that early learning outcomes are adequately monitored.

Estonia has gathered extensive evidence from PISA on how well their 15-year-old students are doing internationally. As mentioned, their overall performance in mathematics, reading and science is excellent. However, PISA data also show that 15-year-old students in Estonia's rural schools score 20 points less in science than their peers in city schools, although rural schools score 35 points more than urban schools after accounting for students' and schools' socio-economic status (Echazarra and Radinger, 2019[27]). In other words, students from a rural background in Estonia would outperform students in urban areas if they and their schools had the same socio-economic status (Echazarra and Radinger, 2019[27]). These results are aligned with Estonian national examinations, which show that students' learning outcomes in rural areas are usually lower than those of their peers in urban areas (Serbak and Valk, 2016[28]). PISA data also show that the performance gap between students with an immigrant background compared to their native peers in Estonia, in favour of students with the non-immigrant background, is greater than the OECD average, and has remained stable between 2006 and 2015 (the last year with available information).

There is much less evidence on younger students in Estonia. For example, Estonia does not participate in the Progress in International Reading Literacy Study (PIRLS) (fourth grade) or the Trends in International Mathematics and Science Study (TIMMS) (eighth grade). Internationally, there is little available information on the quality of children's early learning. However, it is common to find differences in ECEC quality provision within and between countries, between private and public settings, between age groups (children aged under three and those between three and six), and between urban and rural or remote areas (Vandenbroeck, Lenaerts and Beblavý, 2018[12]). High-quality early learning positively predicts well-being across a range of indicators in adulthood, including general well-being, physical and mental health, educational attainment, and employment (Schleicher, 2019[29]). The success of Estonia in PISA may likely be associated with strong early learning foundations.

Providing all children with a strong early start contributes to achieving more equitable outcomes across families and communities. The assessment of crucial early learning domains such as numeracy and emergent literacy, self-regulation skills, and social-emotional skills provides an essential opportunity to understand whether governments, communities, schools and families are adequately supporting children's early learning. IELS is the first international study that provides benchmarking data on children's early learning and a framework to foster the growing interest in, and commitment to, early childhood.

References

Browne, J. et al. (2018), "Faces of Joblessness in Estonia: A People-centred perspective on employment barriers and policies", *OECD Social, Employment and Migration Working Papers*, No. 206, OECD Publishing, Paris, https://dx.doi.org/10.1787/6d9cd656-en. [24]

Echazarra, A. and **T. Radinger** (2019), *Learning in Rural Schools: Insights from PISA, TALIS, and the Literature*, http://www.oecd.org/edu/workingpapers (accessed on 11 April 2019). [27]

European Commission/EACEA/Eurydice (2019), *Key Data on Early Childhood Education and Care in Europe – 2019 Edition*, Luxembourg: Publications Office of the European Union., http://dx.doi.org/10.2797/966808. [17]

Eurostat (2019), *Migration and migrant population statistics - Statistics Explained*, https://ec.europa.eu/eurostat/statistics-explained/index.php/Migration_and_migrant_population_statistics (accessed on 11 April 2019). [7]

Eurostat (2019), *Formal Childcare by Age Group and Duration – % Over the Population of Each Age Group*, http://ec.europa.eu/eurostat/product?code=ilc_caindformal&language=en&mode=view (accessed on 11 April 2019). [26]

Eurostat (2019), *Formal Childcare by Age Group and Duration – % Over the Population of Each Age Group*, http://ec.europa.eu/eurostat/product?code=ilc_caindformal&language=en&mode=view (accessed on 11 April 2019). [27]

Kutsar, D., K. Raid and **K. Soo** (2018), *International Survey of Children's Well-Being – an opportunity to develop child-centred statistics*, Statistics Estonia. [21]

Ministry of Education and Research (2018), *Summary of the annual analysis*, Ministry of Education and Research, https://www.hm.ee/sites/default/files/moer_-_annual_analysis_2018_-_summary.pdf (accessed on 9 April 2019). [15]

Ministry of Education and Research (2014), *The Estonian Lifelong Learning Strategy 2020*, Ministry of Education and Research, https://www.hm.ee/sites/default/files/estonian_lifelong_strategy.pdf (accessed on 11 April 2019). [8]

Ministry of Social Affairs (2011), *Strategy of Children and Families 2012-2020*, Ministry of Social Affairs, https://www.sm.ee/sites/default/files/content-editors/Lapsed_ja_pered/lpa_fulltxt_eng_83a4_nobleed.pdf (accessed on 11 April 2019). [9]

OECD (2019), *Encouraging Quality in Early Childhood Education and Care (ECEC)*, http://www.oecd.org/education/school/48483436.pdf (accessed on 18 April 2019). [18]

OECD (2019), *Fertility rates* (indicator), https://dx.doi.org/10.1787/8272fb01-en (accessed on 11 April 2019). [6]

OECD (2019), *Gross domestic product (GDP)* (indicator), https://dx.doi.org/10.1787/dc2f7aec-en (accessed on 11 April 2019). [4]

OECD (2019), *Income inequality* (indicator), https://dx.doi.org/10.1787/459aa7f1-en (accessed on 11 April 2019). [2]

OECD (2019), *PISA 2018 Results (Volume I): What Students Know and Can Do*, PISA, OECD Publishing, Paris, https://dx.doi.org/10.1787/5f07c754-en. [19]

OECD (2019), *PISA 2018 Results (Volume III): What School Life Means for Students' Lives*, PISA, OECD Publishing, Paris, https://dx.doi.org/10.1787/acd78851-en. [20]

OECD (2019), *Poverty rate* (indicator), https://dx.doi.org/10.1787/0fe1315d-en (accessed on 11 April 2019). [3]

OECD (2018), *Education at a Glance 2018: OECD Indicators*, OECD Publishing, Paris, https://dx.doi.org/10.1787/eag-2018-en. [14]

OECD (2016), *PISA 2015 Results (Volume I): Excellence and Equity in Education*, PISA, OECD Publishing, Paris, https://dx.doi.org/10.1787/9789264266490-en. [25]

Raid, K. and **A. Tammur** (2018), *Quarterly Bulletin of Statistics Estonia 4/2018*, Statistics Estonia. [5]

Riigi Teataja (2018), *Preschool Child Care Institutions Act*, https://www.riigiteataja.ee/en/eli/517062014005/consolide (accessed on 11 April 2019). [10]

Riigi Teataja (2008), *National curriculum for pre-school child care institution*, https://www.riigiteataja.ee/akt/13351772 (accessed on 11 April 2019). [11]

Santiago, P., A. Levitas and **C. Shewbridge** (2016), *OECD Reviews of School Resources Estonia*, https://www.oecd-ilibrary.org/docserver/9789264251731-en.pdf?expires=1554814595&id=id&accname=ocid84004878&checksum=B46711F6AAC944D03D40A39B1790D494 (accessed on 9 April 2019). [22]

Schleicher, A. (2019), *International Summit on the Teaching Profession Helping our Youngest to Learn and Grow POLICIES FOR EARLY LEARNING*, https://istp2019.fi/documents/10810921/10916646/OECD+report/df4eff65-6d14-94ff-aec5-2d549364b249/OECD+report.pdf (accessed on 11 April 2019). [29]

Schreyer, I. and **P. Oberhuemer** (2017), *Estonia - Key Contextual Data*, http://www.seepro.eu/English/Country_Reports.htm (accessed on 19 April 2019). [16]

Schreyer, P. (ed.) (2018), *Estonia ECEC Workforce Profile*, http://www.seepro.eu\Country_Reports\ (accessed on 9 April 2019). [13]

Serbak, K. and **A. Valk** (2016), *Võrdne ligipääs kvaliteetsele haridusele ja tõhus hariduskorraldus. Koolivõrk ja erakoolide rahastamine*, http://www.hm.ee/ (accessed on 9 April 2019). [28]

Statistics Estonia (2019), *Statistical Database*, http://andmebaas.stat.ee/Index.aspx?lang=en&SubSessionId=da2e6b42-6b36-4f33-87cc-e7e993bae966&themetreeid=6 (accessed on 10 April 2019). [1]

Tavits, G. (2018), "Minority policy and social rights: the case of Estonia", in *Citizenship in Segmented Societies*, Edward Elgar Publishing, http://dx.doi.org/10.4337/9781788112697.00012. [23]

Vandenbroeck, M., K. Lenaerts and **M. Beblavý** (2018), *Benefits of Early Childhood Education and Care and the conditions for obtaining them*, European Union, http://dx.doi.org/10.2766/20810. [12]

Notes

1. The Gini coefficient is a measure of income or wealth distribution, where 1 corresponds to maximal inequality and 0 represents perfect equality.
2. The poverty rate is the ratio of the number of people (in a given age group) whose income falls below the poverty line; taken as half the median household income of the total population.
3. A person was considered to be living in relative poverty if his/her equalised monthly disposable income was below EUR 523 (EUR 467 in 2016) and in absolute poverty if their equivalised monthly disposable income was smaller than EUR 207 (EUR 200 in 2016).
4. The total fertility rate in a specific year is defined as the total number of children that would be born to each woman if she were to live to the end of her child-bearing years and give birth to children in alignment with the prevailing age-specific fertility rates.
5. Children with an immigrant background as those with a father and mother who were born in a country or economy other than that in which the child participated.
6. It is calculated as the unweighted mean of the data values of the 22 countries that are members of both the European Union and the OECD.
7. According to the Common European Framework of Reference for Languages.

Children's emergent literacy and emergent numeracy skills in Estonia

This chapter presents findings on the emergent literacy and emergent numeracy of five-year-olds in Estonia. It describes how children's scores in each of these early learning domains relate to their individual characteristics, family backgrounds, and home learning environments.

THE IMPORTANCE OF EARLY LITERACY AND NUMERACY DEVELOPMENT

The cognitive skills developed in early childhood are important for children's well-being in the present, and foundational to their future success in life. Decades of longitudinal research have shown that early literacy and numeracy outcomes strongly predict later cognitive and educational outcomes (Duncan et al., 2007[1]). Early literacy and numeracy skills are also associated with a range of social-emotional and economic outcomes throughout life. Gaps in cognitive skills between children determined by their individual characteristics, home environments, and early childhood education and care (ECEC) experiences are observable by the time children start school and, once they exist, become increasingly difficult and costly to close. There is ample research evidence to suggest that when societies intervene early, the cognitive skills of children are amenable to improvement.

Gaps in literacy skills require early attention

The consequences of not addressing cognitive skills gaps early are serious. Adequate literacy skills are integral to successful functioning in most societies worldwide; however, approximately 33% of 15-year-old students across OECD countries in the 2018 Programme for International Student Assessment (PISA) did not reach a baseline level of proficiency[1] in reading, including 11% of 15-year-olds in Estonia (OECD, 2019[2]). Similarly, 20% of adults, on average, across OECD countries have low reading performance,[2] including 13% of adults in Estonia (OECD, 2013[3]). These adults have poorer labour-market outcomes and poorer self-reported health than their peers with higher levels of literacy proficiency. They are also more likely to feel that they have little impact on the political process and are less likely to report that they have trust in others (OECD, 2013[3]).

The roots of low adult literacy are found in childhood. As skills beget skills, children who fall behind early in their literacy and language skills are likely to fall further behind over time (Kautz et al., 2014[4]; Rigney, 2010[5]). Measuring the early literacy skills of children can provide important information on where societies should focus attention and resources in order to promote quality and equity in early literacy development and, in turn, in children's life chances. Assessing emergent literacy skills comprises an integral part of the International Early Learning and Child Well-being Study (IELS).

Early numeracy outcomes are strongly predictive of a range of later outcomes

Although emergent numeracy has been subject to less research attention than emergent literacy, longitudinal research has also identified numeracy skills in early childhood as important for outcomes throughout schooling and into adulthood. Studies have shown that numeracy competence as assessed at school entry is the strongest predictor of later mathematical achievement and strongly predicts achievement in other academic domains (Duncan et al., 2007[1]). Better numeracy skills in childhood are associated with higher socio-economic status in adulthood (Ritchie and Bates, 2013[6]) and with better self-reported health outcomes (OECD, 2016[7]).

On average, 24% of adults in OECD countries do not develop numeracy skills that go beyond the ability to undertake the most basic numerical operations,[3] although the corresponding proportion in Estonia is lower, at 14% (OECD, 2013[3]). In most countries, adults with less developed information processing skills, including numeracy skills, are less likely to be employed and, when employed, tend to earn lower wages. While the cost of innumeracy to individuals and societies is high now, it is likely to grow even higher in an increasingly technological and scientific world (Raghubar and Barnes, 2017[8]). Given its established importance for later outcomes, emergent numeracy was selected as an important learning domain to be assessed in IELS.

A comprehensive assessment of early cognitive outcomes should consider a range of skills that are predictive of later competence

Emergent cognitive skills can be broadly categorised as constrained or unconstrained. Constrained skills are those that are finite, such as alphabet knowledge, and these are typically easily assessed. Unconstrained skills are not limited in the same way and include aspects of literacy such as vocabulary knowledge. Unconstrained skills develop over a longer period and draw on constrained skills in their formation (Snow and Matthews, 2016[9]). A comprehensive assessment of emergent literacy skills should include an assessment of both types of skill, which is the approach taken in IELS. While unconstrained emergent literacy skills are generally more challenging to assess, they tend to be more strongly associated with later reading success and were therefore the primary focus of the IELS emergent literacy assessment.

IELS assessed a range of constrained and unconstrained early cognitive skills

IELS assessed three skills deemed fundamental to later literacy competence: the unconstrained skills of listening comprehension and vocabulary knowledge, and the constrained skill of phonological awareness. The assessment of listening comprehension in IELS involved two main components: story-level listening comprehension and sentence-level listening comprehension. The former involved children listening to a story and responding to a series of audio-supported items relating to that story, while the latter involved listening to a series of standalone sentences and responding to a single item about the meaning of each one.

Each vocabulary item in IELS required children to identify from a range of very common everyday word options (Tier 1 words[4]) the synonym of a more complex (Tier 2) word. Phonological awareness assessments required children to identify the first, middle and final phonemes (sounds) of short words. Print knowledge was not assessed in IELS, with the focus instead on the pre-reading literacy and language skills that are predictive of later reading success.[5]

The general principle of focusing on the assessment of unconstrained skills in IELS was also applied to the assessment of emergent numeracy skills. Emergent numeracy was defined in the study as the ability to recognise numbers and to undertake numerical operations and reasoning in mathematics. The emphasis in the assessment was on simple problem solving and the application of concepts and reasoning in the following content areas: numbers and counting, working with numbers, shape and space, measurement, and pattern. As with literacy, the emergent numeracy assessment was delivered on a tablet and involved children engaging with game-like activities. The emergent numeracy assessment used a mixture of drag-and-drop technology, where children moved items around the screen to construct solutions to problems, and hot-spot technology, where children tapped objects to indicate their preferred option when responding to an item.

This chapter presents the outcomes of the IELS cognitive assessments of children in Estonia. The metric for all learning outcome scales in IELS is the same. There is theoretically no minimum or maximum score in IELS. The results are instead scaled to have approximately normal distributions, with means around 500 and standard deviations around 100. The overall mean of 500 score points represents the average of the means of all participating countries.

In addition to directly assessing emergent literacy and emergent numeracy skills, the study collected indirect information on the children's emergent literacy and emergent numeracy development through questionnaires administered to the children's parents and educators, and this information is also presented in this chapter. Where parent and educator reports on aspects of children's development are compared in tables, figures or text, these analyses are based on the children for whom both parent and educator ratings were available. Parent and educator questionnaires also collected contextual information about the children's lives at home and at school. This chapter reports how children's emergent literacy and emergent numeracy skills relate to their individual characteristics, family background characteristics, and home learning environments in Estonia. It also considers the relationships between children's emergent literacy and emergent numeracy outcomes and their outcomes in other learning domains assessed in IELS. Similarities and differences between the outcomes of IELS in Estonia and those in the other participating countries, the United States and England, are highlighted throughout. The chapter concludes with summary and conclusions.

EMERGENT LITERACY AND EMERGENT NUMERACY SKILLS OF FIVE-YEAR-OLDS IN ESTONIA

Five-year-olds in Estonia score at or close to the overall averages for emergent literacy and emergent numeracy in IELS

The mean score of children in Estonia on the IELS direct assessment of emergent literacy was 508 points, which was significantly higher than the mean score in the United States (477 points), but not significantly different from the mean in England (515). The score of children at the 25th percentile of emergent literacy in Estonia was 440 points (414 in the United States and 452 in England) and at the 75th percentile was 576 points (541 in the United States and 584 in England).

The mean score of five-year-olds in Estonia on the direct assessment of emergent numeracy was 500 points, the same as the overall IELS mean. Estonia's mean emergent numeracy score was significantly higher than the mean score in the United States (471), significantly lower than the mean score in England (529), and equidistant from both. The score of children at the 25th percentile in emergent numeracy in Estonia was 435 points (409 in the United States, 465 in England), and at the 75th percentile was 567 points (537 in the United States, 599 in England). The distributions of the emergent literacy and emergent numeracy scores in Estonia are shown in Figure 3.1.

Parent and educator evaluations of children's language development are broadly in line with children's assessed early literacy skills, although parents tend to rate their children's development more highly

Both parents and educators are important sources of information on the development of five-year-olds. Parents know most about their child's developmental pathways and educators are trained professionals who work with young children on a daily basis. In IELS, both parents and educators were asked to indicate whether they deemed the child's language and numeracy development to be less than average (either much less or somewhat less), average, or more than average (either somewhat more or much more).

Figure 3.1 **Distribution of emergent literacy and emergent numeracy scores, Estonia**

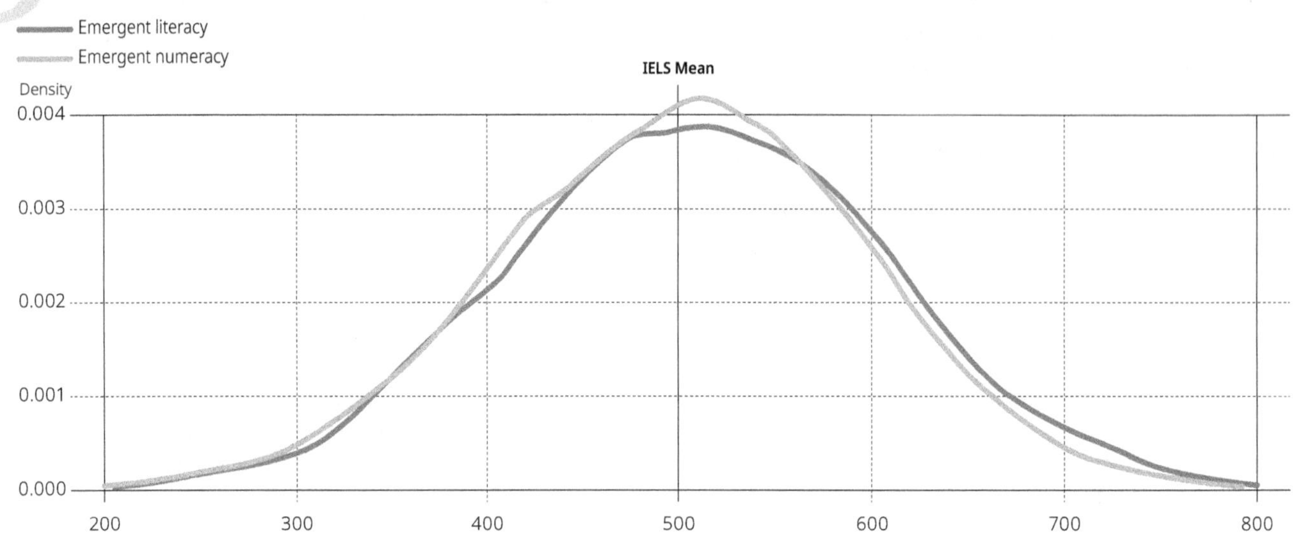

Note: Distributions produced using the first plausible value only.

Just 4% of children in Estonia had parents who described their receptive language development (defined as the extent to which the child understands, interprets and listens) as being below average, and over two-thirds (68%) had parents who assessed their development as above average. Additionally, over half (57%) of children were rated as having above average receptive language skills by their educators, approximately one third (31%) as having average skills, and just 12% as having below average skills (Table 3.1). Children evaluated by either parents or educators as having below average receptive language development had significantly lower mean emergent literacy scores than those rated as average, while those rated above average had significantly higher mean emergent literacy scores than those rated as average.

Table 3.1 **Receptive language development as reported by parents and educators and emergent literacy scores, Estonia**

	Parents		Educators	
	% of children	Mean score	% of children	Mean score
Below average	4	**431**	12	**435**
Average (reference category)	28	479	31	494
Above average	68	**533**	57	**541**

Note: Mean scores in **bold** are significantly different from those of children in the "average" category. The table is based on the subsample of children for whom both parent and educator ratings were available.
StatLink https://doi.org/10.1787/888934106116

In terms of expressive language development in Estonia (i.e. the degree to which the child uses language effectively, can communicate ideas, etc.), 8% of five-year-olds had parents who assessed their skills as below average, and 15% had educators who assessed their skills as below average. A majority of children (67%) had parents who rated their child's expressive language development as above average, while 54% had educators who assessed them as having above average expressive language skills. Children rated as having average expressive language development by their parents or educators had significantly higher mean emergent literacy scores than children rated as below average, and significantly lower mean scores than children rated as above average (Table 3.2).

Most five-year-olds in Estonia have mastered key language skills, according to their parents and educators

In addition to providing overall ratings of children's language development, parents and educators were asked to indicate whether children had mastered a number of specific language and literacy-related skills. In Estonia, 93% of children had parents who indicated that their child could draw inferences after listening to a story about how a character felt or about what might happen next. Additionally, 97% of children had parents who indicated that their five-year-old could speak in multiple sentences (at least three) to explain something that had happened to him or her. A lower proportion (80%) of children had parents who indicated that their child could recognise the sounds of words that rhyme. Educators were less likely than parents were to indicate that children had mastered each skill (Figure 3.2), as was also the case in England and the United States. However, the gaps between parent and educator reports were smaller in Estonia than in any other country. In each case, children whose parents indicated that they had not mastered the skill had a significantly lower mean emergent literacy score than other children (Figure 3.3), with gaps ranging from 34 to 76 points, depending on the skill and informant in question.

Table 3.2 **Expressive language development as reported by parents and educators and emergent literacy scores, Estonia**

	Parents		Educators	
	% of children	Mean score	% of children	Mean score
Less than average	8	**440**	15	**446**
Average (reference category)	26	478	31	495
More than average	67	**536**	54	**544**

Note: Mean scores in **bold** are significantly different from those of children in the "average" category. The table is based on the subsample of children for whom both parent and educator ratings were available.

StatLink https://doi.org/10.1787/888934106135

Figure 3.2 **Mastery of key language and literacy-related skills as reported by parents and educators, Estonia**

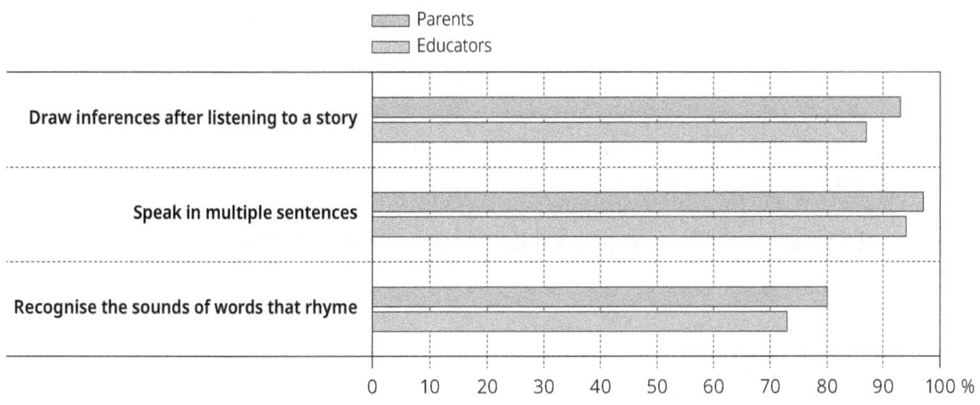

StatLink https://doi.org/10.1787/888934106154

Figure 3.3 **Emergent literacy scores by reported mastery of key language and literacy-related skills, Estonia**

Score-point differences between children who have and have not mastered each language skill, according to their parents and educators

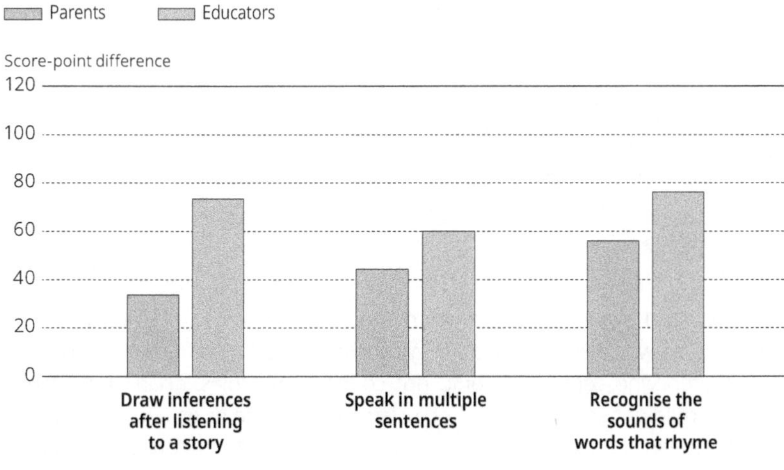

Note: All differences are statistically significant.

StatLink https://doi.org/10.1787/888934106173

Similar proportions of children were reported as having below average, average and above average numeracy development by their parents and educators

Children whose numeracy development was rated as average by their parents or educators had significantly higher mean emergent numeracy scores than children whose development was rated as below average, and significantly lower mean scores than children whose development was rated as above average (Table 3.3).

Table 3.3 **Numeracy development as reported by parents and educators and emergent numeracy scores, Estonia**

	Parents		Educators	
	% of children	Mean score	% of children	Mean score
Less than average	10	**421**	11	**396**
Average (reference category)	36	483	39	492
More than average	54	**533**	49	**538**

Note: Mean scores in **bold** are significantly different from those of children in the "average" category. The table is based on the subsample of children for whom both parent and educator ratings were available.

StatLink https://doi.org/10.1787/888934106192

Parents and educators were asked to indicate whether each child had mastered a series of numeracy or mathematics-related skills. In all cases, parents were more likely than educators to indicate that their child had mastered the skill (Figure 3.4). Children were most likely to be reported by their parents and educators as being able to sort a group of objects by size, shape or colour (98% by both parents and educators), and to identify at least three different shapes (97% by parents and 96% by educators). Children were least likely to be reported by their parents and educators as being able to count in multiples (43% and 31%, respectively, the largest gap between parent and educator reports).

Figure 3.4 **Mastery of key early mathematics skills as reported by parents and educators, Estonia**

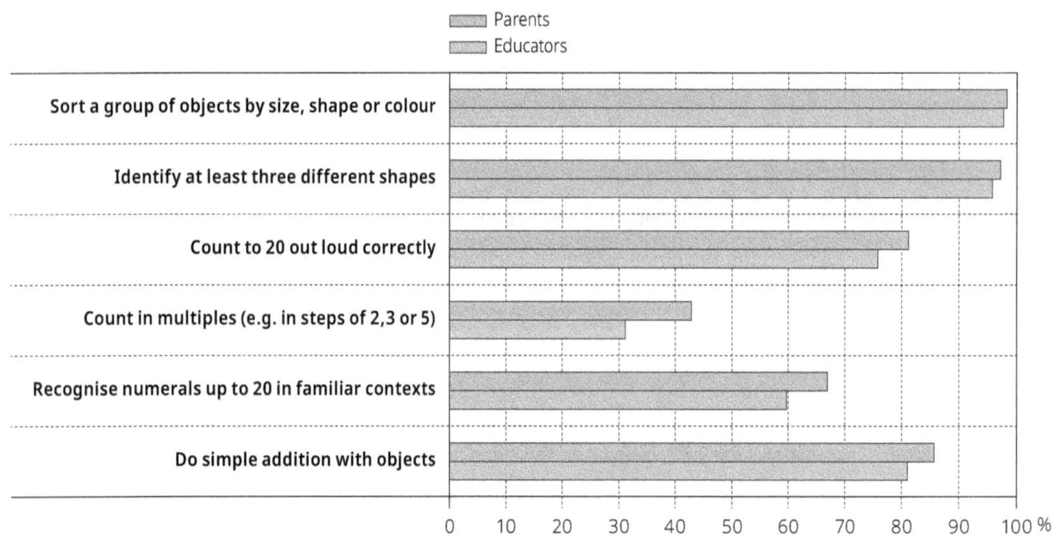

StatLink https://doi.org/10.1787/888934106211

In all cases, children reported as having mastered a particular skill had significantly higher mean emergent numeracy scores than children reported as not having mastered this skill, as was also the case in England and the United States. Significant score-point gaps ranged from 16 points (between children who could and could not count in multiples, according to their parents) to 139 points (between children who could and could not sort a group of objects by size, shape or colour, according to their educators; Figure 3.5). The difference between the mean scores of children who could and could not count in multiples, according to their parents, was not statistically significant.

Figure 3.5 **Emergent numeracy scores by reported mastery of key early mathematics skills, Estonia**

Score-point differences between children who have and have not mastered each early numeracy skill, according to their parents and educators

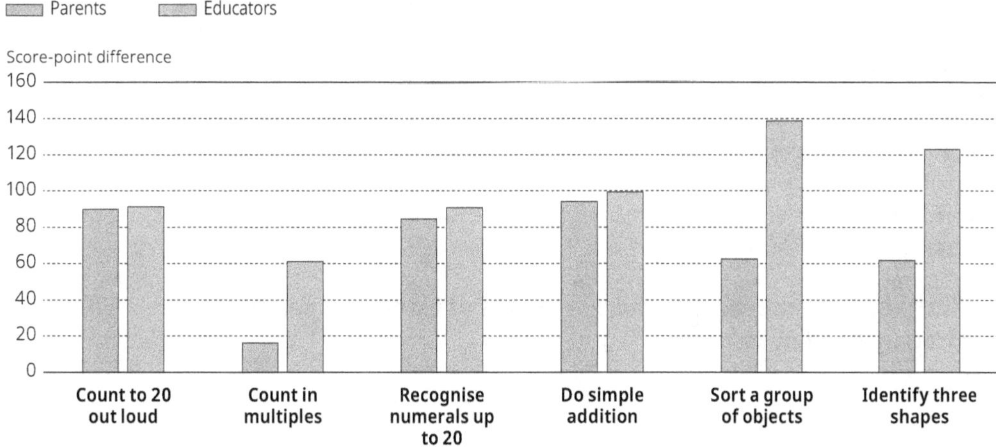

Note: All differences are statistically significant.

StatLink https://doi.org/10.1787/888934106230

INDIVIDUAL CHARACTERISTICS AND EMERGENT LITERACY AND EMERGENT NUMERACY SKILLS

Russian-speaking children have better early literacy and numeracy skills at age five than Estonian-speaking children despite being, on average, of lower socio-economic status

In Estonia, 21% of children took the IELS assessment in Russian. These children had a mean emergent literacy score significantly higher than the mean score for those who took the assessments in Estonian (Figure 3.6), despite Russian-speaking children having significantly lower socio-economic status (SES) scores than Estonian-speaking children. The SES index constructed for use in IELS was based on household income, parent occupation and parental educational attainment.[6]

The mean emergent numeracy score of Russian-speaking children was also significantly higher than that of Estonian-speaking children and the gap increased after accounting for socio-economic status.

Figure 3.6 **Emergent literacy and emergent numeracy scores by children's language, Estonia**

Score-point differences between Russian-speaking children and Estonian-speaking children, before and after accounting for socio-economic status

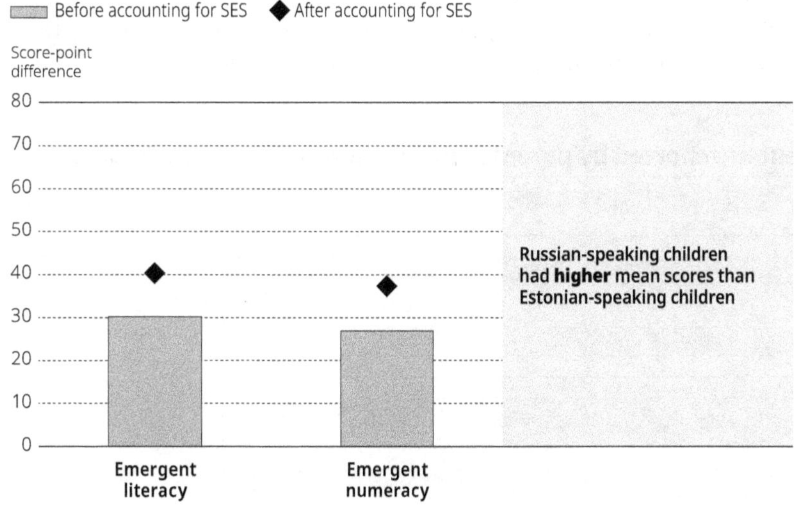

Note: All differences are statistically significant. 'Russian-speaking children' refers to children who took the assessment in Russian.

StatLink https://doi.org/10.1787/888934106249

Russian-speaking girls have better early literacy and numeracy outcomes than Russian-speaking boys, but there are no significant gender gaps among Estonian-speaking children

There was a statistically significant gender gap in emergent literacy among Russian-speaking children, with girls outperforming boys by an average of 37 score points. In contrast, there was no significant gender gap in emergent literacy outcomes among Estonian-speaking children. Significant gender differences in emergent literacy (in favour of girls) were found in both England and the United States. In PISA 2018, the gender gap in reading in Estonia was 31 points, in favour of girls, similar to the 30-point gap on average across OECD countries (OECD, 2019[2])

Russian-speaking girls also had a mean emergent numeracy score that was significantly higher than that of Russian-speaking boys, but again, there was no significant gap between the mean emergent numeracy scores of Estonian girls and Estonian boys (Figure 3.7). In PISA 2018, boys in Estonia outperformed girls in mathematics by eight score points, while across OECD countries, boys outperformed girls by five points (OECD, 2019[2])

Figure 3.7 **Mean emergent literacy and emergent numeracy scores of Estonian-speaking and Russian-speaking children by gender, Estonia**

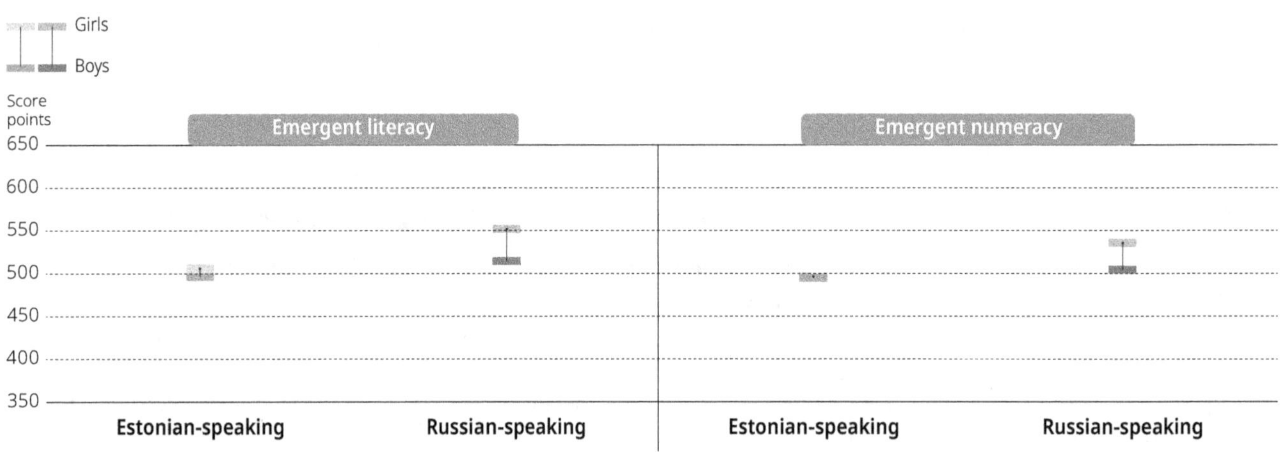

Note: Significant differences are shown in a darker tone. Russian-speaking children' refers to children who took the assessment in Russian.

StatLink https://doi.org/10.1787/888934106268

Girls are more likely than boys to have above average receptive and expressive language skills, according to their parents and educators

In line with their better average score on the IELS emergent literacy assessment, girls in Estonia were more likely than boys to have parents and educators who rated their receptive and expressive language development as above average. Girls were also less likely to have their language development rated as below average by their educators (Figure 3.8 and Figure 3.9).

Figure 3.8 **Receptive language development as reported by parents and educators by gender, Estonia**

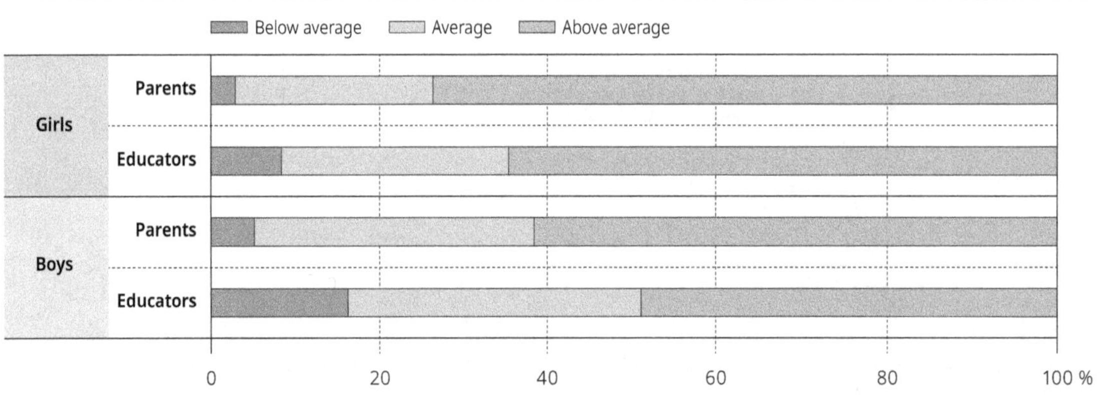

StatLink https://doi.org/10.1787/888934106287

Figure 3.9 **Expressive language development as reported by parents and educators by gender, Estonia**

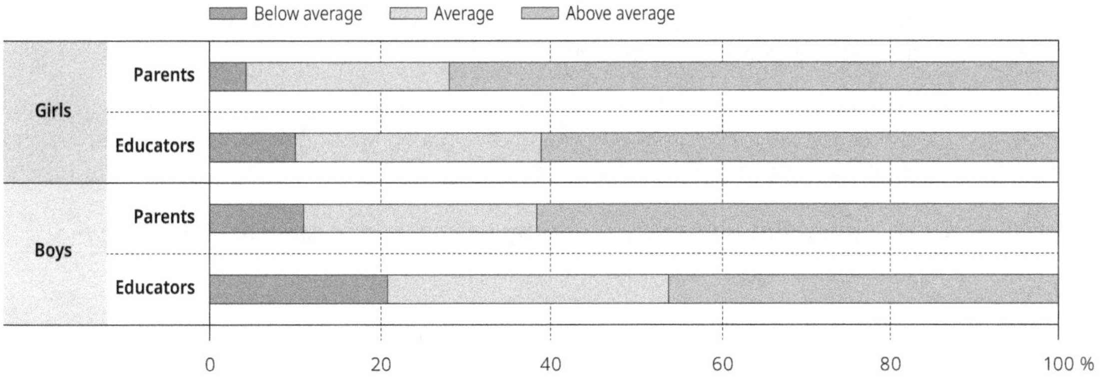

StatLink https://doi.org/10.1787/888934106306

Girls and boys are equally likely to have average numeracy development, according to their parents and educators

Similar proportions of girls and boys were rated as having average numeracy development by their parents and educators, although girls were somewhat more likely to be rated as above average by their educators than boys. (Figure 3.10)

Figure 3.10 **Numeracy development as reported by parents and educators by gender, Estonia**

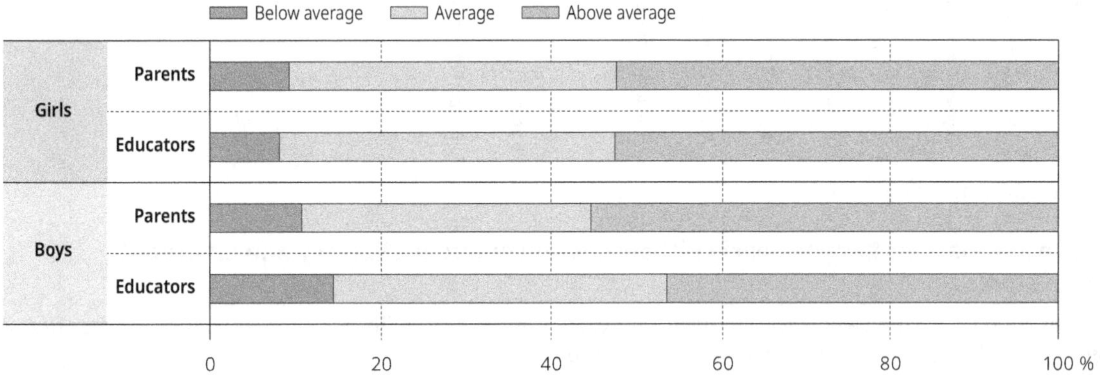

StatLink https://doi.org/10.1787/888934106325

Age is positively related to emergent literacy and emergent numeracy skills in Estonia

For both emergent literacy and emergent numeracy there were significant positive correlations between children's age in months and their scores on the assessments. In Estonia, the correlation between age and emergent skills was 0.20 for emergent literacy and 0.24 for emergent numeracy. For emergent literacy, the score-point difference between the oldest children (6 years 0 months)[7] in the sample and the youngest children in the sample (5 years 0 months) was 78 points. For emergent numeracy, the corresponding gap was 94 points (Figure 3.11).

The difference in the mean emergent literacy scores of children between the ages of five years one month[8] and six years of age was 59 points in Estonia, 87 in England, and 92 in the United States. For emergent numeracy, the difference was 74 points in Estonia, 126 in England, and 110 in the United States.

Having had low birth weight or premature birth, learning difficulties, or social, emotional or behavioural difficulties is associated with lower emergent literacy and emergent numeracy scores

Parents were asked to indicate whether their child had ever experienced a number of potential challenges or difficulties. In Estonia, 8% of children were reported by their parents as having had low weight at birth or premature birth (compared to 10% in the United States and 11% in England).[9] These children had mean emergent numeracy scores that were significantly lower than those of their peers who did not have low birth weight and were not born prematurely, but there was no significant difference in mean emergent literacy scores. One in ten children (10%) in Estonia had experienced learning difficulties, according to their parents (13% in the United States, 10% in England). These children scored significantly lower in both emergent literacy and emergent numeracy, on average, than other children. Additionally, 10% of five-year-olds in Estonia had social, emotional or behavioural difficulties, according to their parents (12% in the United States, 8% in England). Again, these children had significantly lower mean emergent literacy and emergent numeracy scores than other children.

When each of the difficulties was examined in combination (i.e. examining the effect of one difficulty after accounting for the effects of other early difficulties) and after accounting for socio-economic status, having learning difficulties remained the only significant predictor of both emergent literacy and emergent numeracy scores (Figure 3.12).

Figure 3.11 **Emergent literacy and emergent numeracy scores by age of child in months, Estonia**

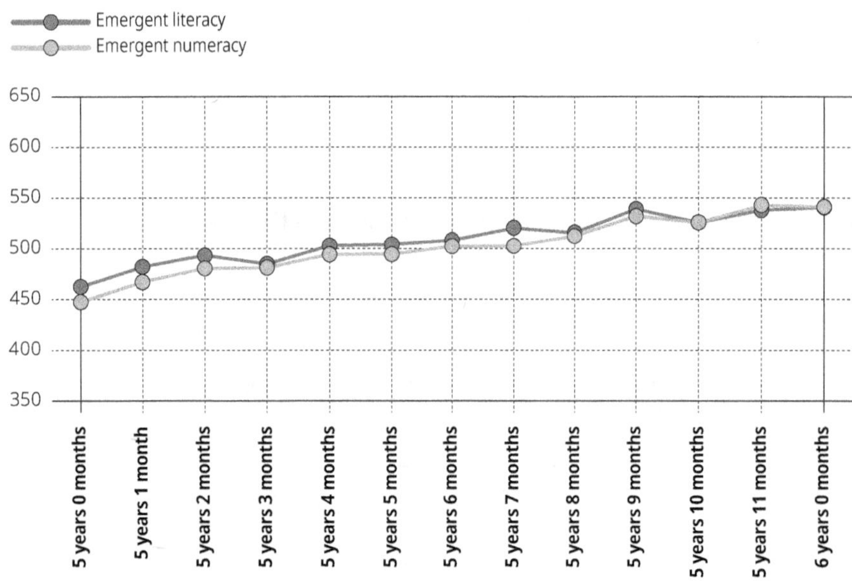

StatLink https://doi.org/10.1787/888934106344

Figure 3.12 **Relative associations between early difficulties and emergent literacy and emergent numeracy scores, Estonia**

Score-point differences between children who have and have not experienced an early difficulty, after accounting for the effects of other early difficulties, and before and after accounting for socio-economic status

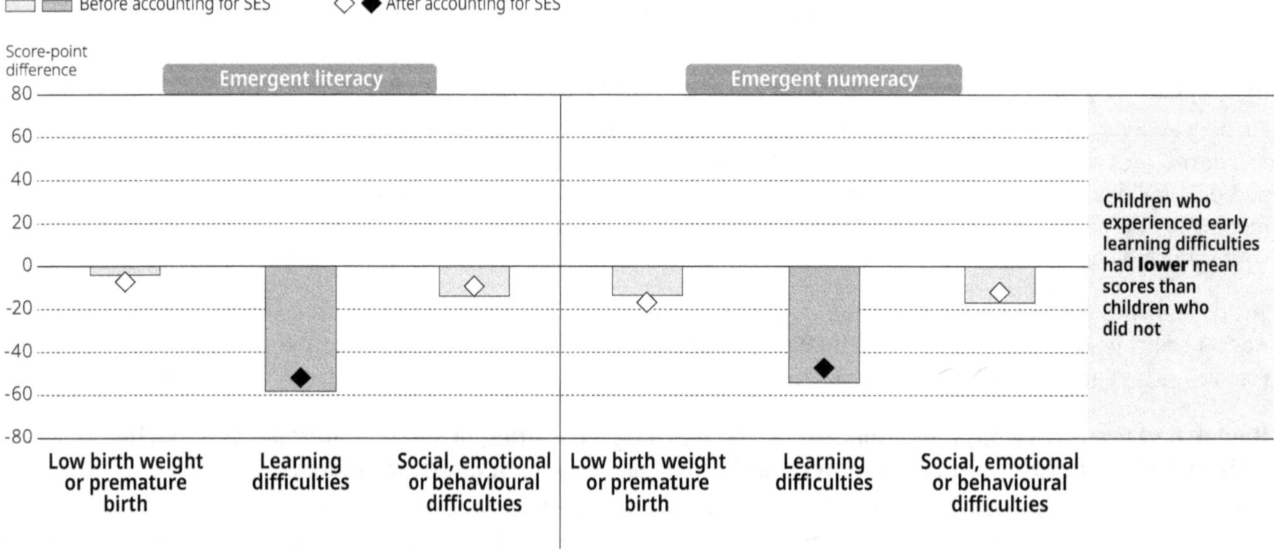

Note: Statistically significant differences are shown in a darker tone.

StatLink https://doi.org/10.1787/888934106363

There were statistically significant associations between gender and having learning difficulties or having social, emotional or behavioural difficulties in Estonia. Boys were twice as likely as girls to be reported as having learning difficulties (6.5% of girls and 13% of boys), and were also significantly more likely to have had social, emotional or behavioural difficulties (7% of girls and 14% of boys), according to their parents. These gender associations were also present in the United States and England. No significant gender differences were observed in relation to birth weight or premature birth.

There were also statistically significant associations between having experienced each of these challenges or difficulties and socio-economic status. In Estonia, 15% of children in the lowest SES quartile had learning difficulties, according to their parents, compared to 7% of children in the top SES quartile. Additionally, 15% of children in the lowest SES quartile in Estonia had social, emotional or behavioural difficulties, according to their parents, compared to 8% of children in the top SES quartile. There was no significant association between low birth weight/premature birth and socio-economic status in Estonia (such an association was present in the United States). Russian-speaking and Estonian-speaking children were equally likely to have experienced low birth weight or premature birth, learning difficulties, and social, emotional or behavioural difficulties.

Overall, 17% of children in Estonia had experienced one of the three challenges, according to their parents, 4% of children experienced two, and fewer than 1% experienced all three. In other words, 78% of five-year-olds in Estonia had experienced none of the challenges, which is similar to the percentage in England and the United States.

HOME AND FAMILY CHARACTERISTICS AND EMERGENT LITERACY AND EMERGENT NUMERACY SKILLS

Socio-economic status is less strongly associated with emergent literacy and emergent numeracy scores in Estonia than in the other two countries that participated in the study

Socio-economic status was significantly positively correlated with emergent literacy (r = 0.20) and emergent numeracy (r = 0.23) outcomes in Estonia, but correlations were weaker than in England (r = 0.37 for emergent literacy and 0.34 for emergent numeracy) and the United States (r = 0.36 and 0.45, respectively).

The gap between the mean emergent literacy scores of children in the top and bottom SES quartiles in Estonia was 56 points, which is smaller than the corresponding gaps in England (93 points) and the United States (84 points). The gap between the mean emergent numeracy scores of those in the top and bottom SES quartiles in Estonia was 56 points, which is around half the size of the corresponding gap in the United States (110 points), and smaller than the 86-point gap in England.

Figure 3.13 **Emergent literacy and emergent numeracy scores by socio-economic quartile, Estonia**

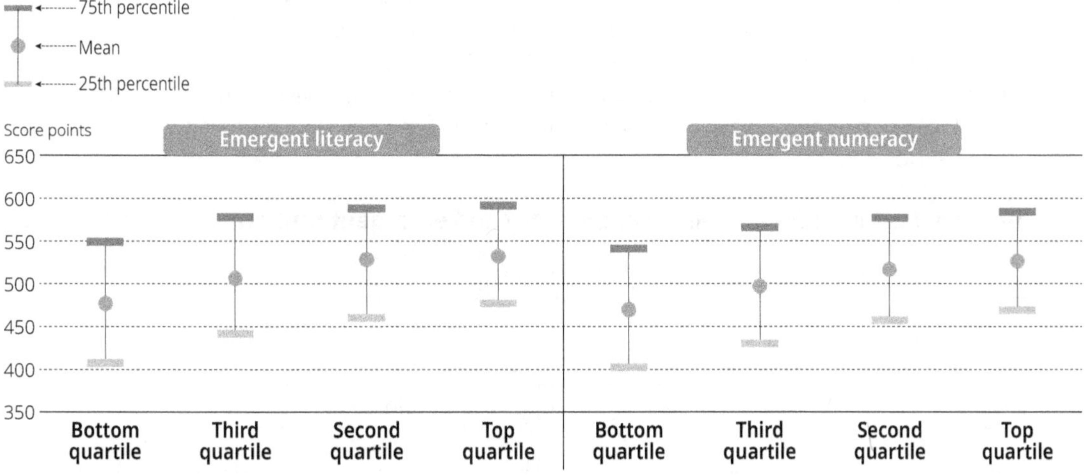

StatLink https://doi.org/10.1787/888934106382

Children with at least one parent who mainly speaks a language other than the assessment language have lower emergent literacy scores

At the time of the assessment in Estonia, 6% of five-year-olds lived in homes where at least one parent mostly spoke a language other than the language through which they took the assessment (either Russian or Estonian). These children had significantly lower mean emergent literacy scores before and after accounting for socio-economic status (Figure 3.14). There was no significant difference between the mean emergent numeracy scores of children with at least one parent who spoke mainly a language other than the IELS assessment language and children whose parents mainly spoke the assessment language, after accounting for socio-economic status.

Figure 3.14 **Emergent literacy and emergent numeracy scores by home language, Estonia**

Score-point differences between children with at least one parent who speaks mainly a language other than the assessment language at home and those whose parent(s) speak mainly the assessment language, before and after accounting for socio-economic status

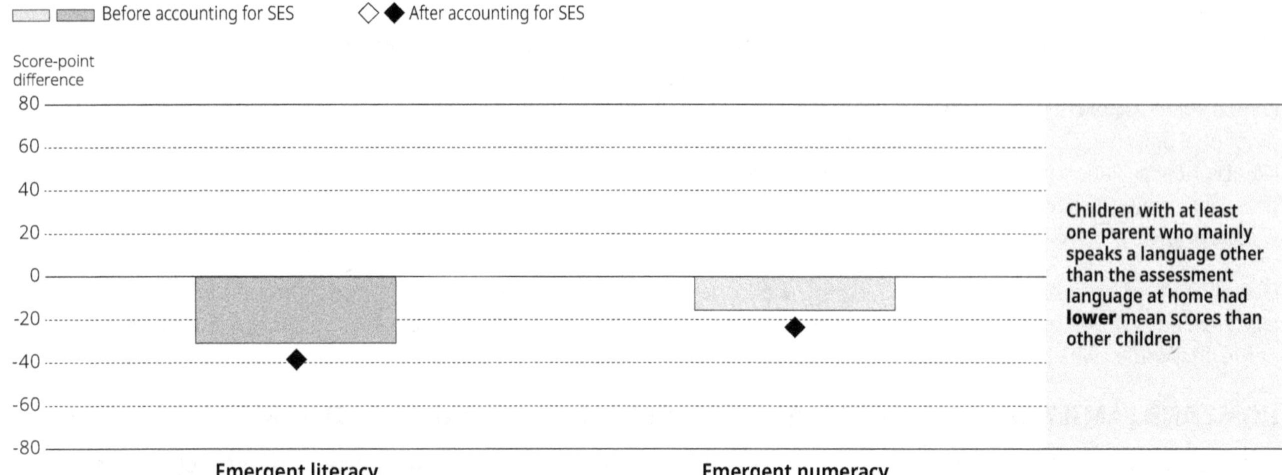

Note: Statistically significant differences are shown in a darker tone.
StatLink https://doi.org/10.1787/888934106401

Family structure is not related to children's emergent literacy and emergent numeracy skills in Estonia

In Estonia, 12% of five-year-olds lived in one-parent households. These children had similar levels of emergent literacy and emergent numeracy as children who lived in two-parent households. One in five (20%) five-year-olds in Estonia had no siblings, half (50%) had one sibling, one in five had two siblings (21%) and the remaining 9% had more than two siblings. The mean emergent literacy and emergent numeracy scores of children with one sibling did not differ significantly from those of children with no siblings or children with more siblings.

Children whose mothers have higher educational attainment have better early literacy and numeracy skills

In Estonia, as in the two other participating countries, mothers' educational attainment was significantly positively related to children's early literacy and numeracy outcomes (Table 3.4). In Estonia, 53% of children had mothers who had completed a bachelor's degree or higher (compared with 39% in the United States and 40% in England). These children had higher mean emergent literacy and emergent numeracy scores than children whose mothers had completed less formal education, even after accounting for household income (Figure 3.15).

Table 3.4 **Maternal educational attainment and emergent literacy and emergent numeracy scores, Estonia**

	% of children	Literacy	Numeracy
Lower secondary	8	474	467
Upper secondary	19	495	484
Post-secondary, non-tertiary	8	496	494
Short-cycle tertiary	12	509	497
Bachelor's degree	32	527	516
Masters degree, doctorate or equivalent	20	533	530

Note: There were too few children whose mothers' highest level of educational attainment was primary school to present their mean scores in this report.
StatLink https://doi.org/10.1787/888934106420

Figure 3.15 **Emergent literacy and emergent numeracy by mother's educational attainment, Estonia**

Score-point differences between children whose mothers have at least a bachelor's degree and those whose mothers do not, before and after accounting for household income

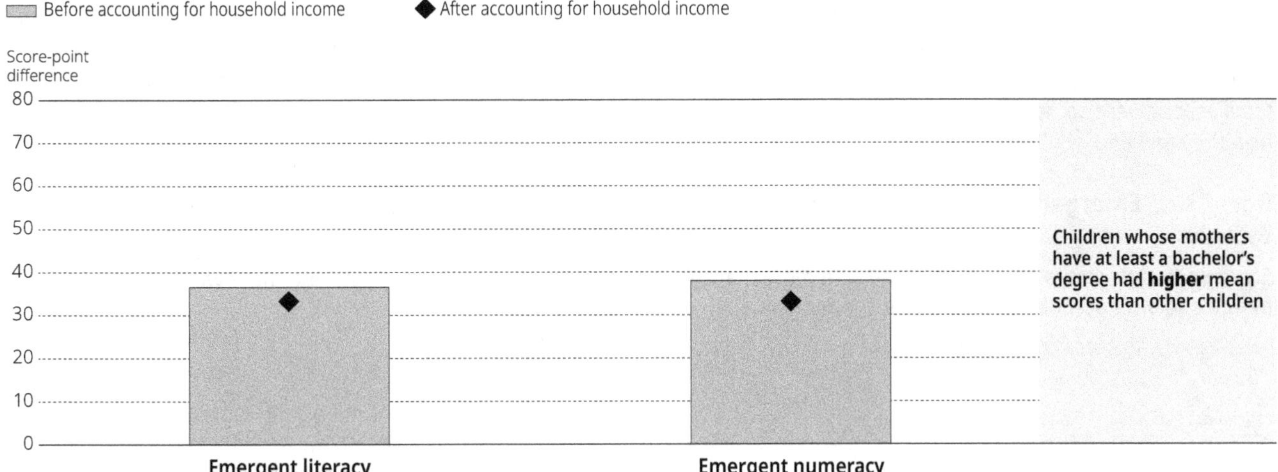

Note: All differences are statistically significant.

StatLink https://doi.org/10.1787/888934106439

HOME LEARNING ENVIRONMENT AND EMERGENT LITERACY AND EMERGENT NUMERACY SKILLS

The home is the first major context in which children learn, develop and grow. A home environment that is supportive of early learning, in terms of both stimulating resources and interactions, is an important determinant of children's early cognitive outcomes. Collecting information on children's home learning environments was an important focus of IELS.

Children from homes with a greater number of children's books have higher average emergent literacy and emergent numeracy scores

Children in homes with more children's books had, on average, higher emergent literacy and emergent numeracy scores than children with fewer books (Table 3.5). Children in Estonia were less likely to come from homes with more than 100 books (10%) than in the United States (26%) or England (29%), but roughly equally likely to be in homes with 10 books or fewer (13%) as the United States (12%) and England (9%). The gap in emergent literacy between children with 10 books or fewer and those with more than 100 children's books was 84 points (64 after accounting for socio-economic status). The corresponding gap for numeracy was 85 points (64 after accounting for socio-economic status; Figure 3.16).

Table 3.5 **Number of books in the home and emergent literacy and emergent numeracy scores, Estonia**

	%	Literacy	Numeracy
0-10	13	465	458
11 to 25	23	503	488
26 to 50	32	512	503
51 to 100	21	535	531
More than 100	10	548	543

StatLink https://doi.org/10.1787/888934106458

Children whose parents read books to them more frequently have better emergent literacy skills than those whose parents read to them less frequently

Figure 3.17 shows the percentage of children whose parents engaged in a range of language and literacy-related activities at home with varying frequency. Having a back-and-forth conversation with the child about how they feel and why was the activity most likely to be engaged in on at least five days each week (48% of children had parents who did this), followed by reading to the child from a book (38% of children). There were no significant associations between a child's gender and the frequency with which their parents engaged in any of these activities with them at home. There were, however, significant associations between socio-economic status and the frequency with which the child was read to from a book, had back-and-forth conversations with the parent, and was sang to by a parent. For example, in Estonia, 18% of children in the bottom SES quartile were read to from a book on at least five days a week, compared to 57% of children in the top SES quartile. Similarly, 38% of children in the bottom SES quartile had back-and-forth conversations with their parents five to seven days a week, compared to 55% of children in the top SES quartile. Finally, 10% of children in the bottom SES quartile had parents who sang songs or nursery rhymes to them five to seven days a week, compared to 15% of children in the top SES quartile. Children from Russian-speaking families were somewhat more likely to be told stories (not from a book) on multiple days a week than children from Estonian-speaking families, but were somewhat less likely to have back-and-forth conversations with their parents on multiple days a week about how they feel and why.

Figure 3.16 **Emergent literacy and emergent numeracy scores by number of children's books in the home, Estonia**

Score-point differences between children with more than 100 children's books or more at home and those with 10 or fewer, before and after accounting for socio-economic status

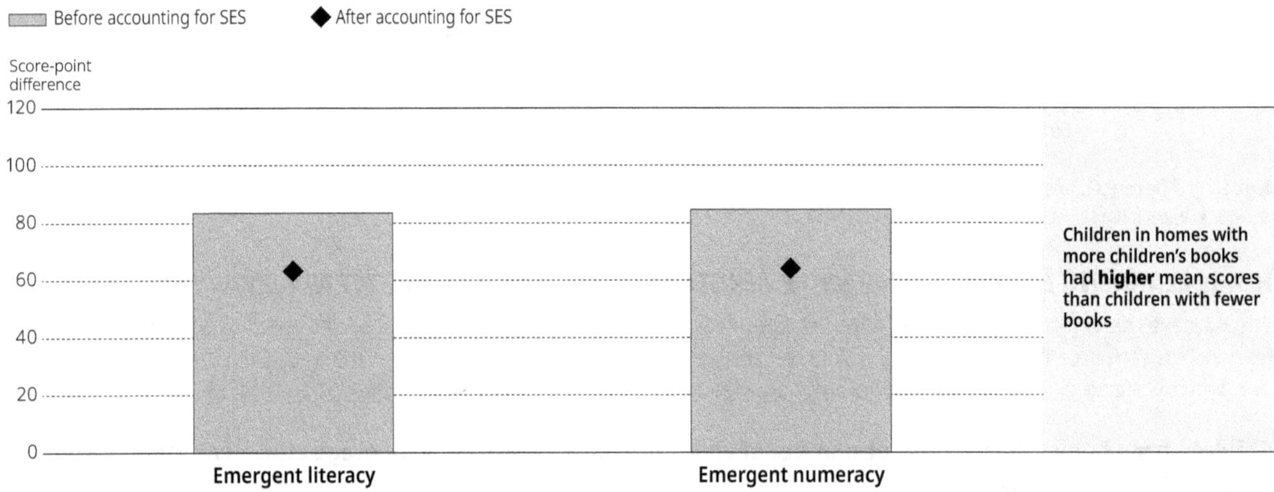

Note: All differences are statistically significant.

StatLink https://doi.org/10.1787/888934106477

Figure 3.17 **Frequency of engagement in literacy-related activities at home, Estonia**

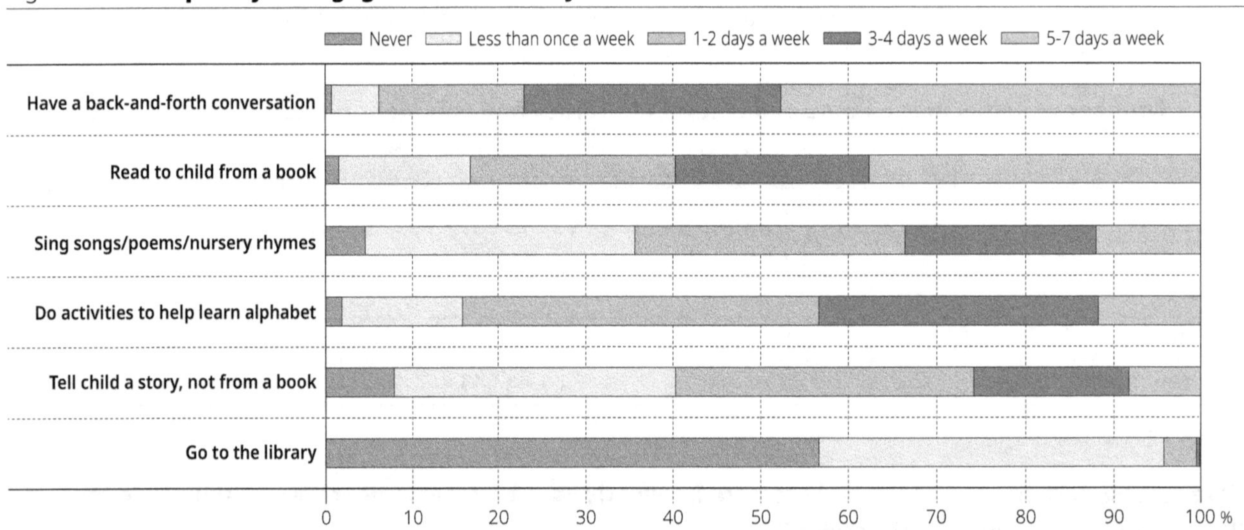

StatLink https://doi.org/10.1787/888934106496

Children whose parents read to them from a book on at least five days a week had a significantly higher mean emergent literacy score than children whose parents did so less than once a week, holding socio-economic status constant (Figure 3.18). This was the only activity that was significantly associated with children's emergent literacy scores in IELS after accounting for socio-economic status.

Figure 3.18 **Emergent literacy scores by how often a child is read to from a book at home, Estonia**

Score-point differences between children whose parents read to them from a book on one or more days a week and those whose who do so less than once a week, before and after accounting for socioeconomic status

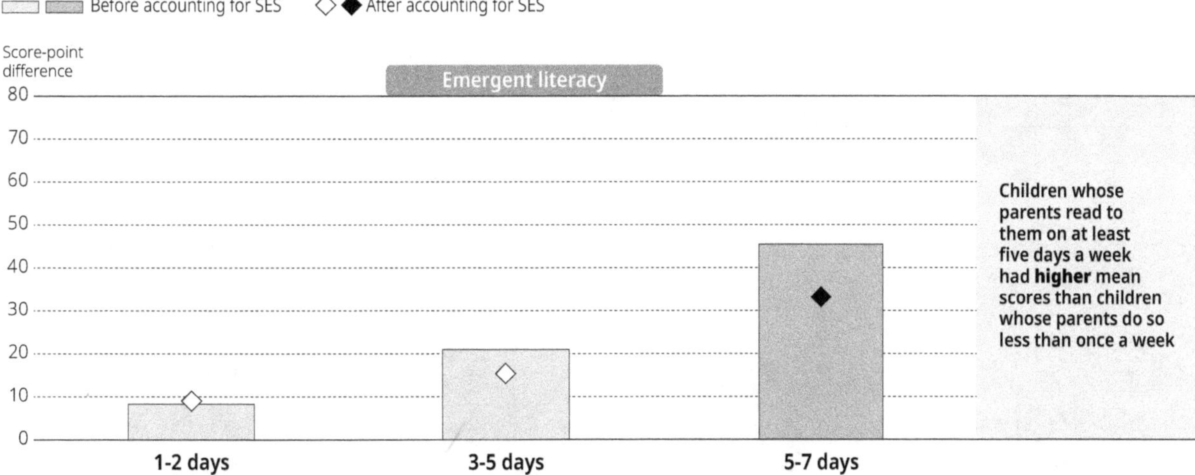

Note: Statistically significant differences are shown in a darker tone.

StatLink https://doi.org/10.1787/888934106515

Most children have parents who engage in numeracy-related activities with them at home at least once a week

Figure 3.19 shows the percentages of children whose parents engaged in numeracy-related activities at home with them with varying frequency. In Estonia, 25% of children had parents who said they played with numbers, counters, measuring or shapes less often than one day a week with their child, and 15% had parents who said they engaged in activities designed to help them learn numbers less than once a week. These percentages are higher than in England or the United States. There was a statistically significant association between a child's gender and the frequency with which parents engaged in activities with the child involving numbers, counters, measuring or shapes, with boys somewhat more likely to have parents engage in these activities with them more frequently. There were no significant associations between frequency of engagement with these activities and socio-economic status, or with being from an Estonian- or Russian-speaking background.

Children whose parents engaged with them in activities at home involving numbers, counters, measuring or shapes less often than once a week had a significantly lower mean emergent numeracy score than children whose parents did so more frequently, even after accounting for socio-economic status (Figure 3.20).

Figure 3.19 **Frequency of engagement in numeracy-related activities at home, Estonia**

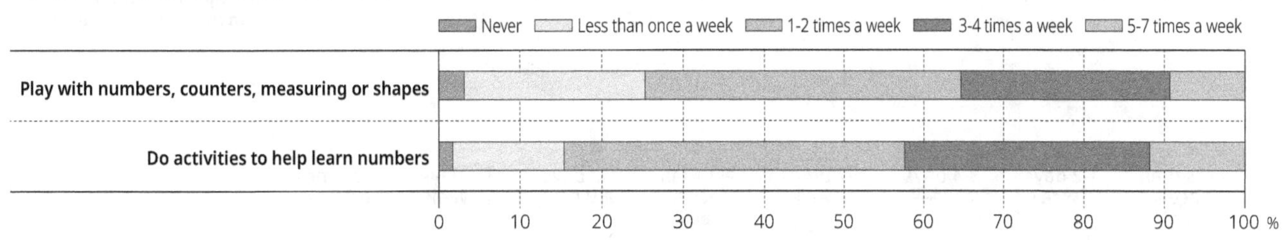

StatLink https://doi.org/10.1787/888934106534

Attendance of special or extra-cost activities outside of the home is associated with higher emergent literacy and emergent numeracy scores

Parents were also asked how often their five-year-old child attended a special or extra-cost activity outside of the home (such as a sports activity, dance, scouts, swimming lessons, language lessons) In Estonia, 22% of five-year-olds never attended a special or extra-cost activity, 14% did so less than once a week, 40% on one or two days a week, 20% on three to four days a week, and 5% on five or more days a week. Generally, children who attended these activities had significantly higher mean scores than children who never did, even after accounting for socio-economic status (Figure 3.21).

Figure 3.20 **Emergent numeracy scores by frequency of numeracy-related activities at home, Estonia**

Score-point differences between children whose parents engage them in activities involving numbers, counters, measuring or shapes on one or more days a week and those who do so less than once a week, before and after accounting for socioeconomic status

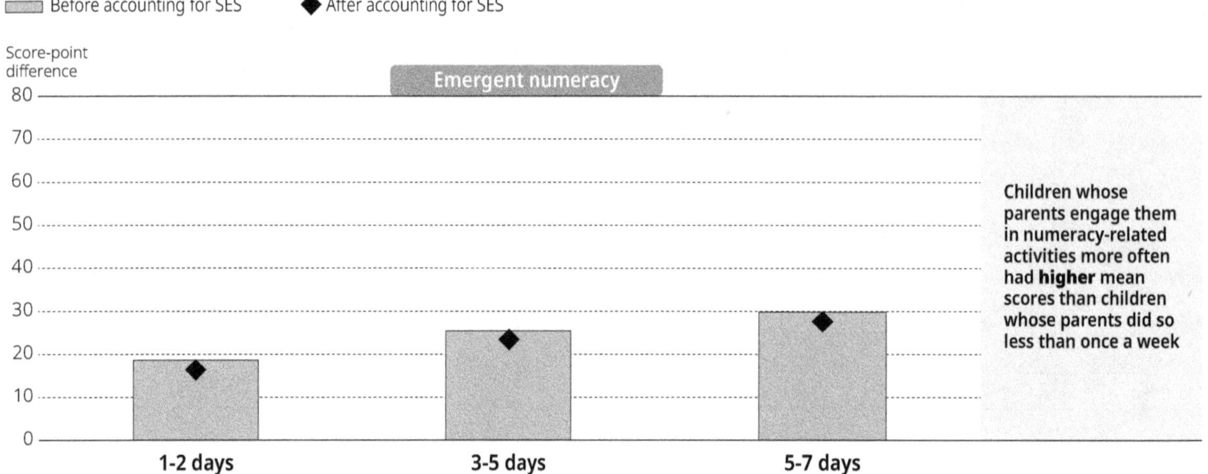

Note: All differences are statistically significant.

StatLink https://doi.org/10.1787/888934106553

Figure 3.21 **Emergent literacy and emergent numeracy by frequency of participation in special or paid activities outside the home, Estonia**

Score-point differences between children who never attend special or paid activities outside the home and those who do so with varying frequency, before and after accounting for socio-economic status

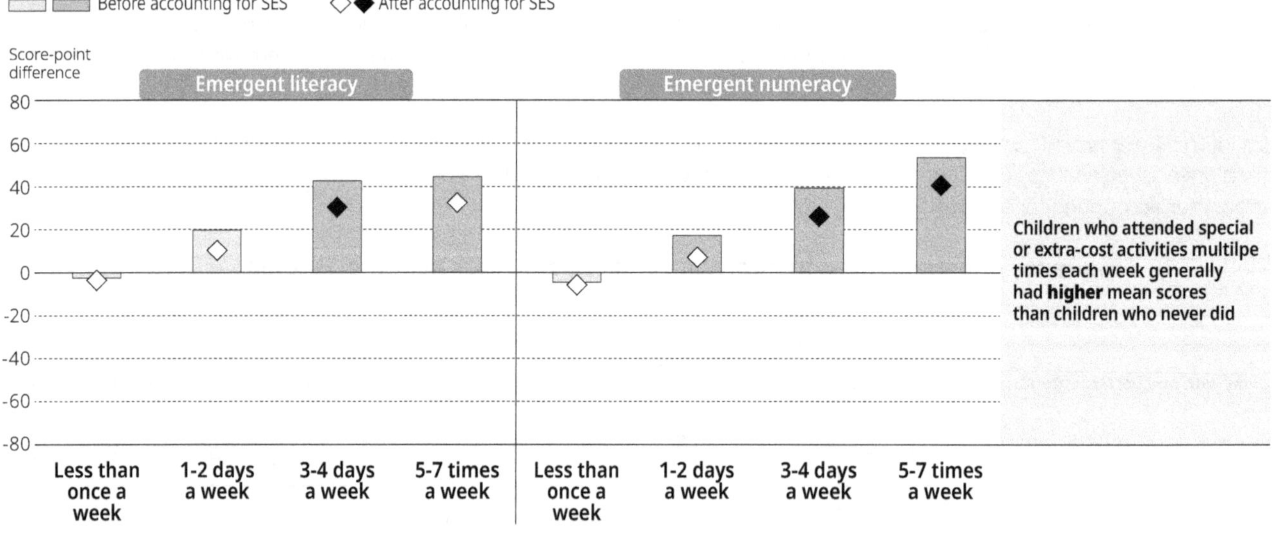

Note: Statistically significant differences are shown in a darker tone.

StatLink https://doi.org/10.1787/888934106572

Children whose parents are more strongly involved in preschool activities have higher scores, on average, than other children

In Estonia, 80% of five-year-olds had parents who were either moderately or strongly involved in their preschool institution (according to educators), a higher percentage than in England (69%) or the United States (65%). These children had a mean emergent literacy score that was significantly higher than the 20% of children whose educators indicated that their parents were not involved or were only slightly involved in the preschool institution, after accounting for socio-economic status. Similarly, children whose parents were more involved had a significantly higher mean emergent numeracy score than those whose parents were less involved, even after accounting for socio-economic status (Figure 3.22).

Figure 3.22 **Emergent literacy and emergent numeracy scores by parental involvement in preschool activities, Estonia**

Score-point differences between children whose parents are moderately or strongly involved in activities at preschool and those whose parents are slightly or not involved, according to their teachers, before and after accounting for socio-economic status

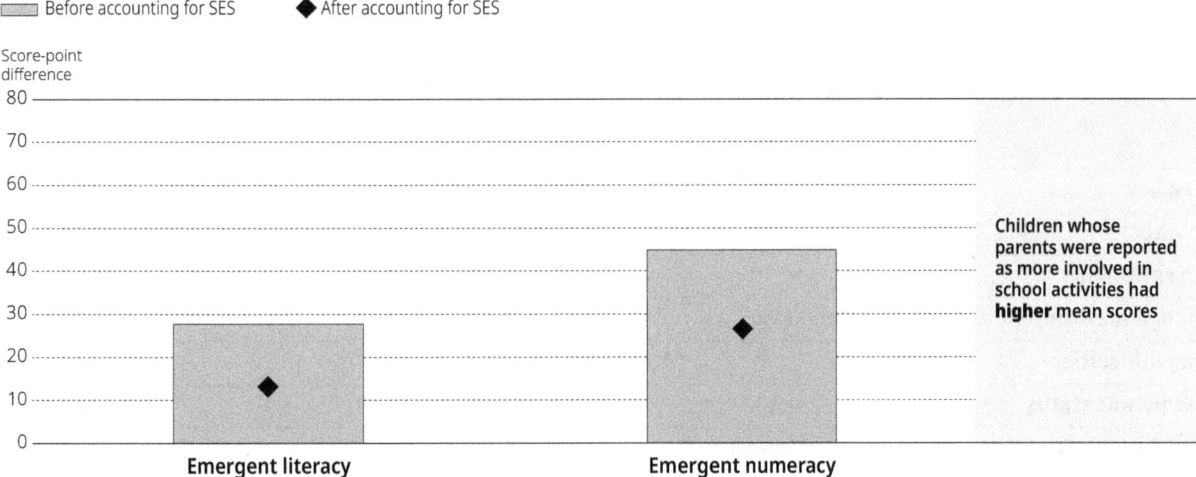

Note: All differences are statistically significant.

StatLink https://doi.org/10.1787/888934106591

The mean emergent literacy and emergent numeracy scores of children who never used digital devices are not significantly different from those of children who did use them, regardless of frequency of use

In Estonia, 39% of five-year-olds used a desktop or laptop computer, tablet device or smartphone every day, similar to the proportion in England and lower than the 49% in the United States. A further 39% used at least one of these devices at least once a week; 13% at least once a month, but not weekly; and 9% never or hardly used such devices. In Estonia, 4% used a digital device for educational activities five to seven days a week, 8% did so three to four days a week, 20% did so one to two days a week, 36% did so less than once a week, and 31% never did. The mean emergent literacy and emergent numeracy scores of children who never used devices were not significantly different from those of children who did, regardless of frequency (before or after accounting for socio-economic status). However, children who used digital devices every day had a significantly lower mean emergent literacy score than those children who used them at least once a week but not every day, after accounting for socio-economic status.

ASSESSING THE COMBINED EFFECTS OF CHILD AND FAMILY CHARACTERISTICS ON EMERGENT LITERACY AND EMERGENT NUMERACY SCORES

Analyses in this chapter have so far looked at relationships between emergent literacy and emergent numeracy outcomes and a series of background characteristics individually, or often after accounting for the effects of a third variable (such as socio-economic status). This section examines the effects of these characteristics in combination. In order to do this, variables that were significantly related to emergent literacy and emergent numeracy outcomes when examined individually were used in two regression models (one for emergent literacy and one for emergent numeracy) to assess how well they explained variation in the outcomes. It should be noted that no causal attribution can be made on the basis of these analyses. Variables that were not significant in the models were removed one at a time[10] until all remaining variables were significantly related to the outcome.

A range of individual characteristics and contextual factors significantly predict the emergent literacy scores of children in Estonia when examined in combination

Eight variables were significant predictors in the final model of emergent literacy in Estonia (Table 3.6). All else being equal, boys in Estonia had an emergent literacy scores that was 14 points lower than that of girls. Each month of increasing age was associated with an increase in emergent literacy scores of 5.4 points. Children with learning difficulties scored almost half a standard deviation lower (45 points) than other children, holding all other variables in the model constant. All else being equal, children from Estonian-speaking ECEC centres had a mean score that was 32 points lower than children from Russian-speaking centres. Children with at least one parent who spoke a language other than the language of the ECEC centre at home scored an average of 32 points lower than other children, all else being equal. Children whose parents read books to them five to seven times a week had a score that was 23 points higher than children whose parents did so less than once a week, holding all other variables in the model constant. A one standard deviation increase in socio-economic status was associated with an increase of 15 score points in emergent literacy. Children with more than 100 children's books at home had an advantage of 54 points, on average, over children with 10 children's books or fewer at home, all else being equal. The final model explains 15% of the variance in emergent literacy outcomes in Estonia.

Table 3.6 **Results of the multiple regression model of emergent literacy, Estonia**

Variable	B	SE	*p*
Child is a boy	-14.3	7.06	**.043**
Age (months)	5.4	0.85	**.000**
Russian speaking	31.5	10.47	**.003**
Home language different to assessment language	-31.9	12.44	**.010**
Learning difficulties	-45.0	13.33	**.001**
Socio-economic status	14.8	3.40	**.000**
Books in the home (reference category: 10 or fewer)			
11 to 25	26.2	9.49	**.006**
26 to 50	27.3	10.19	**.007**
51 to 100	44.9	10.96	**.000**
More than 100	54.4	14.09	**.000**
Frequency of being read to from a book (reference category: less than once a week/never)			
1-2 days a week	7.3	9.88	.463
3-4 days a week	4.6	9.97	.644
5-7 days a week	22.5	8.64	**.009**
Intercept	461.7	19.70	

Note: p-values in **bold** indicate statistical significance. B = regression coefficients. SE = Standard Error.
The intercept is the estimated score of a child in the reference category of each categorical variable, aged 5 years 0 months, and with a mean value for socio-economic status.

StatLink https://doi.org/10.1787/888934106610

A range of individual characteristics and contextual factors significantly predict the emergent numeracy scores of children in Estonia when examined in combination

Seven explanatory variables were significant in the final model of emergent numeracy (Table 3.7). Each month of increasing age was associated with an average increase of 6 points in emergent numeracy. All else being equal, children from Russian-speaking families had a mean emergent numeracy score that was 31 points higher than children from Estonian-speaking families. The gap between the scores of children with 10 or fewer children's books and those with more than 100 children's books at home was equivalent to 59 points on the emergent numeracy scale, all else being equal. A one standard deviation increase in socio-economic status was associated with an increase in the emergent numeracy score of 15 points. The frequency with which parents engaged in activities at home with the child involving numbers, counters, shapes or measuring was also a significant predictor of children's early numeracy outcomes. Children whose parents did so most frequently had a mean emergent numeracy score that was 30 points higher than those whose parents did so less frequently, after accounting for the effects of the other variables in the model. Finally, children whose parents were described as moderately or strongly involved in activities at the child's ECEC centre had a mean numeracy score that was 16 points higher than children whose parents were not involved or only slightly involved. The final model explains 19% of the variance in children's emergent numeracy outcomes in Estonia.

Table 3.7 **Results of the multiple regression model of emergent numeracy, Estonia**

Variable	B	SE	*p*
Age (months)	6.4	.84	**.000**
Russian-speaking	31.1	11.27	**.006**
Socio-economic status	15.4	3.89	**.000**
Learning difficulties	-49.3	10.35	**.000**
Books in the home (reference category: 10 or fewer)			
11 to 25	18.2	8.89	**.040**
26 to 50	28.2	8.29	**.001**
51 to 100	51.4	9.24	**.000**
More than 100	59.0	11.70	**.000**
Frequency of activities at home with numbers, counters, shapes, measuring (reference category: less than once a week/never)			
1-2 days a week	18.8	6.29	**.003**
3-4 days a week	25.7	7.62	**.001**
5-7 days a week	29.6	9.55	**.002**
Parent moderately/strongly involved in ECEC	15.8	6.28	**.012**
Intercept	405.5	10.90	

Note: p-values in **bold** indicate statistical significance. B = regression coefficient. SE = standard error.
The intercept is the estimated score of a child in the reference category of each categorical variable, aged 5 years 0 months, and with a mean value for socio-economic status.

StatLink https://doi.org/10.1787/888934106629

RELATIONSHIP BETWEEN EARLY LITERACY AND NUMERACY SCORES AND OUTCOMES IN OTHER LEARNING DOMAINS

Children's early language and numeracy skills are developing at the same time as children are developing a host of other skills, including self-regulation and a range of social-emotional competencies. Development in each of these areas is theorised to be mutually reinforcing. Young children with better language ability, for example, may be better able to engage successfully with their peers in interactions that support their prosocial development. Better prosocial skills may lead to further opportunities to interact with others in ways that support children's vocabulary development and oral comprehension. As IELS assessed a broad range of children's early learning outcomes, it enables relationships between these learning domains at the age of five to be examined.

Emergent literacy and emergent numeracy skills are strongly related to each other, as well as positively related to self-regulation skills and social-emotional skills

Figure 3.23 shows the correlations between emergent literacy scores and scores in other learning domains assessed in IELS in Estonia. Emergent literacy and emergent numeracy were strongly positively correlated ($r = .73$). Moderate to strong correlations were also observed between emergent literacy and the self-regulation skills of working memory and mental flexibility. Correlations between emergent literacy and most social-emotional skills were weaker, although still statistically significant and positive.

Emergent numeracy scores correlated most strongly with working memory, mental flexibility and emotion identification. Correlations between emergent numeracy and educator assessments of prosocial behaviour, non-disruptive behaviour and trust were weaker (Figure 3.24).

Figure 3.23 **Correlations between emergent literacy scores and other learning domains, Estonia**

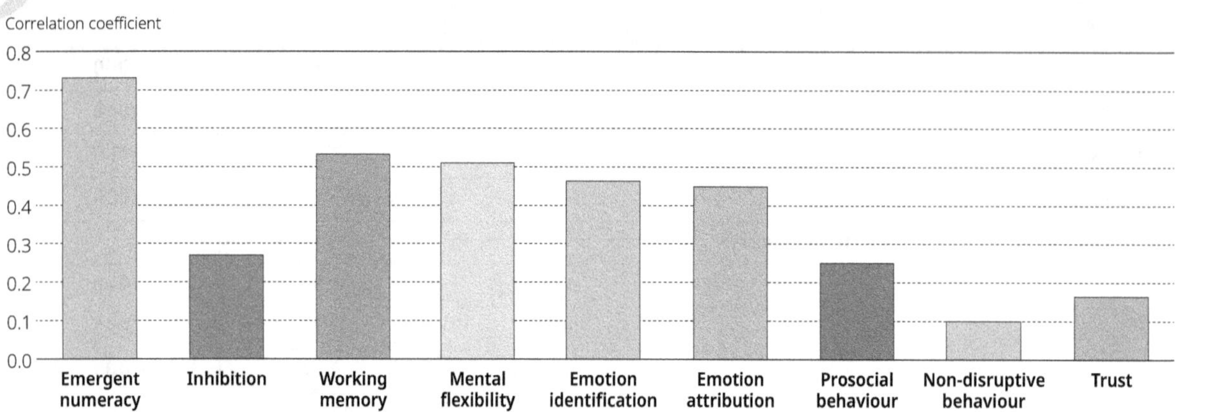

Note: All correlations are statistically significant.

StatLink https://doi.org/10.1787/888934106648

Figure 3.24 **Correlations between emergent numeracy scores and other learning domains, Estonia**

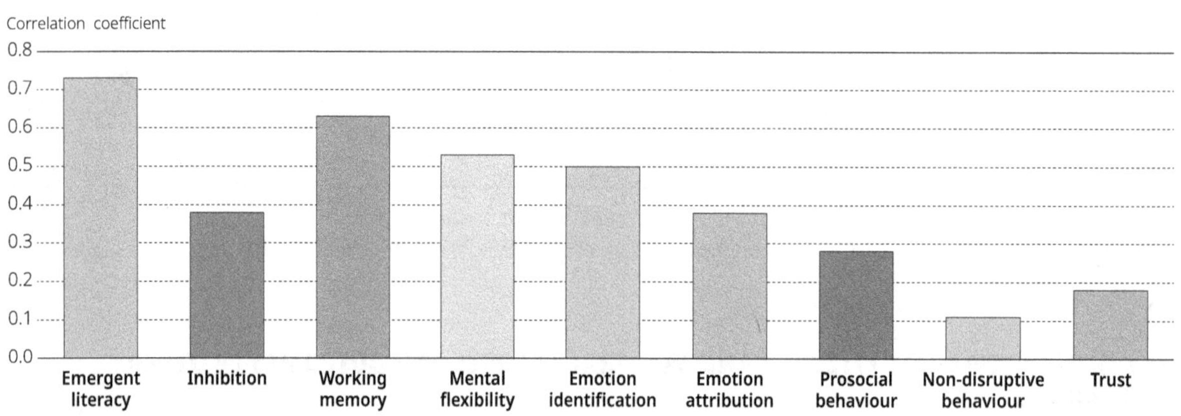

Note: All correlations are statistically significant.

StatLink https://doi.org/10.1787/888934106667

SUMMARY AND CONCLUSIONS

Five-year-old children in Estonia score at or close to the overall averages for emergent literacy and emergent numeracy in IELS

Overall, children in Estonia had mean emergent literacy and emergent numeracy skills that were close to the overall IELS averages. In emergent literacy, five-year-olds in Estonia had a mean score that was similar to the mean of children in England and significantly higher than the mean of children in the United States. In emergent numeracy, the mean score of children in Estonia was significantly higher than that of children in the United States, and significantly lower than that of children in England.

Russian-speaking children, especially girls, have better early literacy and numeracy outcomes than Estonian-speaking children

Russian-speaking children in Estonia had significantly higher mean scores than Estonian-speaking children in both emergent literacy and emergent numeracy, despite being of lower socio-economic status, on average.

In Estonia there was an overall gender gap in favour of girls in emergent literacy, but no equivalent gap for emergent numeracy. This is in line with the patterns in England and the United States. Looking at children from Estonian and Russian language backgrounds separately, however, revealed that the gap was only significant among Russian-speaking children: Estonian-speaking boys and girls had similar emergent literacy outcomes. While there was no significant difference in the mean emergent numeracy scores of Estonian-speaking boys and girls, Russian-speaking girls had a significantly higher mean emergent numeracy score than Russian-speaking boys.

Children who have experienced difficulties before the age of five have lower literacy and numeracy skills at age five

Children with learning difficulties and social, emotional or behavioural difficulties had significantly lower mean literacy and numeracy scores than children who did not. However, when all difficulties were examined in combination, only learning difficulties remained significantly associated with lower emergent literacy and emergent numeracy scores. Roughly similar proportions of children in Estonia were identified by their parents as having had low birth weight or premature birth, learning difficulties, and social, emotional or behavioural difficulties as children in England and the United States. As in those other countries, boys were significantly more likely to have learning difficulties and social, emotional or behavioural difficulties than girls. Children in the bottom SES quartile were also significantly more likely to experience these challenges, but there was no significant association with whether the child was Estonian-speaking or Russian-speaking.

Relationships between early literacy and numeracy outcomes and socio-economic background are weaker in Estonia than in either England or the United States

Score-point gaps between children in the top and bottom SES quartiles in Estonia were considerably smaller than those in England and the United States. Children with a home language other than the assessment language had similar emergent numeracy scores to other children, but had lower emergent literacy scores.

A higher proportion of children in Estonia had mothers with a bachelor's degree or higher than in either England or the United States. Children whose mothers had obtained degrees had better emergent literacy and emergent numeracy outcomes than other children, even after accounting for household income.

A child's home learning environment is related to their emergent literacy and emergent numeracy scores

The frequency with which children were read to by their parents was significantly related to their emergent literacy skills, even after accounting for SES. Children from low-SES backgrounds were less likely to have parents who read to them frequently, sang songs to them frequently and had back-and-forth conversations with them frequently. Children who attended special, extra-cost activities (such as sport, dance lessons, scouts) more frequently had higher mean scores in emergent literacy and emergent numeracy than those who never did, after accounting for socio-economic status.

In Estonia, a higher proportion of parents was described as being strongly or moderately involved in their children's education than in either England or the United States. Children whose parents were more involved had higher mean emergent literacy and emergent numeracy scores than children whose parents were less involved, even after accounting for socio-economic status.

Children who never used digital devices at home did not differ significantly in their mean emergent literacy and emergent numeracy scores from children who did so, regardless of the frequency with which they were used. However, children who used digital devices every day had a significantly lower mean literacy score than those children who used them at least once a week but not every day, after accounting for socio-economic status.

A range of individual characteristics and contextual factors predict children's emergent literacy and emergent numeracy outcomes in Estonia when examined in combination

There were several factors that when analysed in combination were found to be significant predictors of five year olds' emergent literacy scores in Estonia. These were: gender, whether the child is Estonian-speaking or Russian speaking, having at least one parent at home who speaks a language other than the assessment language, learning difficulties, socio-economic status, age, number of children's books at home, and frequency of being read to from a book.

There were also several factors that when analysed in combination were found to be significant predictors of five year olds' emergent numeracy scores in Estonia. These were: whether the child is Estonian-speaking or Russian speaking, socio-economic status, age, number of children's books at home, frequency of activities at home involving numbers, counters, shapes or measuring, learning difficulties, and level of parental involvement in activities at the ECEC centre.

Whether the child is Estonian-speaking or Russian-speaking, the child's age, socio-economic status, learning difficulties, and number of children's books at home were significant predictors in the final models of both emergent literacy and emergent numeracy. Having a language other than the assessment language at home, gender, and the frequency of being read to from a book were significant only in the emergent literacy model, while level of parental involvement at the ECEC centre and the frequency of engaging in activities at home involving numbers, counters, shapes or measuring were only significant in the model of emergent numeracy.

Early learning outcomes in Estonia are interrelated

Five-year-olds' emergent literacy and emergent numeracy scores in Estonia were also positively related to their social-emotional scores and their self-regulation scores, in line with previous research that suggests that these skills are mutually reinforcing. The scores in these other learning domains of five-year-olds in Estonia are described in the following two chapters.

References

Beck, I., M. McKeown and **L. Kucan** (2013), *Bringing words to life : robust vocabulary instruction*, The Guilford Press. [10]

Duncan, G. et al. (2007), "School Readiness and Later Achievement", *Psychological Association*, Vol. 43/6, pp. 1428-1446, http://dx.doi.org/10.1037/[0012-1649.43.6.1428].supp. [1]

Kautz, T. et al. (2014), "Fostering and measuring skills: Improving cognitive and non-cognitive skills to promote lifetime success", *NBER Working Paper Series*, No. 20749, National Bureau of Economic Research, Cambridge, MA, http://dx.doi.org/10.3386/w20749. [4]

OECD (2019), *PISA 2018 Results (Volume I): What Students Know and Can Do*, PISA, OECD Publishing, Paris, https://dx.doi.org/10.1787/5f07c754-en. [2]

OECD (2016), *Skills Matter: Further Results from the Survey of Adult Skills*, OECD Skills Studies, OECD Publishing, Paris, https://dx.doi.org/10.1787/9789264258051-en. [7]

OECD (2013), *OECD Skills Outlook 2013: First Results from the Survey of Adult Skills*, OECD Publishing, Paris, https://dx.doi.org/10.1787/9789264204256-en. [3]

Raghubar, K. and **M. Barnes** (2017), "Early numeracy skills in preschool-aged children: A review of neurocognitive findings and implications for assessment and intervention", *Clinical Neuropsychology*, Vol. 31/2, pp. 329-351, http://dx.doi.org/10.1080/13854046.2016.1259387. [8]

Rigney, D. (2010), *The Matthew Effect: How Advantage Begets Further Advantage*, Columbia University Press. [5]

Ritchie, S. and **T. Bates** (2013), "Enduring links from childhood mathematics and reading achievement to adult socioeconomic status", *Psychological Science*, Vol. 24/7, pp. 1301-1308, http://dx.doi.org/10.1177/0956797612466268. [6]

Snow, C. and **T. Matthews** (2016), *Reading and Language in the Early Grades*, http://www.futureofchildren.org (accessed on 5 December 2019). [9]

Notes

1. Scoring at or below proficiency level 1 in the Programme for International Student Assessment (PISA) reading.
2. Scoring at or below proficiency level 1 in the Programme for the International Assessment of Adult Competencies (PIAAC) reading.
3. Scoring at or below proficiency level 1 in PIAAC numeracy.
4. Beck, McKeown and Kucan (2013[10]) propose a three-tier model of vocabulary development, where Tier 1 words are common words used in everyday speech (e.g. table, blue), Tier 2 words are high-frequency words that occur across contexts and are more common in written than spoken language (e.g. compare, coincidence). Tier 3 words are low-frequency words used in domain-specific contexts (e.g. thesis, ecosystem).
5. For more information, see the IELS assessment framework (OECD, 2020).
6. Where educational attainment information was available for two parents, the higher of the two was used.
7. While small numbers of children in the sample were aged 4 years 11 months or 6 years 1 month at the time of the assessment, there were too few to meet criteria for reporting and so their mean scores are not considered in this analysis.
8. There were too few children aged 5 years 0 months in the United States to reliably estimate their mean scores. Therefore, when comparing the size of score-point differences between older and younger children across all three participating countries, 5 years 1 month is the youngest age for which these comparisons can reliably be made.
9. A birth weight lower than 2.5 kg was defined as low.
10. In order of descending p-value.

Children's self-regulation skills in Estonia

This chapter presents findings on the self-regulation outcomes of five-year-olds in Estonia. It describes how children's scores in inhibition, mental flexibility and working memory relate to their individual characteristics, family backgrounds and home learning environments.

THE IMPORTANCE OF SELF-REGULATION DEVELOPMENT

Self-regulation describes the mental processes that allow individuals to focus attention, remember instructions and handle multiple tasks successfully. These skills allow the brain to filter out distractions, prioritise tasks and control impulses. The ability to regulate and manage reactions and impulses is essential for personal and professional success (Diamond, 2013[1]; Eisenberg, Spinrad and Eggum, 2010[2]; McClelland et al., 2015[3]).

The brain functions that make up self-regulation include the capacity to use inhibition, mental flexibility and working memory – among other skills – to manage thoughts and actions (Zelazo, Blair and Willoughby, 2016[4]). Together, these three skills are referred to as executive function. They describe the ability to inhibit impulse responses, direct and sustain short-term attention, revise initial plans and retrieve rules from memory.

Self-regulation is a strong predictor of later health, education and labour-market outcomes

The development of self-regulation skills in early childhood is associated with a wide range of outcomes later in life. These include facilitating the transition into – and success in – school (Blair and Raver, 2015[5]; Mcclelland et al., 2007[6]; Morrison, Cameron and Mcclelland, 2010[7]), higher academic achievement in adolescence, better labour-market outcomes as adults – including on employment and earnings – and better health outcomes (Duckworth, Quinn and Tsukayama, 2012[8]; Tangney, Baumeister and Boone, 2004[9]).

Self-regulation skills are important for a child's transition to and participation in school (Blair and Peters Razza, 2007[10]; Neuenschwander et al., 2012[11]). Starting school is a time of major change in the physical surroundings and people – including both new peers and educators – that children are accustomed to. It also presents a new set of learning expectations and routines to follow (Dockett, 2001[12]). Children must manage competing stimuli to navigate classroom activities. Self-regulation skills facilitate the learning of new concepts and allow children to engage successfully in classroom activities. These skills also allow them to interact productively with their teachers and peers while managing their own responses (Shonkoff, Phillips and Council, 2000[13]).

A child's ability to self-regulate is associated with the development of social-emotional, literacy and numeracy skills (Blair and Peters Razza, 2007[10]). For example, working memory (Raghubar, Barnes and Hecht, 2010[14]), inhibition and mental flexibility (Clark, Pritchard and Woodward, 2010[15]) are associated with the development of pre-arithmetic, simple and more complex mathematical skills. These skills allow children to better integrate information they receive in the classroom, and play an important role in academic achievement through late childhood and adolescence (Best, Miller and Naglieri, 2011[16]; Duncan et al., 2007[17]).

Children with more developed self-regulation skills in childhood also demonstrate better long-term health outcomes (Caspi et al., 1998[18]; Daly et al., 2015[19]; Moffitt et al., 2011[20]). This includes lower rates of obesity in adolescence (Evans, Fuller-Rowell and Doan, 2012[21]) and lower levels of anxiety and depression (Blair and Peters Razza, 2007[10]; Buckner, Mezzacappa and Beardslee, 2009[22]). Children and adolescents with more developed self-regulation skills are also less likely to use drugs or receive a criminal conviction (Ayduk et al., 2000[23]; Caspi et al., 1998[18]; Duckworth, Tsukayama and May, 2010[24]; Moffitt et al., 2011[20]).

Children's environments are associated with their development of self-regulation skills

A combination of genetic and environmental factors shape self-regulation skills (Bridgett et al., 2015[25]; McClelland et al., 2015[3]). Children exposed to poverty, low economic status, abuse or neglect in their home environment are more likely to display deficits in their self-regulation skills than children living in more enabling environments (Noble, Norman and Farah, 2005[26]; Raver, Blair and Willoughby, 2013[27]).

Difficult childhood experiences and toxic stress can significantly impair the self-regulation development of children. Exposure to adverse home environments can limit their opportunities to develop self-regulation skills. Negative early experiences, including multiple and chronic environmental stressors, can cause structural changes in the neural connections of the areas of the brain that control self-regulation (Nelson et al., 2007[28]; McEwen, Nasca and Gray, 2016[29]). Children exposed to cumulative risks are also more likely to have parents who do not provide them with opportunities to practice their self-regulation skills (Wachs, Gurkas and Kontos, 2004[30]; Fuller et al., 2010[31]).

Disparities in socio-economic background are associated with differences in the physical structure and functioning of the parts of the brain that control self-regulation (Hackman and Farah, 2009[32]). The functioning of the prefrontal cortex in children from low socio-economic status backgrounds who are exposed to chronic environmental stressors, for example, is similar to that of individuals with damage to the prefrontal cortex (Kishiyama et al., 2009[33]).

Emotionally positive parenting, an encouraging home environment and high-quality early childhood education and care experiences enable the development of self-regulation skills

Self-regulation skills are malleable. While adverse childhood experiences and toxic stress impede the development of self-regulation skills, positive home environments and early childhood education and care (ECEC) experiences promote these skills.

Emotionally positive parent-child relationships contribute to self-regulation skills across the early years. Parenting styles that include clear and consistent rules and expectations encourage the positive development of self-regulation skills (Blair and Raver, 2012[34]). For example, parenting styles that focus on child autonomy within set limits predict stronger self-regulation in children compared to parenting styles focused on compliance (Bernier, Carlson and Whipple, 2010[35]).

Organised and predictable home environments provide children with a context to develop their self-regulation skills (McClelland et al., 2018[36]). Interactions between children and their parents and caregivers facilitate the regulation of emotions and behaviour. These interactions help children understand their emotions and express them more productively. This, in turn, allows children to regulate their responses to distracting stimuli in their environment (Heatherton and Wagner, 2011[37]).

As with the home environment, structured and predictable environments in ECEC centres are important for children's self-regulation, engagement and academic outcomes (Ponitz et al., 2009[38]). High-quality ECEC environments enable children to develop self-regulation skills. Examples of high-quality ECEC include stimulating learning environments and positive interactions with teachers and peers.

The International Early Learning and Child Well-being Study (IELS) defines self-regulation skills as inhibition, mental flexibility and working memory

Although the precise definition of which skills and processes make up self-regulation varies across studies and disciplines (Booth, Hennessy and Doyle, 2018[39]), self-regulation skills are highly integrated and influence one another (Anderson and Reidy, 2012[40]). Completing everyday tasks requires adequate development in all of the interdependent parts.

A large body of literature has emphasised a number of key self-regulation skills (Diamond and Lee, 2011[41]; Garon, Bryson and Smith, 2008[42]). These have mostly centred on the influence of inhibition, mental flexibility and working memory skills on later outcomes (McClelland et al., 2010[43]). These three skills together are often referred to as executive function. Executive function skills make up the cognitive component of self-regulation.[1] Accordingly, IELS defines self-regulation in the direct assessment as: 1) inhibition – the ability to control impulses and reactions; 2) mental flexibility – the ability to shift between rules according to changing circumstances; and 3) working memory – the ability to retain and process information (Figure 4.1).

Figure 4.1 **The three key components of self-regulation**

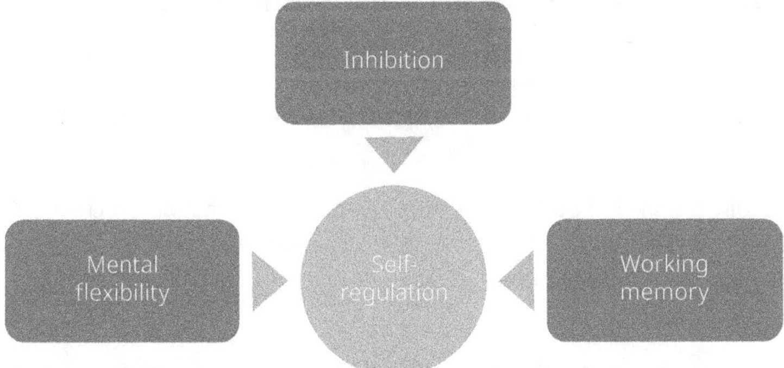

IELS measures self-regulation outcomes through developmentally appropriate and engaging activities

The IELS assessment explores how children's early learning experiences – including their individual characteristics, home learning environment, and their families' socio-economic contexts – relate to their self-regulation development. Each of the skills that make up self-regulation in IELS were measured using a single task, which was made up of a number of different items. There was, therefore, a separate task to measure inhibition, mental flexibility and working memory (Table 4.1). Audio and engaging illustrations guided the children through activities on a tablet under the supervision of a study administrator.

Table 4.1 **The three skills assessed in the self-regulation domain**

Content component	Description	Assessment task
Inhibition	Ability to resist impulsive responses based on new information	Stop/go task
Mental flexibility	Ability to shift between rules according to changing circumstances or to apply different rules in different settings	Switching task
Working memory	Ability to store information and manipulate it to complete a given task	Odd-one-out task

Inhibition

The inhibition activity assessed a child's ability to inhibit a learned response in favour of an alternative response. The assessment introduced the child to an image and asked them to touch a button on the screen whenever this image appeared. It then introduced the child to a visually similar image and asked them to touch a different button whenever the new image appeared. Their ability to touch the different button whenever each different image appeared reflected their ability to inhibit their learned response. In sum, the task required the child to respond differently to each of two similar images, presented one after another in a pre-determined but unpredictable sequence.

Mental flexibility

The mental flexibility activity assessed a child's ability to respond to rules that changed during the activity. The assessment introduced the child to two distinct animals and asked them to touch a different shape on the screen depending on which animal appeared. The assessment then introduced a new rule where the child was asked to touch the alternative shape when each animal appeared. Their ability to adapt to the new inverse rule indicated their mental flexibility.

Working memory

The working memory activity assessed a child's ability to recall short visual sequences. The child was introduced to a visually distinct zebra placed in one of three rows on a bus. The other two rows on the bus were occupied by other animals. The child was then asked to remember in which of the three rows the zebra was seated and touch the corresponding row in a following image. The assessment was divided into several sections of increasing levels of difficulty involving more rows to remember. If the child did not complete the higher difficulty tasks, the assessment automatically proceeded to the next section.

IELS assesses how children's self-regulation abilities relate to their individual characteristics, family backgrounds and home learning environments

This chapter presents the outcomes of the IELS assessments of the inhibition, mental flexibility and working memory outcomes of children in Estonia. The chapter details how children's self-regulation outcomes relate to their individual characteristics, family backgrounds and home learning environments.

The self-regulation outcomes of children were measured directly through the assessments. Indirect information on children's self-regulation development was also collected through questionnaires administered to children's parents and educators. Parents and educators were asked to assess each child's overall self-regulation development, defined as whether the child was attentive, organised or in control of their actions.

The chapter presents the results of both the direct assessment of children's inhibition, mental flexibility, and working memory outcomes, as well as how parents and educators perceived children's overall self-regulation development. It highlights similarities and differences between outcomes in Estonia and those in England and the United States.

SELF-REGULATION SKILLS OF FIVE-YEAR-OLDS IN ESTONIA

On average, the self-regulation skills of children in Estonia are above the overall mean of participating countries

On average, five-year-olds in Estonia were about 20 points above the overall mean of participating countries (500 IELS points) on inhibition (520), 11 points above on mental flexibility (511) and 21 points above on working memory (521).

Average inhibition outcomes in Estonia were about equal to those in the United States and significantly higher than those in England. Average mental flexibility and working memory outcomes in Estonia were about equal to those in England and significantly higher than those in the United States.

The spread between the outcomes of the bottom quartile and those of the top quartile of children in Estonia was greater for mental flexibility (141 points) than for inhibition (130 points) or working memory (128 points). The spread in mental flexibility outcomes was also greater in Estonia than in the United States, meaning that the difference in outcomes between the top and bottom quartiles in Estonia was greater than in the United States. The spread in working memory outcomes was greater in Estonia than in England, meaning that the differences in outcomes between the top and bottom quartiles in Estonia are greater than in England. The spread in inhibition outcomes was about the same across the three countries.

The distribution of inhibition and working memory outcomes in Estonia was generally to the right of the overall mean of participating countries, reflecting Estonia's higher average outcomes on inhibition and working memory at age five (Figure 4.2). There was greater distribution in the mental flexibility outcomes. The lower tail of the distribution was smaller than the upper tail, which results in an average score above the overall mean.

Figure 4.2 **Distribution of self-regulation scores, Estonia**

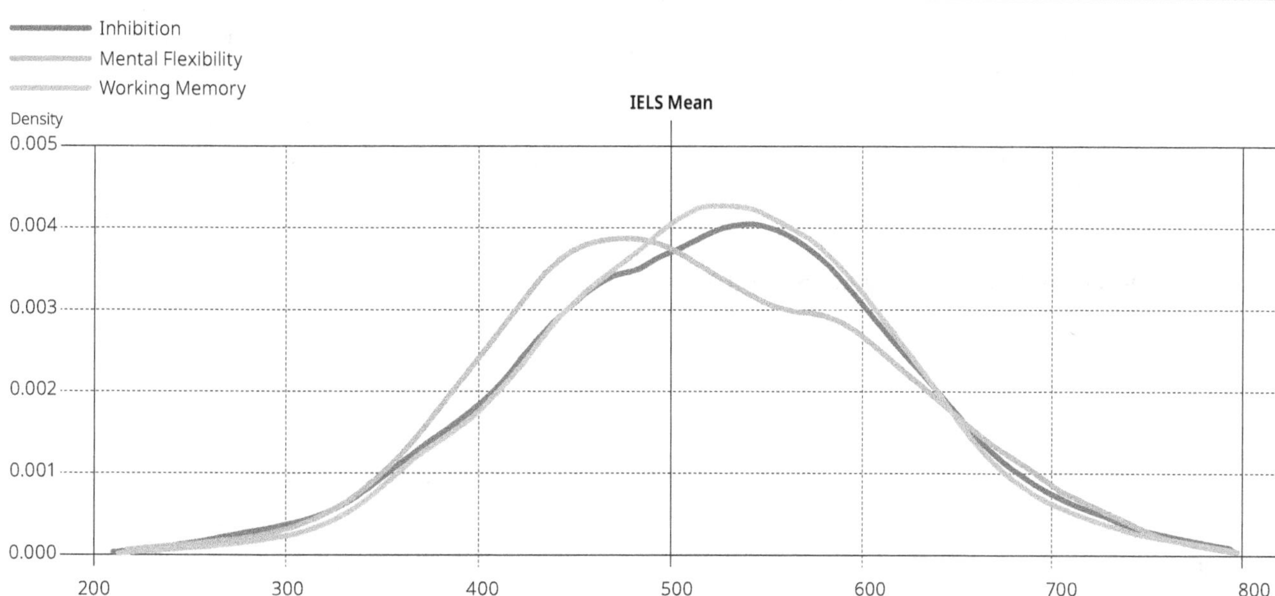

Note: Distributions produced using the first plausible value only.

Parents in Estonia are less likely than educators to report that their child, or the child they teach, is developing below average self-regulation skills

Parents and educators were asked to comment on a child's overall self-regulation development (e.g. attentiveness, organisation, in control of actions), which differed from self-regulation sub-domains measured by the IELS direct assessments of children. Parents in Estonia were about as likely as educators to report that their child, or the child they teach, was developing above average self-regulation skills. However, they were significantly less likely to rate their child as developing below average self-regulation skills: about 12% of parents compared to about 19% of educators (Figure 4.3).

This may be partly due to children behaving differently in a home environment than they would in an ECEC environment. Educators may also have more experience assessing the level of development of a child as they have access to a bigger group of children to provide a comparison, among other factors.

Figure 4.3 **Self-regulation development as reported by parents and educators, Estonia**

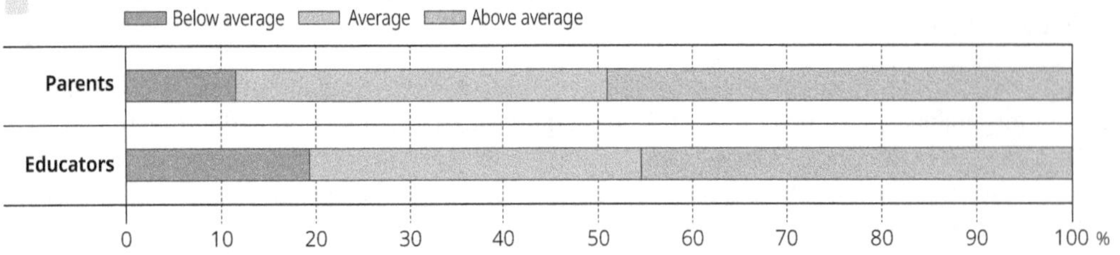

StatLink https://doi.org/10.1787/888934106686

INDIVIDUAL CHARACTERISTICS AND SELF-REGULATION SKILLS

Girls have higher self-regulation outcomes than boys

A child's individual characteristics are associated with their early learning outcomes. The self-regulation outcomes of girls were significantly higher than those of boys in Estonia. The gender gap was a statistically significant 24 IELS points on inhibition outcomes, 23 IELS points on mental flexibility outcomes and 12 IELS points on working memory outcomes (Figure 4.4). This gender difference in outcomes is consistent with the pattern observed for emergent literacy and numeracy skills, as well as the perceptions of parents and educators.

In the United States there were also significant gaps in the inhibition and working memory outcomes of girls and boys, although no differences in their mental flexibility outcomes. In England, the gender gap on inhibition outcomes was reversed, with the outcomes of boys in England higher than those of girls. There were no differences in the outcomes of boys and girls on mental flexibility and working memory.

Figure 4.4 **Self-regulation scores by gender, Estonia**

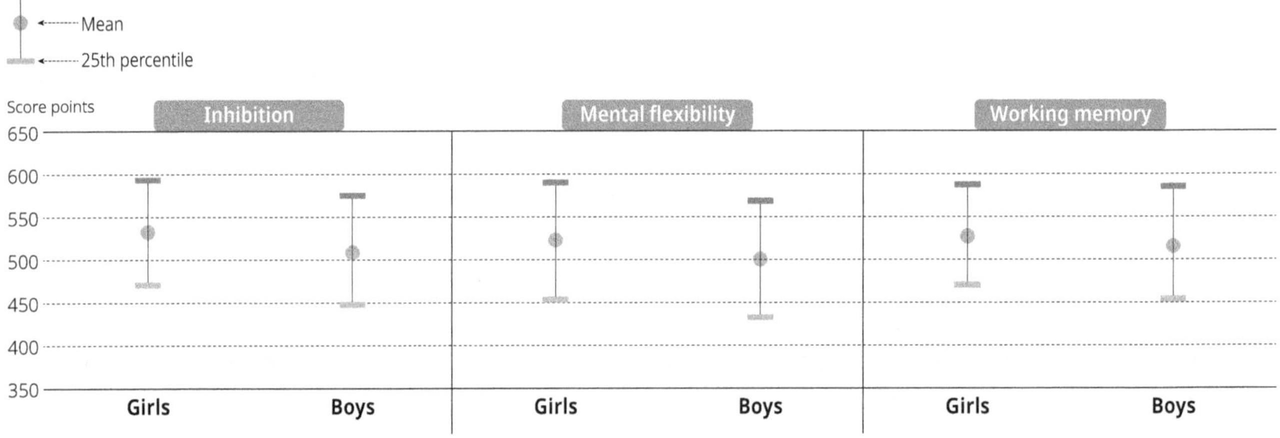

Note: Differences are statistically significant, except for working memory scores at the 75th percentile

StatLink https://doi.org/10.1787/888934106705

Parents and educators perceive girls as more likely than boys to have developed above average self-regulation skills

When asked to report on how they perceived children's overall self-regulation development, both parents and educators in Estonia were, on average, more likely to report girls rather than boys as developing above average skills. Educators perceived about 56% of girls as developing above average skills compared to 35% of boys (Figure 4.5).

Educators and parents also perceived boys as more likely to be developing below average self-regulation skills, with educators perceiving about 28% of boys and 11% of girls as developing below average self-regulation skills. The gender gap in parent and educator reports of self-regulation development was consistent with the outcomes of the direct assessment, where the inhibition, mental flexibility and working memory outcomes of girls were higher than those of boys.

Figure 4.5 **Self-regulation development as reported by parents and educators by gender, Estonia**

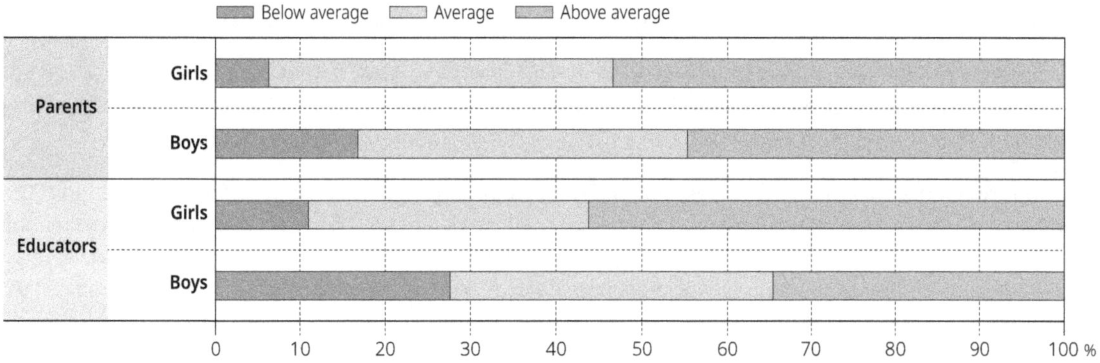

StatLink https://doi.org/10.1787/888934106724

A child's self-regulation outcomes increase with every month between their fifth and sixth birthday

Children's self-regulation skills develop as they grow older. Between the ages of five and six, the average inhibition outcomes of children in Estonia increased by 69 IELS points, their mental flexibility outcomes by 55 points and their working memory outcomes by 86 points (Figure 4.6). By the age of five years four months, the average self-regulation skills of children in Estonia were higher than the overall mean of participating countries for each of the assessed skills.

The average difference in the inhibition and mental flexibility outcomes of children between the ages of five years one month and six years were similar across the three countries participating in IELS. The average difference working memory outcomes in that year of growth were similar in both England and the United States, but significantly lower in Estonia.

Figure 4.6 **Self-regulation scores by age of child in months, Estonia**

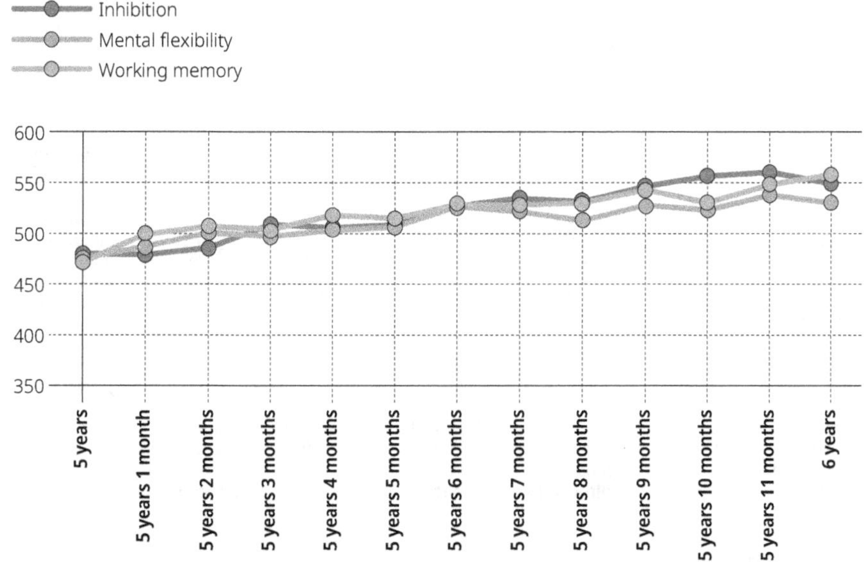

StatLink https://doi.org/10.1787/888934106743

Children who had experienced low birth weight or premature birth, learning difficulties, or social, emotional or behavioural difficulties have lower average self-regulation outcomes than those who had not

IELS asked parents to indicate whether their child had ever experienced a number of potential difficulties that might affect their early learning outcomes. Results indicated that experiencing low birth weight[2] or premature birth, learning difficulties, or social, emotional or behavioural difficulties early in life was negatively related to a child's self-regulation skills at age five.

The inhibition and mental flexibility scores of children who experienced low birth weight or premature birth were lower than those of other children. The inhibition outcomes of children with low birth weight or premature birth were 39 points lower than those of other children, after accounting for socio-economic status and the experience of the other early difficulties (Figure 4.7).

The difference in mental flexibility outcomes was about 27 points. There was no significant difference in the working memory outcomes of children who experienced low birth weight or premature birth and those who did not. The self-regulation outcomes of both girls and boys in Estonia were associated with having experienced low birth weight or premature birth.

The self-regulation outcomes of children who had experienced learning difficulties were lower than those of children who had not experienced such difficulties: 30 points lower on inhibition, 34 points lower on mental flexibility and 29 points lower on working memory, after accounting for socio-economic status and the experience of the other early difficulties (Figure 4.7).

The association of having experienced learning difficulties with self-regulation outcomes was different for boys and girls. The outcomes of girls who had experienced learning difficulties were similar to those of girls who had not. The inhibition and mental flexibility outcomes of boys whose parents identified as having experienced learning difficulties were significantly lower than those of boys whose parents did not after accounting for socio-economic status and the experience of the other early difficulties.

Experiencing social, emotional or behavioural difficulties also had a negative association with mental flexibility and working memory outcomes. The outcomes of children who had experienced such difficulties were 29 points lower on mental flexibility and 36 points lower on working memory than the outcomes of children who had not after accounting for socio-economic status and the experience of the other early difficulties (Figure 4.7).

As with learning difficulties, the gender of the child who had experienced social, emotional or behavioural difficulties also influenced their self-regulation outcomes. There were no differences in the outcomes of girls who had experienced social, emotional or behavioural difficulties and those who had not across the three self-regulation domains. The mental flexibility and working memory outcomes of boys who had experienced social, emotional or behavioural difficulties were lower than those of boys who had not.

Figure 4.7 **Relative associations between early difficulties and self-regulation scores, Estonia**

Score-point differences between children who had and had not experienced early difficulties, after accounting for the effects of other early difficulties, and before and after accounting for socio-economic status

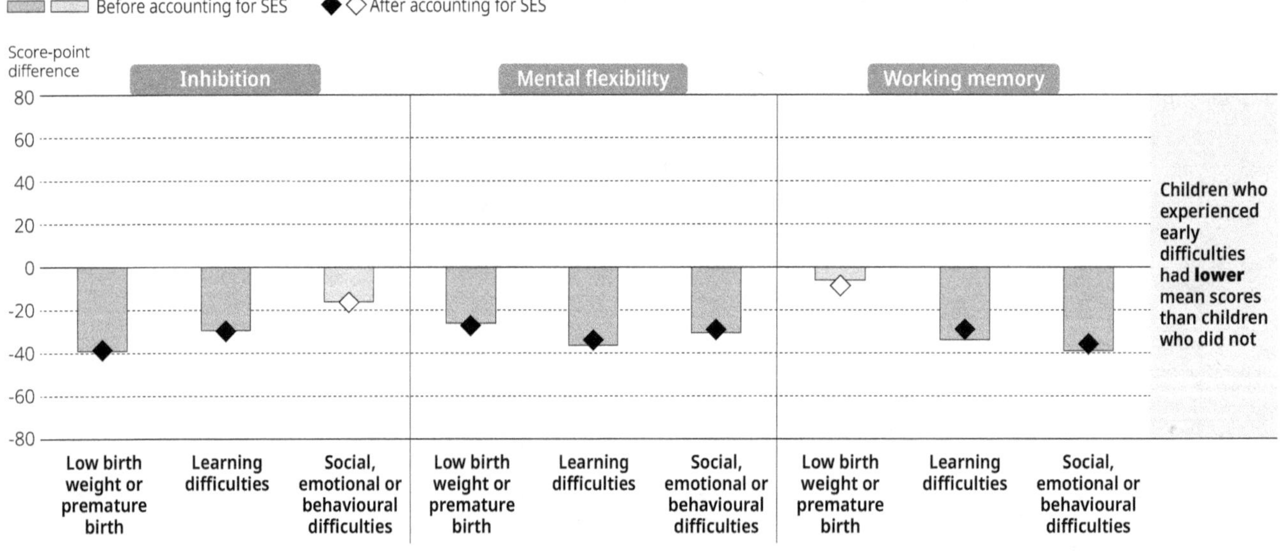

Note: Statistically significant differences are shown in a darker tone.

StatLink https://doi.org/10.1787/888934106762

HOME AND FAMILY CHARACTERISTICS AND SELF-REGULATION SKILLS

A child's parents play an important role in all of aspects of their upbringing, from the context of their home environment to their activities outside the home. The home environment that a child grows up in and their interactions with their parents and environment shape a child's early learning experiences and opportunities.

Family background and socio-economic status were positively associated with a child's self-regulation development. The combination of household income, parental occupation and parental educational completion – that together create the socio-economic index applied in this study – interact with a child's individual characteristics to influence the development of their self-regulation skills. The children of parents with higher levels of education exhibit higher self-regulation skills. Families with higher economic resources are able to spend more money on early learning activities and materials for their children.

Children's working memory outcomes increase with the socio-economic status of their family

The relationship between socio-economic status and self-regulation skills in Estonia, however, was less pronounced than in the other two countries that participated in the study. The socio-economic status of a child's family in Estonia, for example, had no significant association with the inhibition and mental flexibility outcomes of five-year-old children (Figure 4.8).

The socio-economic status of children's families, however, was significantly related to children's working memory outcomes. The outcomes of children in Estonia from families in the lowest quartile of socio-economic status were, on average, 46 points below those of children in the most advantaged quartile (Figure 4.8). There was no difference in the association of socio-economic status with self-regulation outcomes for boys and girls.

Figure 4.8 **Working memory scores by socio-economic quartile, Estonia**

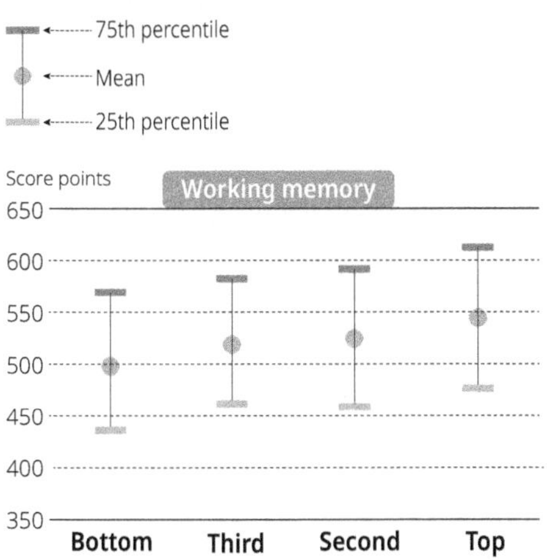

StatLink https://doi.org/10.1787/888934106781

Parents and educators are more likely to report a child as developing above average self-regulation skills if they are from a family in a higher socio-economic quartile

Both parents and educators were more likely to perceive a child from a family in the top quartile of socio-economic status as developing above average self-regulation skills than a child in the bottom quartile (Figure 4.9). They also perceived children from families in the top quartile as less likely to be developing below average self-regulation skills than a child in the bottom quartile.

Figure 4.9 **Self-regulation development as reported by parents and educators by socio-economic quartile, Estonia**

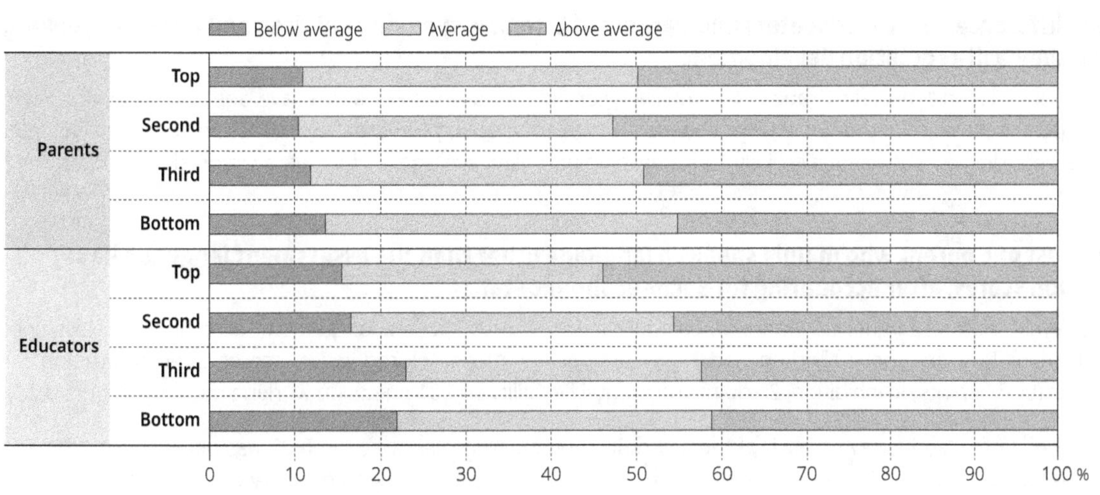

StatLink https://doi.org/10.1787/888934106800

Parents and educators reported fewer differences in self-regulation development between children from families in the second, third and top quartiles, and reported children in those quartiles as about equally likely to be developing both above and below average self-regulation skills. Educators perceived children from families in the second and top quartiles as the groups least likely to be developing below average skills.

The working memory outcomes of Russian-speaking children are higher than those of Estonian-speaking children, after accounting for socio-economic status

The working memory outcomes of Russian-speaking children were significantly higher than those of their Estonian-speaking peers (by about 16 points), after accounting for socio-economic status (Figure 4.10). There were no significant differences in inhibition and mental flexibility outcomes.

There were larger differences in the outcomes of girls than boys based on the child's language. Russian-speaking girls scored 22 points higher on inhibition and 32 points higher on working memory than Estonian-speaking girls after accounting for socio-economic status. There were no significant differences in the outcomes of boys.

Figure 4.10 **Working memory scores by child language, Estonia**

Score-point differences between Russian-speaking children and Estonian-speaking children, before and after accounting for socio-economic status

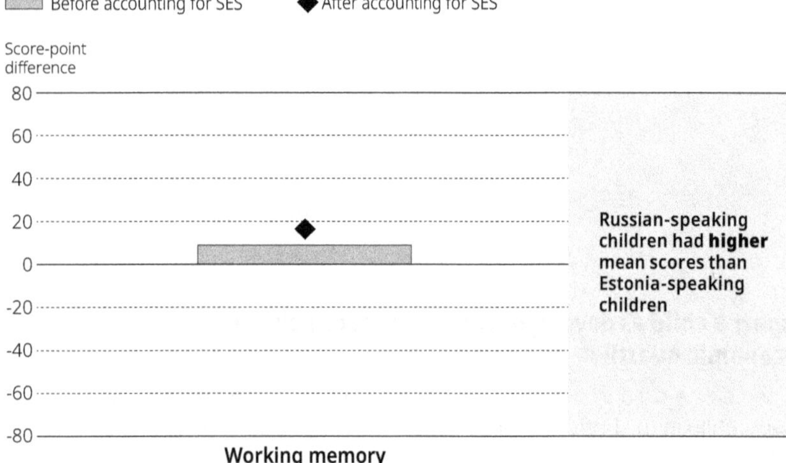

Note: All differences are statistically significant.

StatLink https://doi.org/10.1787/888934106819

There are limited differences in how educators and parents of Estonian-speaking children and Russian-speaking children perceive their self-regulation development

Parents and educators in Estonia perceived about half of five-year-olds as developing above average self-regulation skills (Figure 4.11). This perception did not differ much between Estonian-speaking children and Russian-speaking children. These children were perceived as about equally likely to be developing below average and above average skills by both their parents and educators.

Children with at least one parent who mainly speaks a language other than the assessment language have lower self-regulation scores, after accounting for socio-economic status

In Estonia, 6% of five-year-olds lived in homes where at least one parent mostly spoke a language other than the assessment languages of Estonian or Russian. These children had significantly lower mean self-regulation scores after accounting for socio-economic status (by 31 points on inhibition, 26 points on mental flexibility and 31 points on working memory) (Figure 4.12).

The association between home language and each of the self-regulation outcomes assessed in IELS was different for boys and girls, after accounting for socio-economic status. The inhibition, mental flexibility and working memory outcomes of the boys of parents (or the single parent) who primarily spoke a language other than the assessment language were significantly lower than those of boys whose parents both (or single parent) primarily spoke the assessment language. There were no differences in the outcomes of girls in these two groups.

Figure 4.11 **Self-regulation development as reported by parents and educators by child language, Estonia**

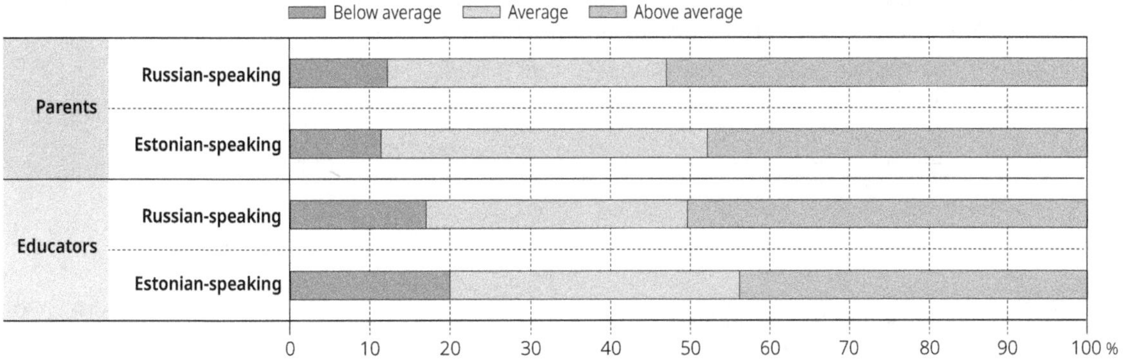

StatLink https://doi.org/10.1787/888934106838

Figure 4.12 **Self-regulation scores by home language, Estonia**

Score-point differences between children with at least one parent who speaks mainly a language other than the assessment language at home and those whose parent(s) speak mainly the assessment language, before and after accounting for socio-economic status

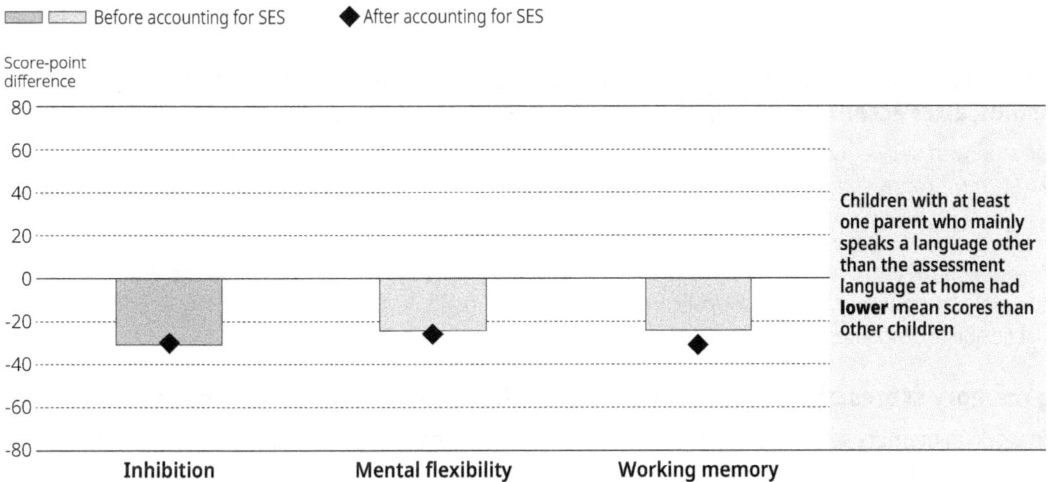

Note: Statistically significant differences are shown in a darker tone.
StatLink https://doi.org/10.1787/888934106857

The working memory outcomes of the children of mothers with at least a bachelor's degree are higher than those of the children of mothers who have not completed any tertiary education

Maternal education was a significant predictor of working memory outcomes. The children of mothers who had completed at least a bachelor's degree had significantly higher working memory outcomes (21 points) than the children of mothers who had not completed tertiary education, after accounting for household income (Figure 4.13). A mother's completion of a bachelor's degree was not related to her children's inhibition or mental flexibility outcomes after controlling for household income.

A mother's completion of at least a bachelor's degree was associated with the working memory outcomes of girls but not boys. The working memory outcomes of the girls of mothers who had completed at least a bachelor's degree were 27 points higher than the girls of mothers who had not, after controlling for household income.

The association between a mother's educational attainment and her child's self-regulation scores was most pronounced in England, where any level of education above lower secondary predicted higher mental flexibility and working memory scores, after accounting for household income. In the United States, mental flexibility scores were higher for children of mothers who had completed at least a bachelor's degree than for children of mothers who had completed only primary education.

Figure 4.13 **Working memory scores by mother's educational attainment, Estonia**

Score-point differences between children whose mothers have completed at least a Bachelor's degree and those whose mothers have not completed a Bachelor's degree, before and after accounting for household income

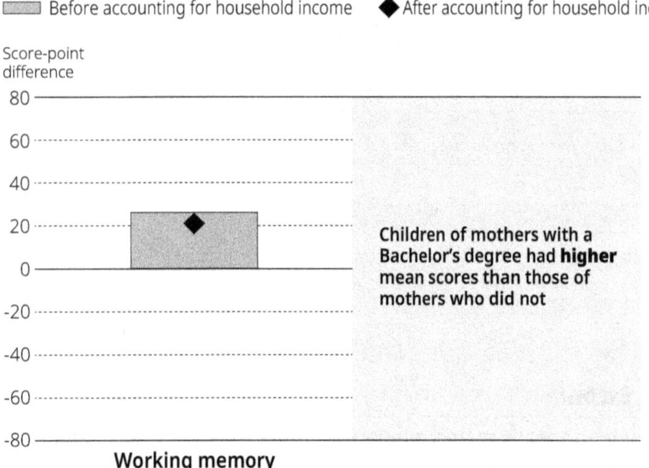

Note: All differences are statistically significant.
StatLink https://doi.org/10.1787/888934106876

The working memory outcomes of children in single-parent households are higher than those of children in two-parent households, after accounting for socio-economic status

Family structure is associated with self-regulation skills in different ways. The presence of two parents in a home may increase the possibility that children have more stimulating interactions. It may also facilitate employment opportunities and increase household income.

In Estonia, however, the working memory outcomes of children in single-parent homes were higher than those of children in two-parent homes by 26 points, after accounting for socio-economic status (Figure 4.14). There were no significant differences in the inhibition and mental flexibility outcomes of children in single- and two-parent households.

Figure 4.14 **Working memory scores of children in single-parent households and two-parent, Estonia**

Score point difference in working memory scores between children in single-parent households and those in two-parent households, before and after accounting for socioeconomic status

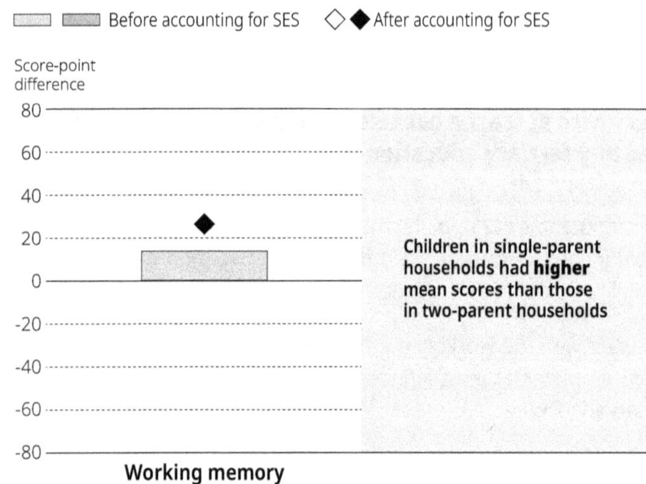

Note: Statistically significant differences are shown in a darker tone.
StatLink https://doi.org/10.1787/888934106895

The relationship between family structure and working memory outcomes was different for boys and girls, after accounting for socio-economic status. There was no difference in the working memory outcomes of boys in single-parent homes and boys in two-parent homes, but there was a significant difference for girls, with the working memory outcomes of girls in single-parent homes 32 points higher than those of girls in two-parent homes.

The inhibition and working memory outcomes of children with one or two siblings are higher than those of children with no siblings

The number of siblings a child had was related to their inhibition and working memory outcomes. The inhibition (15 points) and working memory outcomes (16 points) of children with one sibling were higher than those of children with no siblings, after accounting for socio-economic status (Figure 4.15). The inhibition outcomes of children with two siblings were 17 points higher than those with no siblings.

The inhibition and working memory outcomes were different for boys and girls by number of siblings. The inhibition outcomes of boys with two siblings were 24 points higher than those of boys with no siblings, after accounting for socio-economic status. The outcomes of boys with one sibling or with more than two siblings, however, were no different from the outcomes of boys with no siblings. The working memory outcomes of boys with one or two siblings were 23 and 27 points higher, respectively, than those of boys with no siblings.

The association of siblings with self-regulation outcomes was different in the three countries participating in IELS. The number of siblings did not influence the self-regulation skills of children in England. In the United States, the working memory outcomes of children with one or two siblings were significantly higher than those of children with no siblings.

Figure 4.15 **Inhibition and working memory scores by number of siblings, Estonia**

Score-point differences between children at least one sibling and those with no siblings, before and after accounting for socio-economic status

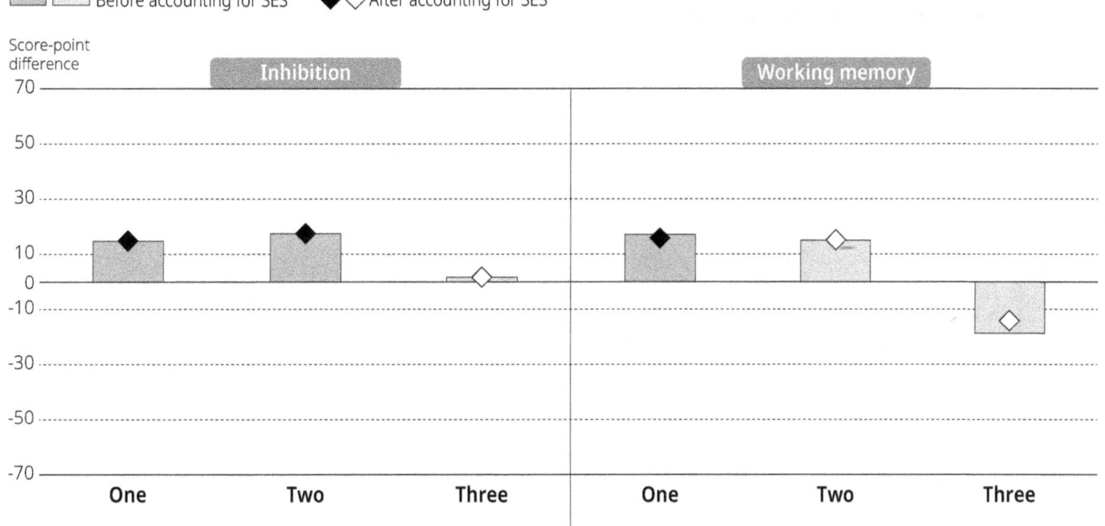

Note: Statistically significant differences are shown in a darker tone.

StatLink https://doi.org/10.1787/888934106914

HOME LEARNING ENVIRONMENT AND SELF-REGULATION SKILLS

A child's home learning environment and the quality of their interactions with their parents influences early learning outcomes. A child's access to developmentally-appropriate books, toys and activities, and the quality of their interactions with their parents, promotes their opportunities for early learning development.

In the context of this report, IELS defines a child's home learning environment as the number of children's books in their home, the frequency with which a child is read to, the frequency with which they are taken to an activity outside of the home and the level of parental involvement in activities taking place at the preschool. Additionally, parents were asked whether their child used a digital device and, if so, the frequency of that usage.

The number of children's books in the home is predictive of a child's mental flexibility and working memory outcomes

In Estonia, the number of children's books that a child had access to in their home – including those from a public or preschool library – predicted their mental flexibility and working memory outcomes. This relationship held even after accounting for the income or socio-economic status of a child's family. The number of books that a child had access to in their home was not related to their inhibition outcomes.

The mental flexibility outcomes of children with access to more than 10 books in their home were significantly higher than those of children with 10 books or fewer, even after accounting for socio-economic status. The gap in development between children with 10 books or fewer in their home and those with between 26 and 50, for example, was 27 points on mental flexibility outcomes (Figure 4.16).

The working memory scores of children with access to over 50 children's books in their home were higher than those of children with access to 10 books or fewer. For example, the gap in working memory outcomes between children with 10 books or fewer in their home and those with between 51 and 100 was 31 points (Figure 4.16).

The number of books a child had access to in their home related differently to the self-regulation outcomes of boys and girls. The self-regulation outcomes of girls with more than 10 books were no different than the outcomes of girls with 10 books or fewer, after accounting for socio-economic status. The self-regulation skills of boys, however, increased with the number of children's books in their home, even after accounting for socio-economic status. The mental flexibility outcomes of boys with access to any number of books above 10 were higher than those of boys with access to 10 books or fewer. Similarly, the inhibition and working memory outcomes of boys with any number of books greater than 25 were higher than those of boys with access to 10 books or fewer.

Figure 4.16 **Self-regulation scores by number of children's books in the home, Estonia**

Score-point difference between children with access to more than 10 children's books in the home and those with access to 10 or fewer, before and after accounting for socio-economic status

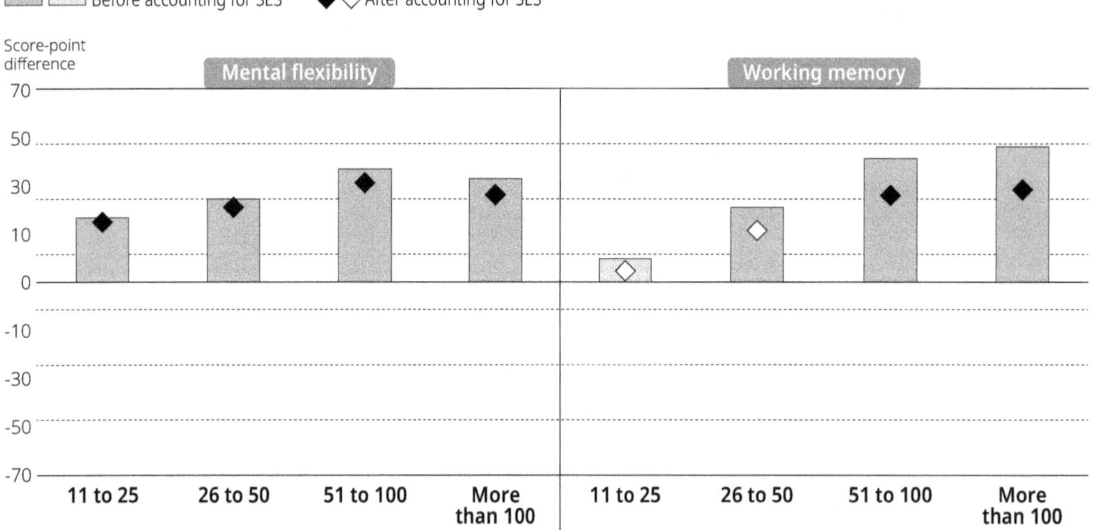

Note: Statistically significant differences are shown in a darker tone.

StatLink https://doi.org/10.1787/888934106933

The inhibition and working memory outcomes of children read to at least once or twice a week are higher than those of children read to less often

The frequency with which a child was read to from a book or e-book was significantly related to their inhibition and working memory outcomes, even after accounting for socio-economic status. It was not related to their mental flexibility outcomes.

The inhibition outcomes of children who were read to once or twice a week were 25 points higher than those of children read to less than once a week (Figure 4.17). The outcomes of children who were read to between three and seven days a week were no different from those of children who were read to once a week.

The working memory outcomes of children read to once or twice a week were 33 points higher than those of children read to less than once a week, after accounting for socio-economic status (Figure 4.17). The outcomes of children read to between three and four days a week were 23 points higher than those of children read to less than once a week, and the outcomes of children read to almost every day were 27 points higher.

While the act of being read to is related to the development of a child's emergent literacy skills, the quality and type of reading experience may be more important for self-regulation development. For example, direct interaction between a child and the reading material – either in the interactivity of the reading material or the reading experience with their caregiver – may be more important for self-regulation outcomes.

Figure 4.17 **Inhibition and working memory scores by frequency child is read to, Estonia**

Score point difference in inhibition and working memory outcomes between children who are read to at least once a week and those read to less, before and after accounting for socioeconomic status

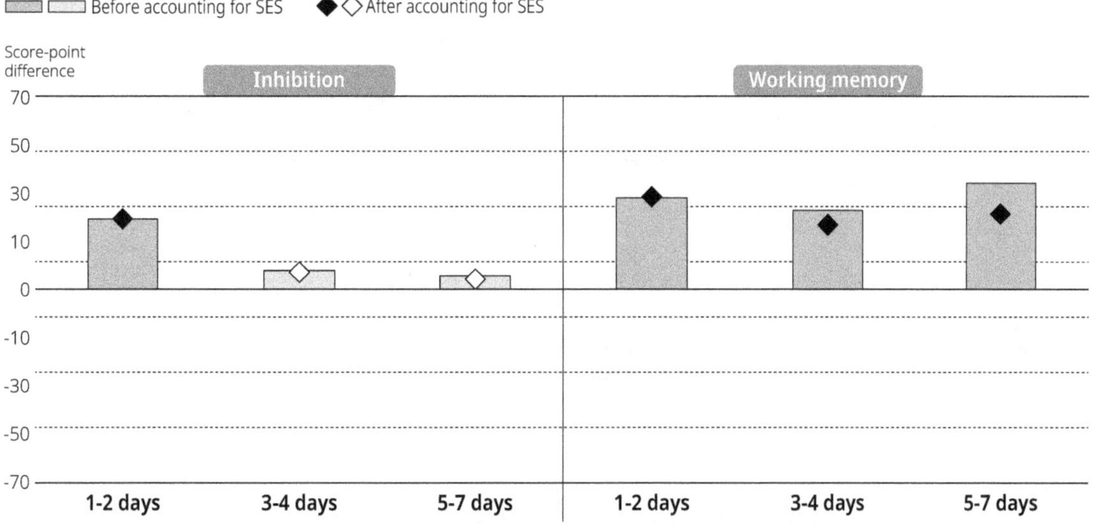

Note: Statistically significant differences are shown in a darker tone.

StatLink https://doi.org/10.1787/888934106952

The mental flexibility outcomes of boys whose parents are moderately or strongly involved in activities taking place at preschool are higher than those of boys whose parents are slightly or not involved, after accounting for socio-economic status

On average, the self-regulation outcomes of children whose parents were perceived by educators as being slightly or not involved in activities taking place at preschool were no different from those whose parents were perceived as being strongly or moderately involved, after accounting for socio-economic status. While differences existed before accounting for socio-economic status, these were driven by the parents of children from higher socio-economic families being more involved in activities at their child's centre.

The benefit of having an involved parent, however, was different for girls and boys. While there were no differences in the self-regulation outcomes of girls, the mental flexibility outcomes of the boys of parents moderately or strongly involved in activities at the centre were 22 points higher than those of the boys of parents slightly or not involved after accounting for socio-economic status.

The frequency with which a child is taken to a special or paid activity outside of the home is related to their inhibition and working memory skills, even after accounting for socio-economic status

Taking a child to a special or paid activity outside of the home – such as a sports club or dance, swimming and language lessons – was positively related to their inhibition and working memory outcomes, even after accounting for socio-economic status.

The inhibition outcomes of children who attended a special activity five to seven days a week were 41 points higher than those of children who never attended an activity, after accounting for socio-economic status (Figure 4.18). Attending activities less frequently than five to seven days a week was not related to a child's inhibition outcomes.

The working memory outcomes of children who attended an activity almost daily were no different from those who never attended an activity. However, the working memory outcomes of children who attended a special activity between three and four days a week were significantly higher (25 points) than those of children who never attended an activity (Figure 4.18).

Figure 4.18 **Inhibition and working memory scores by participation in special or paid activity outside of the home, Estonia**

Score-point differences in inhibition and working memory scores between children who participated in a special or paid activity outside of the home and those who never participated in such activity, before and after accounting for socio-economic status

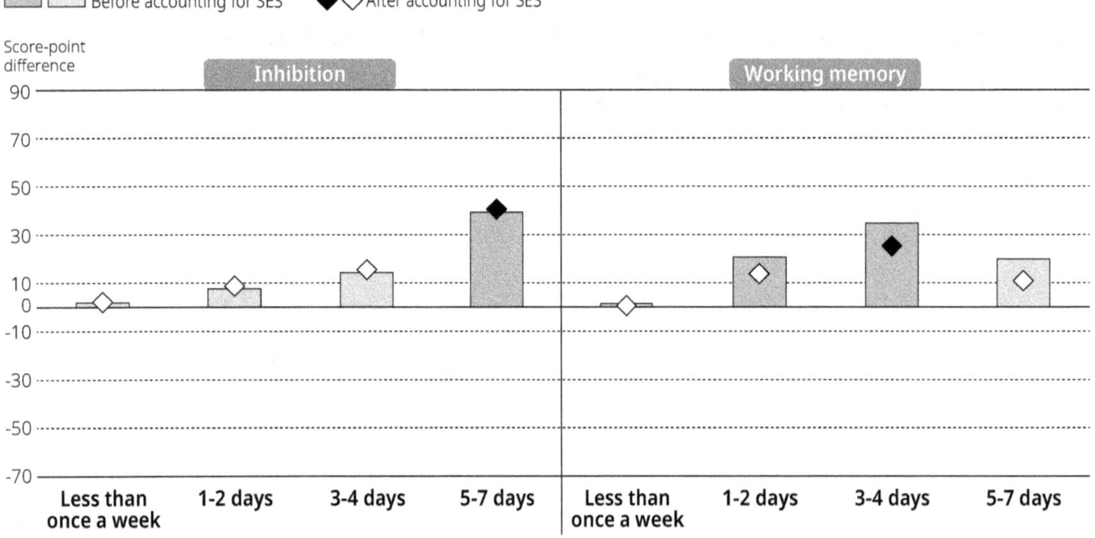

Note: Statistically significant differences are shown in a darker tone.
StatLink https://doi.org/10.1787/888934106971

Figure 4.19 **Inhibition and mental flexibility scores by use of digital devices, Estonia**

Score-point differences between children who use a digital device once a month or more frequently and those who never use a device, before and after accounting for socio-economic status

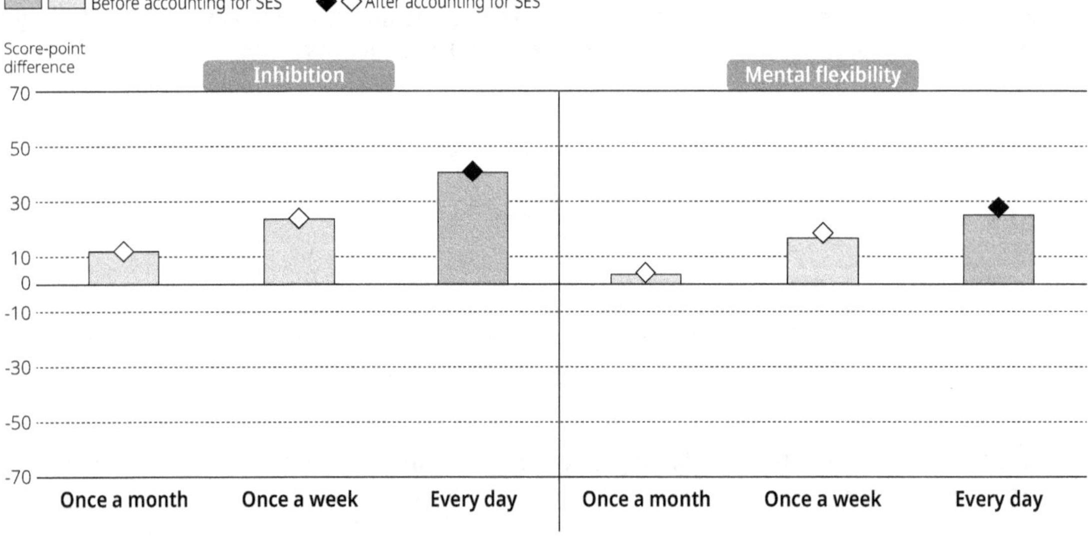

Note: Statistically significant differences are shown in a darker tone.
StatLink https://doi.org/10.1787/888934106990

Five-year olds who use a digital device every day have higher inhibition and mental flexibility outcomes than those who hardly ever use one

The frequency with which a child used a digital device – including a desktop or laptop computer, tablet device or smartphone – was significantly related to their inhibition and mental flexibility outcomes in Estonia, after accounting for socio-economic status, but not related to their working memory outcomes.

The outcomes of children who used a device every day were 41 points higher on inhibition and 28 points higher on mental flexibility than those of children who never or hardly ever used a device, after accounting for socio-economic status (Figure 4.19). While the use of a digital device in and of itself may not have been related to a child's outcomes, the types of activities that a child engaged in while on those devices may have contributed to the development of inhibition and mental flexibility skills.

The observed difference in outcomes based on digital device use may be partly attributable to the assessment of a child's self-regulation skills through a tablet-based direct assessment. However, the frequency of use that predicted different self-regulation outcomes differed by participating countries. Using a device every day predicted higher working memory outcomes in England, after accounting for socio-economic status. In the United States, using a device at least once a week predicted higher mental flexibility and working memory outcomes. The inconsistency with which digital device use predicted self-regulation outcomes implies that differences are more likely to be specific to a child within a given country, rather than to a tablet-based direct assessment.

ASSESSING THE COMBINED EFFECTS OF CHILD AND FAMILY CHARACTERISTICS ON SELF-REGULATION SCORES

Analysing how the variables that predict self-regulation outcomes presented in this chapter also relate to one another through a regression model gives insight into which factors contribute most to the observed outcomes. Such results do not provide a causal explanation of which factors lead to changes in a child's self-regulation outcomes; however, they do provide a better understanding of which child-, family- and home-level variables predict self-regulation outcomes.

Variables that were significantly related to self-regulation scores were included in regression models to assess how well they explained variation in the scores. Variables that were not significant in the models were removed one at a time[3] until all remaining variables were significantly related to the outcome.

The results of the regression models also provide an opportunity to quantify score point differences in terms of months of child development on a given skill. For example, the results of the regression model indicate that children's inhibition scores increase by an average of over 7.5 points a month between the ages of five- and six-years old. This equates to about 93 points for the year between the ages of five- and six-years old. Their mental flexibility scores increase by over 5 points a month—or about 62 points a year—and their working memory scores increase by over 5.5 points a month—or over 67 points a year. This difference will be used to quantify what a score-point difference implies in terms of months of child self-regulation development.

Inhibition outcomes are related to children's gender, experience of early difficulties and the primary language of their parents

A child's individual characteristics and their home background uniquely predicted their inhibition outcomes, after accounting for all variables in the model (Table 4.2). The outcomes of boys were about 20 points lower than those of girls. This translates to a gap of over 2.5 months of inhibition development at the age of five.

Table 4.2 **Results of the multiple regression model of inhibition, Estonia**

Variable	B	SE	*p*
Child is a boy	-20.96	6.00	**0.00**
Age (months)	7.72	0.85	**0.00**
Low birth weight or premature birth	-37.37	9.90	**0.00**
Learning difficulties	-29.25	12.52	**0.02**
Home language*	-25.91	11.93	**0.03**
Information on home language missing	-15.79	22.71	0.487
Intercept	456.62	11.65	

Note: p-values in **bold** indicate statistical significance. B = regression coefficients. SE = Standard Error. The intercept is the estimated score of a child in the reference category of each categorical variable, aged 5 years 6 months, and with a mean value for socio-economic status.
*Variable has a missing indicator to preserve cases in the dataset.

StatLink https://doi.org/10.1787/888934107009

A child's experience of early difficulties also predicted their inhibition outcomes at the age of five. The outcomes of children born prematurely or with a birth weight of under 2.5 kg were about 37 points – or under 5 months of development – lower than those of children who were not. The outcomes of children who had experienced learning difficulties were 29 points lower than the outcomes of those who had not. This equates to over 3.5 months of inhibition development.

As with a child's individual characteristics, their home background was a significant predictor of inhibition outcomes. The inhibition outcomes of children who lived in homes where at least one parent primarily spoke a language other than the assessment language were lower than those of children in homes where both parents (or the single parent) primarily spoke the assessment language, after accounting for all other factors in the model. This gap was of about 26 points – or the equivalent of over 3 months of inhibition development.

Mental flexibility outcomes are related to children's gender, experience of early difficulties and access to children's books

A child's individual characteristics and their home background uniquely predicted their mental flexibility outcomes, after accounting for all variables in the model (Table 4.3). The outcomes of boys were about 18 points lower than those of girls. This represents a gap of about 3.5 months of mental flexibility development at the age of five.

A child's experience of early difficulties also predicted their mental flexibility outcomes at the age of five. The outcomes of children born prematurely or with a birth weight under 2.5 kg were about 26 points – or over 5 months of development – lower than those of other children born. The outcomes of children who had experienced learning difficulties were 28.5 points lower than the outcomes of those who had not. This equates to about 5.5 months of mental flexibility development. Similarly, the mental flexibility scores of children who experienced social, emotional or behavioural difficulties were over 27.5 points lower than those that did not. This equates to over 5 months of mental flexibility development.

A child's home background was a significant predictor of mental flexibility outcomes. The scores of children with access to over 10 books were significantly higher than those of children with access to fewer than 10. For example, the average gap in outcomes between children with access to 10 books or fewer and those with between 26 and 50 books was over 30 points. This equates to about over 6 months of mental flexibility development.

Table 4.3 **Results of the multiple regression model of mental flexibility, Estonia**

Variable	B	SE	*p*
Child is a boy	-18.12	5.98	**0.00**
Age (months)	5.16	0.88	**0.00**
Low birth weight or premature birth	-26.12	10.00	**0.01**
Learning difficulties	-28.50	12.00	**0.02**
Social, emotional or behavioural difficulties	-27.78	10.16	**0.01**
Access to children's books		Reference group	
0 to 10			
11 to 25	23.88	10.98	**0.03**
26 to 50	31.30	9.94	**0.00**
51 to 100	41.59	11.00	**0.00**
More than 100	40.04	12.60	**0.00**
Intercept	447.10	17.14	

Note: p-values in **bold** indicate statistical significance. B = regression coefficients. SE = Standard Error. The intercept is the estimated score of a child in the reference category of each categorical variable, aged 5 years 6 months, and with a mean value for socio-economic status.

StatLink https://doi.org/10.1787/888934107028

Working memory outcomes are related to children's experience of early difficulties, the socioeconomic status of their households, their household structures and their access to children's books

A child's individual characteristics, their family background and their home environment predicted their working memory outcomes, after accounting for all variables in the model (Table 4.4). Unlike their inhibition and mental flexibility outcomes, a child's gender and their experience of low birth weight did not predict their working memory outcomes. However, the socio-economic background of a child's family and being from a single-parent household did predict working memory outcomes.

The outcomes of children reported as having experienced learning difficulties were over 27 points below those of children who had not experienced such difficulties, equating to about 5 months of working memory development. The outcomes of children who had experienced social, emotional or behavioural difficulties were about 39.5 points below those of children who had not experienced such difficulties, equating to over 7 months of development.

The outcomes of children from households in the top quartile of socio-economic status were significantly higher than those of children in the bottom. The gap between the outcomes of children from the least advantaged quartile of families and those from the most advantaged was about 32 points, or about 6 months of working memory development.

Outcomes for children in single-parent homes were about 26 points higher than those of children in two-parent homes, equating to over 4.5 months of working memory development. A child's outcomes also increased with access to more children's books. For example, the average gap in outcomes between children with 10 books or fewer and those with between 51 and 100 was about 32 points. This roughly translates to about 6 months of working memory development.

Table 4.4 **Results of the multiple regression model of working memory, Estonia**

Variable	B	SE	*p*
Age (months)	5.56	0.88	**0.00**
Learning difficulties	-27.73	12.06	**0.02**
Social, emotional or behavioural difficulties	-39.46	11.38	**0.00**
Socio-economic status quartile	Reference group		
Bottom			
3rd	12.15	9.31	0.19
2nd	15.06	10.02	0.13
Top	33.11	11.66	**0.01**
Single parent*	25.84	12.04	**0.03**
Information on number of parents missing	-10.54	15.87	0.51
Access to children's books	Reference group		
0 to 10			
11 to 25	4.05	10.27	0.69
26 to 50	18.02	9.89	0.07
51 to 100	30.58	10.31	**0.00**
More than 100	32.42	14.07	**0.02**
Intercept	463.24	12.54	

Note: p-values in **bold** indicate statistical significance. B = regression coefficients. SE = Standard Error. The intercept is the estimated score of a child in the reference category of each categorical variable, aged 5 years 6 months, and with a mean value for socio-economic status.

StatLink https://doi.org/10.1787/888934107047

SUMMARY AND CONCLUSIONS

The self-regulation outcomes of children in Estonia are above the overall IELS mean of participating countries

The self-regulation outcomes of children in Estonia were higher than the IELS overall mean. The average inhibition outcomes in Estonia were about equal to those in the United States and higher than those in England. The average mental flexibility and working memory outcomes in Estonia were about equal to those in England and significantly higher than those in the United States.

These results suggest that five-years old children in Estonia are relatively more likely to successfully inhibit their responses when presented with a new set of information. These children are also more likely to successfully switch between rules and recall short visual sequences. This set of self-regulation skills is predictive of children's future well-being, including how well they do at preschool and in non-academic activities where concentration and persistence correlate with success.

The self-regulation outcomes of girls, especially Russian-speaking girls, are higher than those of boys

In Estonia, the self-regulation outcomes of girls were significantly higher than those of boys across all self-regulation domains measured by IELS. Parents and educators in Estonia were also, on average, more likely to report girls rather than boys as developing above average skills. Russian-speaking children showed more prominent gender differences than Estonian-speaking children in working memory.

In the United States there were similar gaps in the inhibition and working memory outcomes of girls and boys; however, there was no difference in mental flexibility outcomes. In England, the gender gap on inhibition outcomes was reversed, with the inhibition outcomes of boys higher than those of girls. There were also no differences in the outcomes of boys and girls on mental flexibility and working memory in England.

Children who have experienced difficulties before the age of five have lower average self-regulation scores at age five

Experiencing learning difficulties earlier in life was significantly related to the self-regulation scores of five-year-olds in Estonia across all three self-regulation domains. The self-regulation scores of children who had experienced such difficulties before the age of five were significantly lower than those of children who had not. Experiencing low birth weight or premature birth was also related to the inhibition and mental flexibility skills of five-year-olds in Estonia, even after accounting for all factors in the regression models.

Experiencing learning difficulties before the age of five was a significant predictor of the self-regulation outcomes of five-year-old children, after accounting for all factors in the overall regression model. Experiencing social, emotional or behavioural difficulties early in life was also a significant predictor of a child's working memory and mental flexibility outcomes at age five, when all factors were accounted for.

The socio-economic status of a child's family is associated with their working memory outcomes

The working memory outcomes of five-year-olds from a household in a higher socio-economic bracket in Estonia were higher than those of children from low socio-economic backgrounds, even after accounting for all factors in the overall regression model. This implies that children from households with a lower socio-economic background are less likely to successfully recall short visual sequences than children from households with a higher socio-economic background.

The socio-economic status of a child's household was a significant predictor of self-regulation outcomes in all participating countries – particularly in relation to mental flexibility and working memory – although the strength varied by country. Estonia had the smallest differences in children's skills considering socio-economic status compared to England and the United States.

A child's home learning environment is related to their self-regulation outcomes

A child's home learning environment was predictive of their self-regulation outcomes in Estonia. The number of children's books in their home and the frequency with which a child used a digital device, was read to and was taken to an activity outside of the home all related positively to different aspects of a child's ability to self-regulate. Similarly, the level of parental involvement in activities taking place at the preschool was related to a boy's mental flexibility skills.

References

Anderson, P. and **N. Reidy** (2012), "Assessing executive function in preschoolers", *Neuropsychological Review*, Vol. 22, pp. 345-360, http://dx.doi.org/10.1002/ets2.12148. [40]

Ayduk, O. et al. (2000), "Regulating the interpersonal self: Strategic self-regulation for coping with rejection sensitivity.", *Journal of Personality and Social Psychology*, Vol. 79/5, pp. 776-792, https://psycnet.apa.org/doiLanding?doi=10.1037%2F0022-3514.79.5.776 (accessed on 28 June 2019). [23]

Bernier, A., S. Carlson and **N. Whipple** (2010), "From External Regulation to Self-Regulation: Early Parenting Precursors of Young Children's Executive Functioning", *Child Development*, Vol. 81/1, pp. 326-339, http://dx.doi.org/10.1111/j.1467-8624.2009.01397.x. [35]

Best, J., P. Miller and **J. Naglieri** (2011), "Relations between executive function and academic achievement from ages 5 to 17 in a large, representative national sample", *Learning and Individual Differences*, Vol. 21/4, pp. 327-336, http://dx.doi.org/10.1016/J.LINDIF.2011.01.007. [16]

Blair, C. and **R. Peters Razza** (2007), "Relating Effortful Control, Executive Function, and False Belief Understanding to Emerging Math and Literacy Ability in Kindergarten", *Child Development*, Vol. 78/2, pp. 647-663, https://onlinelibrary.wiley.com/doi/pdf/10.1111/j.1467-8624.2007.01019.x (accessed on 28 June 2019). [10]

Blair, C. and **C. Raver** (2015), "School Readiness and Self-Regulation: A Developmental Psychobiological Approach", *Annual Review of Psychology*, Vol. 66/1, pp. 711-731, http://dx.doi.org/10.1146/annurev-psych-010814-015221. [5]

Blair, C. and **C. Raver** (2012), "Individual development and evolution: Experiential canalization of self-regulation.", *Developmental Psychology*, Vol. 48/3, pp. 647-657, http://dx.doi.org/10.1037/a0026472. [34]

Booth, A., E. Hennessy and **O. Doyle** (2018), "Self-Regulation: Learning Across Disciplines", *Journal of Child and Family Studies*, Vol. 27, pp. 3767–3781, https://doi.org/10.1007/s10826-018-1202-5. [39]

Bridgett, D. et al. (2015), "Intergenerational transmission of self-regulation: A multidisciplinary review and integrative conceptual framework.", *Psychological Bulletin*, Vol. 141/3, pp. 602-654, http://dx.doi.org/10.1037/a0038662. [25]

Buckner, J., E. Mezzacappa and **W. Beardslee** (2009), "Self-Regulation and Its Relations to Adaptive Functioning in Low Income Youths", *American Journal of Olrhopsychrauy*, Vol. 79/1, pp. 19-30, http://dx.doi.org/10.1037/a0014796. [22]

Caspi, A. et al. (1998), "Early failure in the labor market: Childhood and adolescent predictors of unemployment in the transition to adulthood", *American Sociological Review*, Vol. 63/3, pp. 424-451, https://search.proquest.com/openview/a125bf198ee436749889e960111ac591/1?pq-origsite=gscholar&cbl=41945 (accessed on 28 June 2019). [18]

Clark, C., V. Pritchard and **L. Woodward** (2010), "Preschool executive functioning abilities predict early mathematics achievement.", *Developmental Psychology*, Vol. 46/5, pp. 1176-1191, http://dx.doi.org/10.1037/a0019672. [15]

Daly, M. et al. (2015), "Childhood Self-Control and Unemployment Throughout the Life Span", *Psychological Science*, Vol. 26/6, pp. 709-723, http://dx.doi.org/10.1177/0956797615569001. [19]

Diamond, A. (2013), "Executive Functions", *Annual Review of Psychology*, Vol. 64/1, pp. 135-168, http://dx.doi.org/10.1146/annurev-psych-113011-143750. [1]

Diamond, A. and **K. Lee** (2011), "Interventions shown to aid executive function development in children 4 to 12 years old.", *Science*, Vol. 333/6045, pp. 959-964, http://dx.doi.org/10.1126/science.1204529. [41]

Dockett, S. (2001), "Starting School: Effective Transitions.", *Early Childhood Research & Practice*, Vol. 3/2, https://eric.ed.gov/?id=ED458041 (accessed on 3 July 2019). [12]

Duckworth, A., P. Quinn and **E. Tsukayama** (2012), "What No Child Left Behind Leaves Behind: The Roles of IQ and Self-Control in Predicting Standardized Achievement Test Scores and Report Card Grades.", *Journal of educational psychology*, Vol. 104/2, pp. 439-451, http://dx.doi.org/10.1037/a0026280. [8]

Duckworth, A., E. Tsukayama and **H. May** (2010), "Establishing Causality Using Longitudinal Hierarchical Linear Modeling: An Illustration Predicting Achievement From Self-Control", *Social Psychological and Personality Science*, Vol. 1/4, pp. 311-317, http://dx.doi.org/10.1177/1948550609359707. [24]

Duncan, G. et al. (2007), "School Readiness and Later Achievement", *Developmental Psychology*, Vol. 43/6, pp. 1428-1446, http://dx.doi.org/10.1037/[0012-1649.43.6.1428].supp. [17]

Eisenberg, N., T. Spinrad and **N. Eggum** (2010), "Emotion-related self-regulation and its relation to children's maladjustment.", *Annual review of clinical psychology*, Vol. 6, pp. 495-525, http://dx.doi.org/10.1146/annurev.clinpsy.121208.131208. [2]

Evans, G., T. Fuller-Rowell and **S. Doan** (2012), "Childhood Cumulative Risk and Obesity: The Mediating Role of Self-Regulatory Ability", *Pediatrics*, Vol. 129/1, pp. e68-e73, http://dx.doi.org/10.1542/peds.2010-3647. [21]

Fuller, B. et al. (2010), "Maternal practices that influence Hispanic infants' health and cognitive growth.", *Pediatrics*, Vol. 125/2, pp. e324-32, http://dx.doi.org/10.1542/peds.2009-0496. [31]

Garon, N., S. Bryson and **I. Smith** (2008), "Executive function in preschoolers: A review using an integrative framework.", *Psychological Bulletin*, Vol. 134/1, pp. 31-60, http://dx.doi.org/10.1037/0033-2909.134.1.31. [42]

Hackman, D. and **M. Farah** (2009), "Socioeconomic status and the developing brain", *Trends in Cognitive Sciences*, Vol. 13/2, pp. 65-73, http://dx.doi.org/10.1016/J.TICS.2008.11.003. [32]

Heatherton, T. and **D. Wagner** (2011), "Cognitive neuroscience of self-regulation failure", *Trends in Cognitive Sciences*, Vol. 15/3, pp. 132-139, http://dx.doi.org/10.1016/J.TICS.2010.12.005. [37]

Kishiyama, M. et al. (2009), "Socioeconomic Disparities Affect Prefrontal Function in Children", *Journal of Cognitive Neuroscience*, Vol. 21/6, pp. 1106-1115, http://dx.doi.org/10.1162/jocn.2009.21101. [33]

Mcclelland, M. et al. (2007), "Links Between Behavioral Regulation and Preschoolers' Literacy, Vocabulary, and Math Skills", *Developmental Psychology*, Vol. 43/4, pp. 947–959, http://dx.doi.org/10.1037/0012-1649.43.4.947. [6]

McClelland, M. et al. (2018), "Self-Regulation", in *Handbook of Life Course Health Development*, Springer International Publishing, Cham, http://dx.doi.org/10.1007/978-3-319-47143-3_12. [36]

McClelland, M. et al. (2015), "Development and Self-Regulation", in *Handbook of Child Psychology and Developmental Science*, John Wiley & Sons, Inc., http://dx.doi.org/10.1002/9781118963418.childpsy114. [3]

McClelland, M. et al. (2010), "Self-Regulation: Integration of Cognition and Emotion", in *The Handbook of Life-Span Development*, John Wiley & Sons, Inc., http://dx.doi.org/10.1002/9780470880166.hlsd001015. [43]

McEwen, B., C. Nasca and **J. Gray** (2016), "Stress Effects on Neuronal Structure: Hippocampus, Amygdala, and Prefrontal Cortex.", *Neuropsychopharmacology : official publication of the American College of Neuropsychopharmacology*, Vol. 41/1, pp. 3-23, http://dx.doi.org/10.1038/npp.2015.171. [29]

Moffitt, T. et al. (2011), "A gradient of childhood self-control predicts health, wealth, and public safety.", *Proceedings of the National Academy of Sciences of the United States of America*, Vol. 108/7, pp. 2693-8, http://dx.doi.org/10.1073/pnas.1010076108. [20]

Morrison, F., C. Cameron and **M. Mcclelland** (2010), "Self-regulation and academic achievement in the transition to school", in S. D. Calkins & M. Bell (ed.), *Child development at the intersection of emotion and cognition*, American Psychological Association, Washington, DC, http://dx.doi.org/10.1037/12059-011. [7]

Nelson, C. et al. (2007), "Cognitive Recovery in Socially Deprived Young Children: The Bucharest Early Intervention Project", *Science*, Vol. 318/5858, pp. 1937-1940, http://dx.doi.org/10.1126/SCIENCE.1143921. [28]

Neuenschwander, R. et al. (2012), "How do different aspects of self-regulation predict successful adaptation to school?", *Journal of Experimental Child Psychology*, Vol. 113/3, pp. 353-371, http://dx.doi.org/10.1016/J.JECP.2012.07.004. [11]

Noble, K., M. Norman and **M. Farah** (2005), "Neurocognitive correlates of socioeconomic status in kindergarten children", *Developmental Science*, Vol. 8/1, pp. 74-87, http://dx.doi.org/10.1111/j.1467-7687.2005.00394.x. [26]

Ponitz, C. et al. (2009), "A structured observation of behavioral self-regulation and its contribution to kindergarten outcomes", *Developmental Psychology*, Vol. 45/3, pp. 605-619, https://psycnet.apa.org/doiLanding?doi=10.1037%2Fa0015365 (accessed on 9 July 2019). [38]

Raghubar, K., M. Barnes and **S. Hecht** (2010), "Working memory and mathematics: A review of developmental, individual difference, and cognitive approaches", *Learning and Individual Differences*, Vol. 20/2, pp. 110-122, http://dx.doi.org/10.1016/J.LINDIF.2009.10.005. [14]

Raver, C., C. Blair and **M. Willoughby** (2013), "Poverty as a predictor of 4-year-olds' executive function: New perspectives on models of differential susceptibility.", *Developmental Psychology*, Vol. 49/2, pp. 292-304, http://dx.doi.org/10.1037/a0028343. [27]

Shonkoff, J., D. Phillips and **N. Council** (2000), *Executive function in preschoolers: A review using an integrative framework.*, National Acadamies Press, Washington, DC, http://dx.doi.org/10.1037/0033-2909.134.1.31. [13]

Tangney, J., R. Baumeister and **A. Boone** (2004), "High Self-Control Predicts Good Adjustment, Less Pathology, Better Grades, and Interpersonal Success", *Journal of Personality*, Vol. 72/2, pp. 271-324, http://dx.doi.org/10.1111/j.0022-3506.2004.00263.x. [9]

Wachs, T., P. Gurkas and **S. Kontos** (2004), "Predictors of preschool children's compliance behavior in early childhood classroom settings", *Journal of Applied Developmental Psychology*, Vol. 25/4, pp. 439-457, http://dx.doi.org/10.1016/J.APPDEV.2004.06.003. [30]

Zelazo, P., C. Blair and **M. Willoughby** (2016), *Executive Function: Implications for Education (NCER 2017-2000)*, National Center for Education Research, Institute of Education Sciences, U.S. Department of Education, http://ies.ed.gov/. (accessed on 28 June 2019). [4]

Notes

1. Chapter 6 of this report will cover children's socioemotional development
2. A birth weight lower than 5lbs 5oz/2.5 kg was defined as low.
3. In order of descending p-value.

Children's social-emotional skills in Estonia

This chapter presents findings on the social-emotional skills of five-year-olds in Estonia. It shows the differences in social-emotional scores across multiple subgroups of children, considering their individual and family characteristics, as well as their home learning environments. This is based on a direct assessment of children's skills and reports from the children's parents and educators.

THE IMPORTANCE OF SOCIAL-EMOTIONAL DEVELOPMENT

Children develop their capacity to experience and express emotions starting in early infancy, at the same time as they grow physically and cognitively in developing their language and problem-solving skills (Thompson, 2001[1]). Recent developments in neuroscience have shown that the same neural circuits involved in the regulation of emotions overlap with those associated with cognitive processing (Bush, Luu and Posner, 2000[2]; Davidson et al., 2002[3]; Posner and Rothbart, 2000[4]).

Emotions can support cognitive development when they are well-regulated, but that they interfere when they are not. For instance, children who do not feel in control of their emotions are more prone to outbursts, inattention and rapid retreats from stressful situations (Garber and Dodge, 1991[5]). Children's beliefs and their neural mechanisms of attention are interrelated components during childhood development (Schroder et al., 2017[6]).

Early social-emotional skills are strong predictors of later health, educational, social and labour-market outcomes

Understanding emotions is a unique, concurrent predictor of academic competence (Leerkes et al., 2008[7]). Early prosocial behaviour at age eight is shown to be as important as early cognitive ability in predicting educational attainment at age 30 (Schoon et al., 2015[8]), as well as in shaping attainment in adolescence and adulthood (Caprara et al., 2000[9]). Social-emotional skills developed during childhood are linked to educational achievement, even after controlling for early literacy and numeracy skills (Duncan et al., 2007[10]). For example, children's early skills in identifying and responding empathetically to others' emotions have been found to predict concept knowledge and language competence, even after controlling for age, gender and parental income level (Rhoades et al., 2011[11]; Garner and Waajid, 2008[12]).

Underdeveloped skills in identifying others' emotions in early adolescence predict increases in fear, decreases in positive emotions and decreases in the quality and quantity of social support. Amongst boys, low emotion identification skills also predict increases in sadness (Ciarrochi, Heaven and Supavadeeprasit, 2008[13]).

Early empathy, trust and prosocial behaviours are associated with social justice beliefs and a lower likelihood of involvement in crime and delinquency in adulthood (Schoon et al., 2015[8]). Low empathy is associated with antisocial and delinquent behaviours, and increased risk of psychopathology as adults (Fontaine et al., 2011[14]). Sympathy and moral reasoning among six- to nine-year-olds are associated with social justice values at age 12 (Daniel et al., 2014[15]).

Children's emotional health is the strongest predictor of adult life satisfaction at all ages, even more than family economic resources, family psychosocial resources and children's cognitive ability (Flèche, Lekfuangfu and Clark, 2019[16]). Early emotional well-being is linked with mental health in later life, and emotional difficulties at age five are predictors of midlife psychological disorders, such as anxiety and depression (Buchanan, Flouri and Brinke, 2002[17]; Rutter, Kim-Cohen and Maughan, 2006[18]).

IELS included a direct measure of children's emotion identification and attribution, and indirect measures of children's prosocial behaviour, trust in familiar people and non-disruptive behaviour

The International Early Learning and Child Well-being Study (IELS) provides a direct and indirect assessment of social-emotional skills (Box 5.1). Parents and educators responded to survey questions about the child's prosocial behaviour, trust and disruptive behaviours. Children in the study participated in an interactive tablet-based assessment of their empathy skills in a one-on-one setting with a trained study administrator. Reports from educators and parents helped to create a fuller picture of children's early social-emotional skills in both home and early childhood education and care (ECEC) environments than could be ascertained from the direct assessment alone.

Measuring empathy entails the assessment of two skills: emotion identification and emotion attribution in response to a story about a set of characters. Children who participated in the IELS direct assessment responded to hypothetical (story) scenarios designed to measure their empathy skills. Narrated stimulus stories presented cartoon-like children in brief vignettes presented on electronic tablets. The empathy measure required the child to identify an emotion using emoticons representing happy, sad, afraid, angry and surprised. The emotion identification scores reflected children's ability to recognise the emotions of others (i.e. how did the story character feel?). The emotion attribution scores reflected the interaction of concordant emotional response (i.e. when child's responses matched the emotion of the story character) and his or her own emotion attribution (i.e. how the child felt and why s/he felt that way in response to the story).

IELS also measured prosocial, trust and non-disruptive behaviours indirectly through reports from parents and educators, with parents and educators rating the same children on the same set of behaviours. The items for assessing prosocial behaviour and non-disruptive behaviour were based on the Adaptive Social Behaviour Inventory (Hogan, Scott and Bauer, 1992[19]), while those for trust were developed based on previous research (Baumrind, 1968[20]; Roberts, Strayer and Denham, 2014[21]). The prosocial behaviour measure is composed of items such as the child "understands others' feelings, such as when they are happy, sad or angry". The non-disruptive behaviour measure was composed of items such as the child "fights with other children", which was positively inverted for easier interpretation (i.e. the higher the scores the less disruptive). Lastly, the trust measure is composed of items such as the child "approaches familiar adults for comfort when upset".

This chapter compares educators and parents' ratings of children's behaviours related to their social-emotional skills. Parents undoubtedly have a better knowledge of their child in a wider set of situations, while educators have a larger reference group for comparison, but children may also behave differently in different environments.

Educators' ratings on children's behaviours were more closely related to the direct assessment of social-emotional skills and their scores were aggregated into a single score for prosocial behaviour, trust and non-disruptive behaviour, and scaled together with the rest of the study's outcomes. Educators' indirect assessments are, therefore, internationally standardised with a mean of 500 and a standard deviation of 100, and comparable with the scores from other subdomains of the children's direct assessment.

Box 5.1 **Defining social-emotional learning**

Social-emotional learning is the process through which children and adults acquire and effectively apply the knowledge, attitudes, and skills necessary to understand and manage emotions; set and achieve positive goals; feel and show empathy for and towards others; establish and maintain positive relationships; and make responsible decisions (CASEL, 2015[22]; Wessberg et al., 2015[23]).

Social-emotional development is the continuous process of learning social-emotional skills. Similar to literacy and numeracy, developing these skills early on and continuing throughout adulthood is important for their effect on personal, academic and life outcomes over time.

Social-emotional skills are individual characteristics that 1) link biological predispositions and environmental factors; 2) are expressed through consistent patterns of thoughts, feelings and behaviours; 3) develop through formal and informal learning experiences; and 4) influence important socio-economic outcomes throughout life (De Fruyt and Wille, 2015[24]). The term is increasingly prevalent in policy discussions that emphasise improving these skills through learning. Other terms such as "21st century skills", "non-cognitive skills", "employability skills" and "personality characteristics" often refer to the same concept. For further discussion about their overlaps and differences, see Abrahams et al. (2019[25]) and Kankaraš and Suarez-Alvarez (2019[26]).

IELS measures of social-emotional skills are interrelated

An important component of prosocial behaviour and getting along with others is being able to recognise and understand the emotions of others (Strayer, 1987[27]; Strayer, 1993[28]). Both emotion identification and emotion attribution act, therefore, as precursors to engaging in prosocial behaviour in response to another person's emotional state (Hinnant and O'Brien, 2007[29]). At the same time, it is important to note that prosocial behaviour goes one-step further as it also includes the expression of positive social behaviours, such as: the child "tries to comfort others when they are upset".

The central aspect of trust in IELS is the child's expectations that others will be supportive, responsive and kind (Bowlby, 1983[30]). Children develop their first relationships with adults, peers and friends in early childhood. When these first relationships are consistent, predictable and responsive to their needs, children are more likely to develop secure attachments that help them to acquire and reinforce their trust in known people and themselves (Bowlby, 1983[30]). It is important to clarify that trust does not mean that children are indiscriminately developing secure attachments with anybody without judgement, but that they develop trust because of frequent and repetitive patterns with close adults. Reassuring expressions from caregivers (which nurture a child's secure attachment) can support children to continue to play comfortably, while anxious expressions (which nurture a child's insecure attachments) might interfere in children's trust and playful interactions and, ultimately, hamper their development (Baldwin and Moses, 1996[31]). Mistrustful children might be overly wary or fearful of peers or adults; a child might be reluctant to engage with others, or be needy and dependent since s/he does not trust others to be responsive and supportive. As shown in this chapter, children's trust is associated with adaptive social behaviour, such as the expression of prosocial and non-disruptive behaviour.

SOCIAL-EMOTIONAL SKILLS OF FIVE-YEAR-OLDS IN ESTONIA

The average five-year-old child in Estonia exhibit social-emotional skills at the same or higher levels than their counterparts in England and the United States, although educators in Estonia rate five-year-olds as more disruptive than educators in England or the United States rated their respective children.

When presented with a range of stories and situations, children in Estonia were better able to identify the feelings of the characters than children in the United States and England. The mean for five-year-olds in Estonia on emotion identification was 511 points, which is significantly higher than England (497) and the United States (493). Children's ability to recognise emotions is a precursor of their ability to feel empathy for others. In emotion attribution, where the score reflects children's own emotions, children in Estonia scored similar to those in the United States and England.

According to educators, children in Estonia had significantly higher prosocial behaviour (511) than children in the United States (494) and England (495). However, educators in Estonia (470) rated children significantly more disruptive than children in the United States (515) and England (515). Educators in the three countries participating in the study rated children's average levels of trust similarly.

Scores were scaled so that the overall mean in each domain (emotion identification, emotion attribution, prosocial behaviour, trust and non-disruptive) was 500, and the standard deviation 100. Each country contributed equally to the computation of that mean. The distributions of social-emotional scores in Estonia are shown in Figure 5.1.

Figure 5.1 **Distribution of social-emotional learning scores, Estonia**

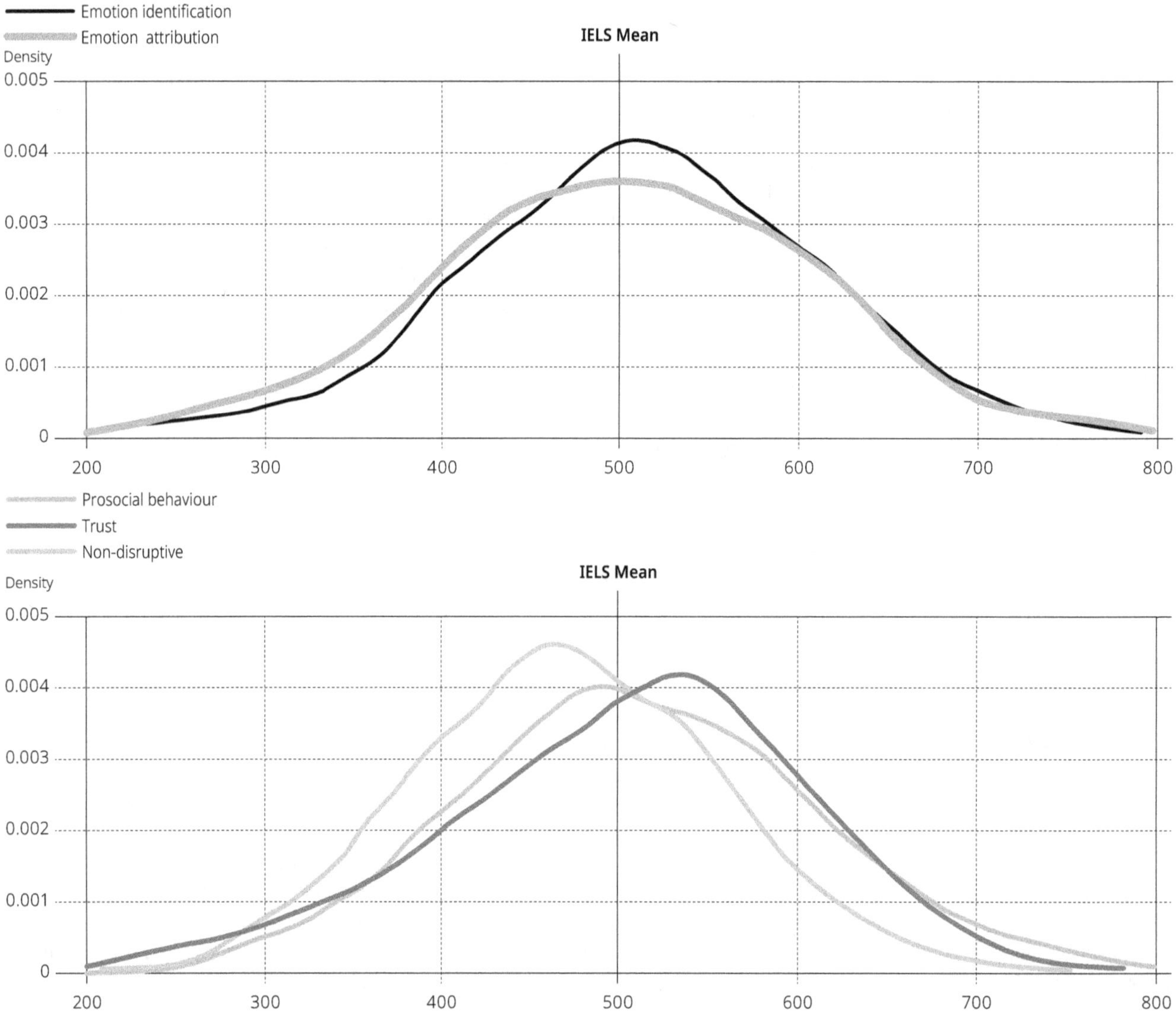

Note: Graphs produced using the first plausible values.

Social-emotional learning scores are interrelated in both the direct and indirect assessments

Table 5.1 shows the correlation coefficients between the social-emotional skills measured as part of IELS for Estonia. For the direct assessment, the scores for emotion identification and emotion attribution were strongly correlated (r=0.54). For the indirect assessments (both educators and parents), the association between prosocial behaviour and non-disruptive behaviour was strong. The strongest association was between ratings of prosocial behaviour and trust. The association between trust and non-disruptive behaviour in Estonia was weaker than in the United States and England. As expected, these results were similar to the overall correlations across participating countries in IELS.

The association between the direct assessment of children and educators' indirect assessment is moderately strong. The direct assessment provides children's scores on emotion identification and emotion attribution, while the indirect assessment provides educator views on children's prosocial behaviour, trust and non-disruptive behaviour. Examples of prosocial behaviour include the child "understands others' feelings" and "tries to comfort others when they are upset". While the first statement is closely associated with the tasks in the direct assessment, the second statement includes a positive behaviour. Examples of trust include the child "approaches familiar adults for comfort when upset" and for disruptive behaviours: the child "fights with other children". Although these behaviours still relate to the tasks presented in the direct assessment, they are slightly more distal behaviours from emotion identification and emotion attribution than prosocial behaviour.

On the other hand, the association between educators' and parents' indirect assessments is moderate while the association between parents' ratings and the direct assessment of children's social and emotional is smaller. As previously mentioned, these domains are conceptually overlapping, but not exactly the same.

Table 5.1 **Correlations between the social-emotional skills in each type of assessment, Estonia**

		Direct assessment		Indirect assessment (educators)			Indirect assessment (parents)	
		Emotion identification	Emotion attribution	Prosocial behaviour	Trust	Non-disruptive	Prosocial behaviour	Trust
Direct assessment	Emotion attribution	0.54 (0.57)						
Indirect assessment (educators)	Prosocial behaviour	0.21 (0.25)	0.16 (0.18)					
	Trust	0.19 (0.17)	0.11 (0.13)	0.67 (0.72)				
	Non-disruptive	0.09 (0.12)	0.09 (0.09)	0.51 (0.49)	0.08 (0.21)			
Indirect assessment (parents)	Prosocial behaviour	0.14 (0.14)	0.10 (0.10)	0.27 (0.23)	0.20 (0.20)	0.16 (0.12)		
	Trust	0.09 (0.10)	0.06 (0.07)	0.14 (0.13)	0.29 0.27)	-0.05 (-0.04)	0.77 (0.80)	
	Non-disruptive	0.01 (0.06)	0.10 (0.11)	0.23 (0.22)	0.00 (0.06)	0.42 (0.35)	0.43 (0.47)	0.31 (0.37)

Note: This table shows the correlation coefficients between the social-emotional skills in Estonia (using child weights). The values in parentheses are the overall values across participating countries in IELS (senate weighted).

StatLink https://doi.org/10.1787/888934107066

Parents give more positive ratings of their children's empathy skills than educators but rate children's emotional control as less developed

In addition to the direct assessment of emotion identification and emotion attribution, parents and educators rated children's development in empathy (e.g. the child is considerate, helpful, caring) and emotional control (e.g. the child controls emotions, waits patiently for something he or she wants). Parents were more likely to rate children's empathy skills as more developed than educators (Figure 5.2). However, parents rated children's emotional control as less developed than educators. Parents in England and the United States also rated children's empathy skills as more developed than educators. However, educators in England and the United States rated children's emotional control similarly to parents.

Figure 5.2 **Social-emotional development as reported by parents and educators, Estonia**

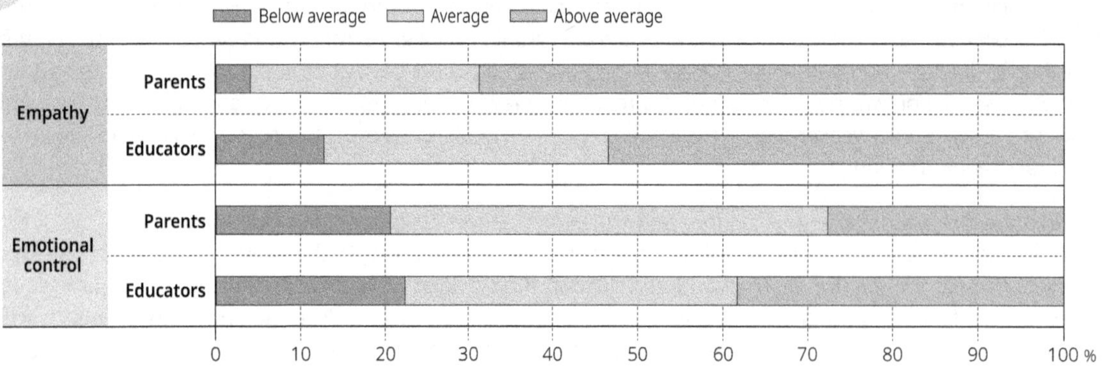

Note: The figure is comparing the same children rated by their educators and parents.
StatLink https://doi.org/10.1787/888934107085

INDIVIDUAL CHARACTERISTICS AND SOCIAL-EMOTIONAL SKILLS

Girls typically have better social-emotional outcomes than boys

Figure 5.3 shows that, on average, girls had better social-emotional scores than boys with respect to emotion identification, emotion attribution, prosocial behaviour, trust and non-disruptive behaviour. Educators reported higher gender differences in prosocial behaviour than were found in the direct assessment. The differences in scores between boys and girls were statistically significant for the direct and indirect assessments. The gender gap in Estonia is significantly larger than in the United States in prosocial behaviour and trust. However, the gender gap in Estonia is not significantly larger than in the United States in emotion identification, emotion attribution, and non-disruptive behaviour or in any of the five social-emotional domains in comparison to England.

Figure 5.3 **Social-emotional scores by gender, Estonia**

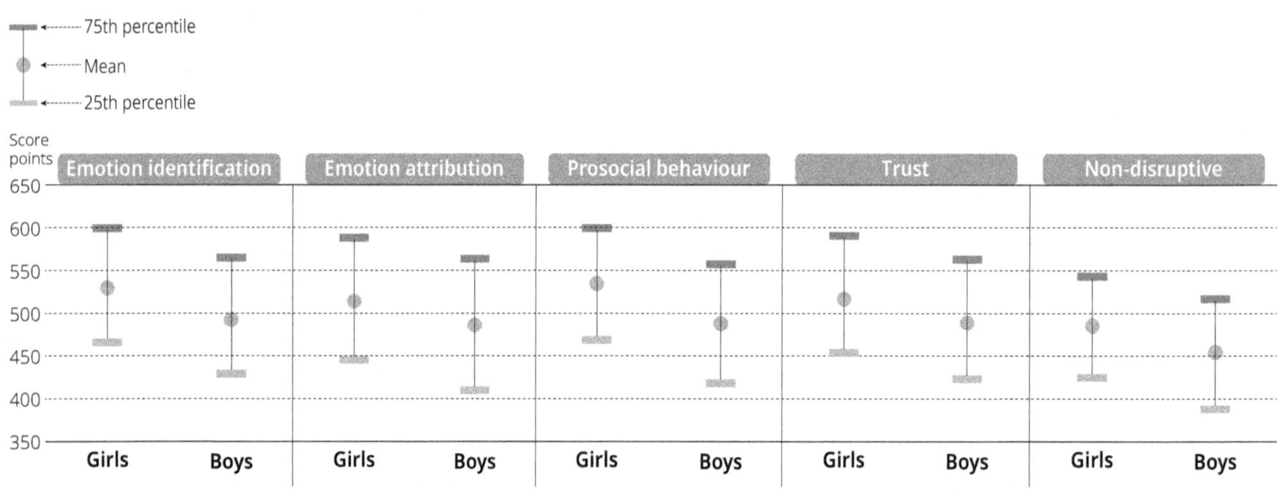

Note: The gender differences in mean scores are statistically significant.
StatLink https://doi.org/10.1787/888934107104

Both parents and educators reported girls as having more developed empathy and emotional control than boys (Figure 5.4). This difference also existed in England and the United States. Parents were also more likely than educators to rate children's empathy skills as better developed regardless of their gender.

Figure 5.4 **Social-emotional development as reported by parents and educators by gender, Estonia**

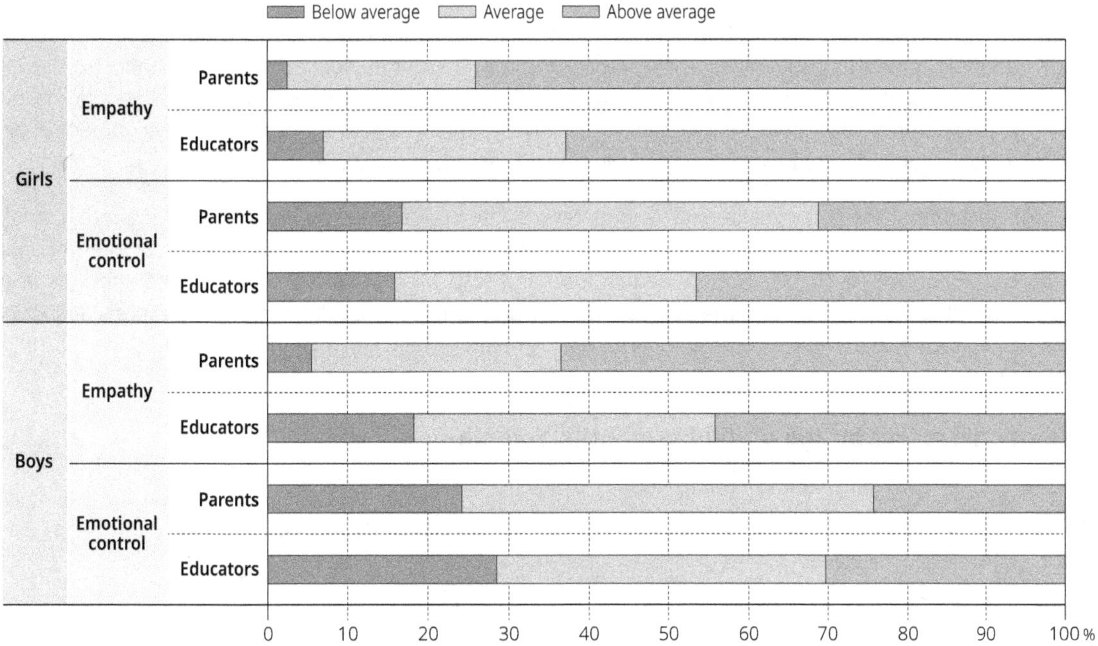

Below average Average Above average

Girls
Empathy: Parents, Educators
Emotional control: Parents, Educators

Boys
Empathy: Parents, Educators
Emotional control: Parents, Educators

0 10 20 30 40 50 60 70 80 90 100 %

Note: The figure is comparing the same children rated by their educators and parents.

StatLink https://doi.org/10.1787/888934107123

The gender gap in social-emotional skills is larger among Russian-speaking children

Figure 5.5 shows the differences between girls and boys by language (i.e. Estonian-speaking children and Russian-speaking children), with girls having, on average, better social-emotional outcomes than boys across both subgroups. However, Russian-speaking children had the highest gender difference in social-emotional scores. In prosocial behaviour, where the highest gap was found, Russian-speaking girls scored 66 points higher than Russian-speaking boys, compared to Estonian-speaking girls who scored 41 points higher than Estonian-speaking boys.

At the same time, Russian-speaking girls scored on average 18 points more than Estonian-speaking girls across all social-emotional skills, , while this difference was 9 points for boys. The following section will provide further analyses of the differences in findings between Estonian and Russian-speaking children.

Figure 5.5 **Social-emotional scores by language and gender, Estonia**

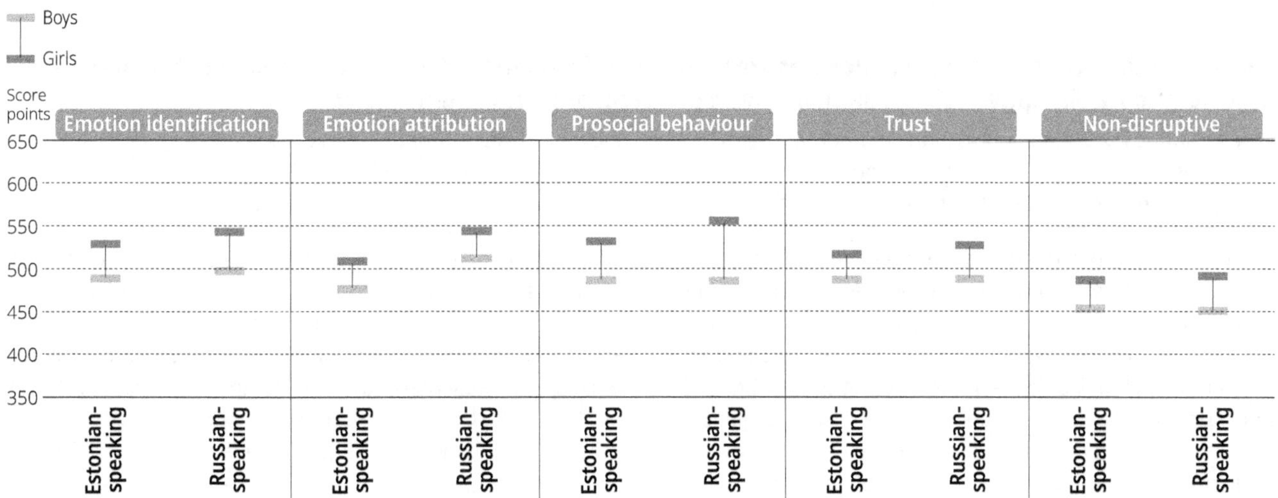

Note: The differences shown in this figure are all statistically significant.

StatLink https://doi.org/10.1787/888934107142

Children's social-emotional skills scores increase slightly with age

In Estonia, the average difference between the oldest and youngest children was 108 points for emotion identification and 71 points for emotion attribution. This means, for every additional month in age, children's emotion identification scores increased by 7 points on average and their emotion attribution scores by 4 points. On average, the oldest children in Estonia (6 years 0 months) scored approximately 80 points more than the youngest children (5 years 0 months) in the direct assessment domains. This means that a score-point difference of 20 points in this report roughly equates to a quarter year in the development of an average 5-years old child in these domains, assuming his/her development is approximately linear.

Figure 5.6 shows the social-emotional scores by children's age in months at the time of assessment. The data indicate a small but significant positive correlation between children's age and their scores on the direct assessment of their social-emotional learning. In Estonia, the correlation was 0.21 for emotion identification and 0.12 for emotion attribution. Differences by age were smaller in educator indirect assessment ratings: the correlation was significant for prosocial behaviour and not statistically significant for trust and non-disruptive behaviour. The data show similar correlations between age and social-emotional learning outcomes for boys and girls.

Figure 5.6 **Social-emotional scores by age of child in months, Estonia**

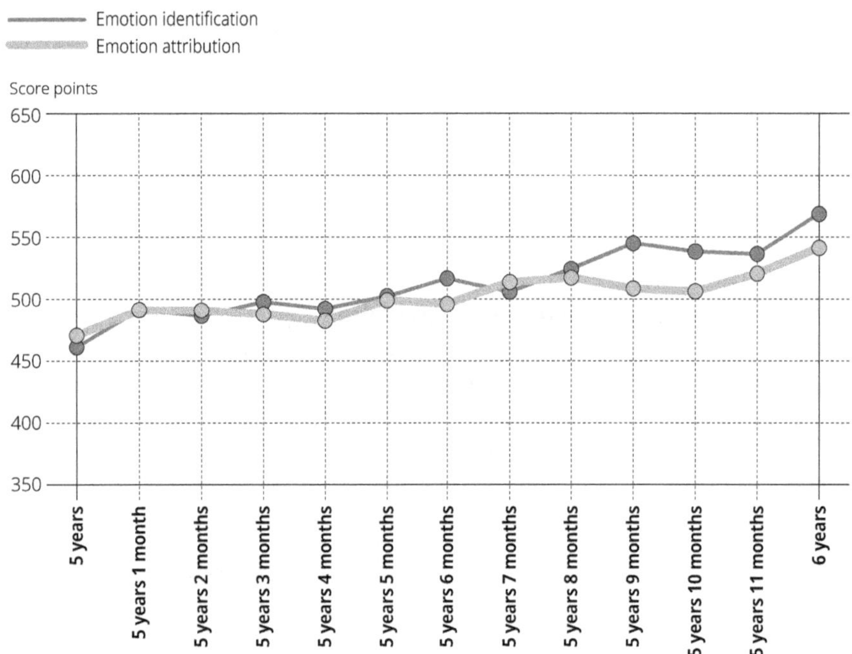

StatLink https://doi.org/10.1787/888934107161

Social, emotional or behavioural difficulties are more strongly associated with lower social-emotional skills, especially more disruptive behaviour, than low birth weight or learning difficulties

Parents in IELS provided information on whether their child had a low birth weight (under 2.5 kg) or premature birth, learning difficulties, or social, emotional or behavioural difficulties. The child's ECEC centre also provided information on whether they were classified as having special educational needs (SEN).

The cause of low birth weight is often premature birth (i.e. born before 37 weeks gestation). Parents of 8% of 5-year-old children in Estonia reported that their children had low birth weight or premature birth, slightly lower to the share in England (11%) and the United States (10%). Children with learning difficulties (e.g. speech or language delay, intellectual disability) in Estonia represented 10% of children, which was 3 percentage points lower than in the United States, and similar to England. Children with emotional difficulties (e.g. social, emotional or behavioural difficulties) represented 10% of children in Estonia, which was approximately 2 percentage points higher than in England and lower than in the United States. Children with SEN (e.g. cognitive, behavioural or emotional disability) represented 5% of children in Estonia, which was less 2 percentage points lower than in England (the United States had no available data).

In Estonia, boys were more likely than girls to be identified by their parents as having learning difficulties (13% for boys and 7% for girls); having social, emotional or behavioural difficulties (14% for boys and 7% for girls); and having SEN (6% of boys and 3%

of girls). However, the data showed no significant gender differences in social-emotional learning scores between children with and without these difficulties, after accounting for socio-economic status (the low number of children with SEN do not allow a robust analysis by gender).

Overall, 17% of children in Estonia had experienced one of these three challenges, as reported by parents, 4% had experienced two and fewer than 1% had experienced all three. In other words, 78% of parents reported that their children had experienced none of these challenges, which is similar to the percentage in England and the United States.

Children who had experienced learning difficulties had lower emotion identification and emotion attribution skills, and were rated by their educators as having lower prosocial behaviour and trust, than children without learning difficulties, after controlling for socio-economic status. Children with social, emotional or behavioural difficulties had lower emotion identification, prosocial behaviour and trust, as well as more disruptive behaviour, after controlling for socio-economic status.

When all of these challenges were analysed together, social, emotional or behavioural difficulties were more highly associated with poor social-emotional outcomes than low birth weight, or learning difficulties – except in the case of emotion identification and trust, where learning difficulties were also highly associated with poorer outcomes. Disruptive behaviour was particularly associated with social, emotional or behavioural difficulties, as might be expected. These associations were significant after controlling for socio-economic status.

When analysed alone, children with a low birth weight or premature birth had lower emotion identification skills than children born weighing over 2.5 kg. However, these differences disappeared when controlling for children's learning and social, emotional or behavioural difficulties.

Figure 5.7 **Relative associations between early difficulties and social-emotional scores, Estonia**

Score-point differences between children who have and have not experienced an early difficulty, after accounting for the effects of other early difficulties, and before and after accounting for socio-economic status

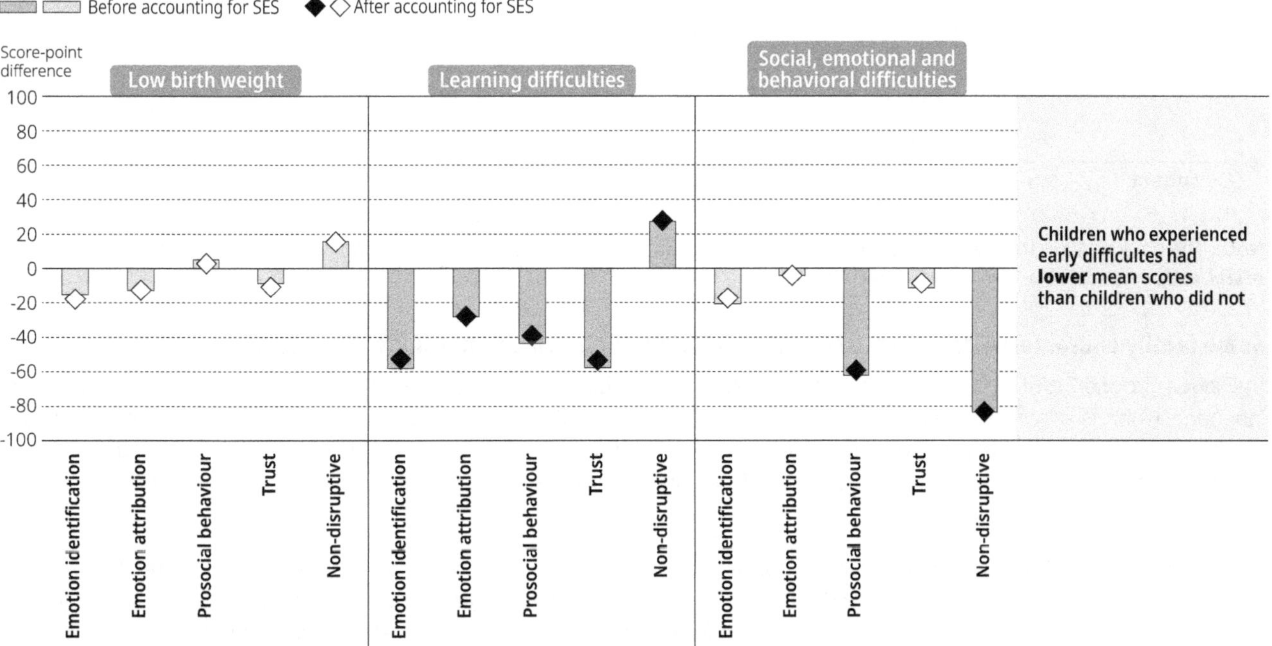

Note: Darker coloured markers indicate that the difference is statistically significant.

StatLink https://doi.org/10.1787/888934107180

HOME AND FAMILY CHARACTERISTICS AND EARLY SOCIAL-EMOTIONAL SKILLS

Children from advantaged socio-economic backgrounds in Estonia have higher social-emotional scores, but the differences were narrower than in the other two countries participating in the study

Figure 5.8 shows the difference in social-emotional learning outcomes between children from the top and bottom quartile of the national socio-economic status (SES) index[1]. IELS defines children from an advantaged socio-economic background as those located in the top quartile of socio-economic status. Children from a disadvantaged socio-economic background are defined as those located in the bottom quartile. The results show that children from advantaged socio-economic backgrounds had higher outcomes than children from disadvantaged socio-economic backgrounds in both direct and indirect assessments.

Nevertheless, the strength of the relationship varied depending on the social-emotional outcome. The direct assessment showed that socio-economic status had a significant relationship with emotion identification, but not on emotion attribution. According to educators, children from an advantaged socio-economic background had higher prosocial behaviour and trust, but similar disruptive behaviour as children from other socio-economic backgrounds.

In Estonia, socio-economic status was significantly positively correlated with emotion identification (r = 0.17), prosocial behaviour (r = 0.16), and trust (r = 0.14), and not significantly associated with emotion attribution and disruptive behaviour. In the United States, socio-economic status was significantly positively correlated with emotion identification (r = 0.18), emotion attribution (r = 0.08), prosocial behaviour (r = 0.15), trust (r = 0.12), and not significantly associated with disruptive behaviour. In England, socio-economic status was significantly positively correlated with emotion identification (r = 0.15), emotion attribution (r = 0.17), prosocial behaviour (r = 0.17), trust (r = 0.11), and non-disruptive behaviour (r = 0.10).

Figure 5.8 **Social-emotional scores by socio-economic quartile, Estonia**

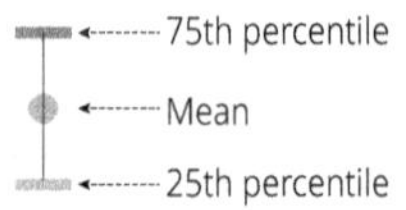

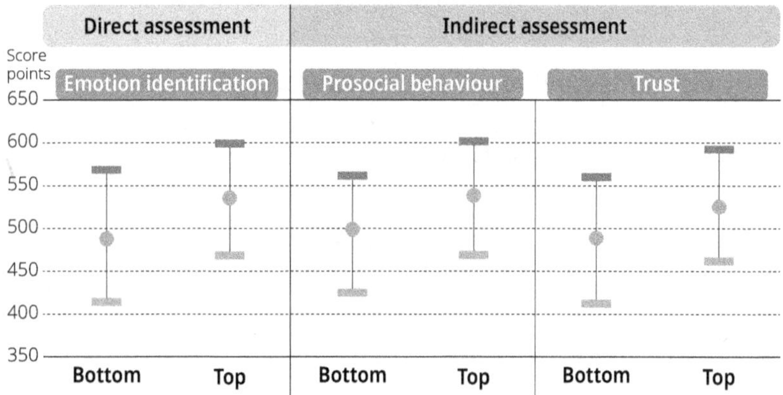

Note: The differences in the mean scores of children in the bottom and top quartiles of socio-economic status are statistically significant.
StatLink https://doi.org/10.1787/888934107199

Some family characteristics are not associated with the social-emotional skills of children.

In Estonia, around 6% of children lived in homes where at least one parent mostly spoke a language other than the assessment language, which is lower than in England (16%) and the United States (20%). In Estonia, the two languages of assessment were Estonian and Russian. The results from both direct and indirect assessments showed no significant differences in the results of children who spoke a language at home other than Estonian or Russian and the results of other children, either before or after controlling for socio-economic status.

In Estonia, 12% of children lived in single-parent households, which was lower than in England (15%) and the United States (15%). The direct and indirect assessments showed no statistically significant differences between one- and two-parent households in terms of children's social-emotional outcomes, either before or after controlling for socio-economic status. Parents' age was also not significantly associated with social-emotional skills after accounting for socio-economic background.

IELS defines an immigrant background as having both parents – or the sole parent if a single parent – born in another country or economy than where the study took place. In Estonia, less than 2% of children had an immigrant background, which is substantially lower than in the United States (18%) and England (18%). The low number of children with an immigrant background in Estonia was not sufficient to provide robust comparative results.

Russian-speaking children have better social-emotional outcomes than Estonian-speaking children

In Estonia, Russian-speaking children represented 21% of the children. Figure 5.9 shows the social-emotional scores of Estonian-speaking children and Russian-speaking children, before and after controlling for socio-economic status. Russian-speaking children had significantly higher outcomes than Estonian-speaking children in emotion identification, emotion attribution, prosocial behaviour and trust. According to educators, however, Russian-speaking children were as disruptive as Estonian-speaking children.

As previously noted, Russian-speaking children showed more prominent gender differences than Estonian-speaking children. However, Russian-speaking girls did not significantly contribute more than boys to the overall differences, after accounting for socio-economic status and the overall gender differences on outcomes.

Figure 5.9 **Social-emotional scores by children's language, Estonia**

Score-point differences between Russian-speaking children and Estonian-speaking children, before and after accounting for socio-economic status

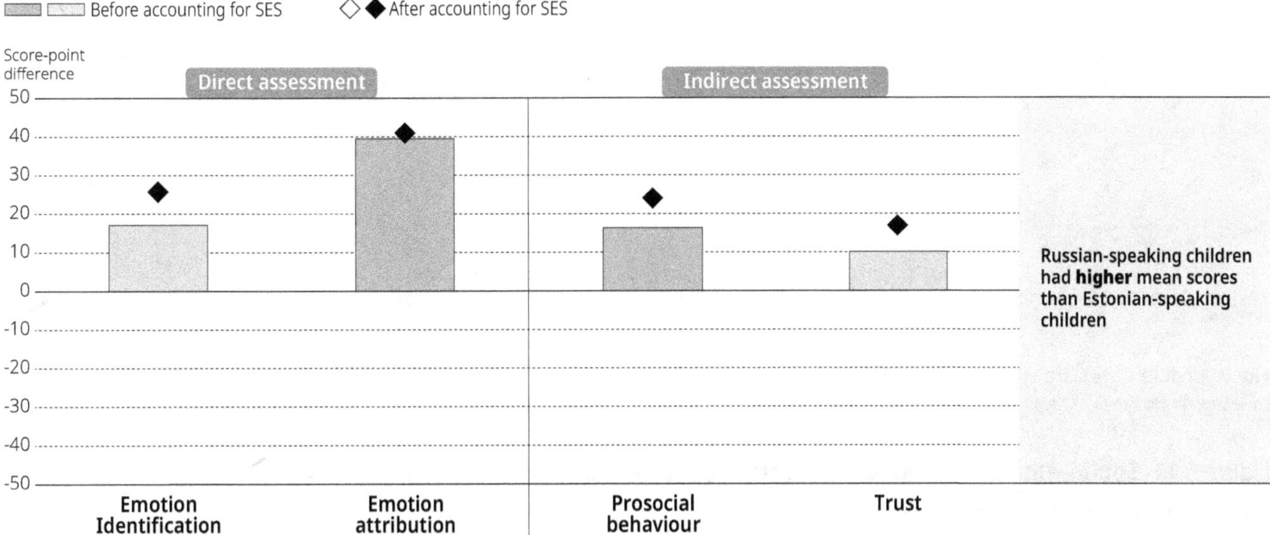

Note: Darker coloured markers indicate that the difference is statistically significant. Russian-speaking children refer to children who took the assessment in Russian.

StatLink https://doi.org/10.1787/888934107218

Children whose mothers had completed tertiary education have better social-emotional outcomes than those whose mothers had not

In Estonia, 53% of mothers with five-year-olds had completed tertiary education (i.e. bachelor's degree or master's degree, professional degree or doctorate), which was higher than in the other two countries participating in the study (40% in England and 39% in the United States). Figure 5.10 shows the social-emotional scores of children whose mothers had completed tertiary education and those whose mothers had not, with results showing that children whose mothers had completed tertiary education had higher emotion identification and higher prosocial behaviour and trust, after accounting for household income. Maternal education is also positively associated with social-emotional scores after accounting household income in England and the United States.

Being an only-child is associated with higher disruptive behaviour and lower emotion identification

In Estonia, approximately 20% of children had no siblings, 50% had one, 21% had two, 6% had three, 1% had four and around 1% had five or more. Across participating countries, most children had one sibling. On average, children in Estonia had a lower number of siblings than in the other two countries: around 8% of children had three or more siblings compared to 12% in England and 20% in the United States.

The average 5-years old child with no siblings in Estonia had higher disruptive behaviour scores than children with one or more siblings and lower mean emotion identification scores than children with one sibling (Figure 5.11). These differences remained significant after controlling for socio-economic background. Children without siblings were also reported by educators in England as having higher disruptive behaviour than children with one or more siblings. However, this result was not found in the United States after controlling for socio-economic status.

Figure 5.10 **Social-emotional scores by mother's educational attainment, Estonia**

Score-point differences between children whose mothers have at least a bachelor's degree and those whose mothers do not, before and after accounting for household income

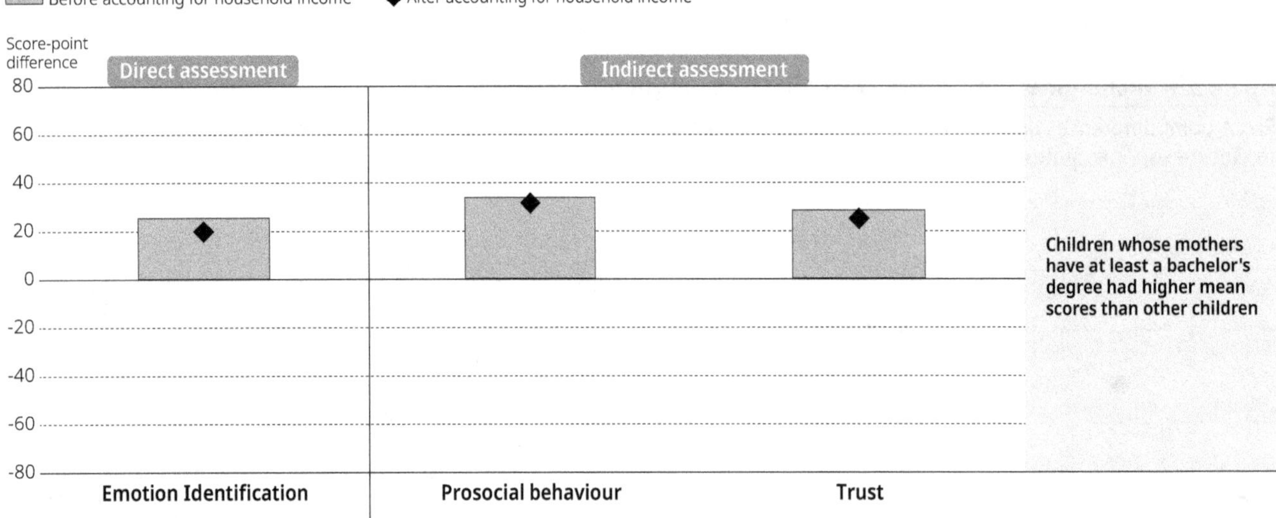

Note: All differences are statistically significant.

StatLink https://doi.org/10.1787/888934107237

Figure 5.11 **Social-emotional scores by number of siblings, Estonia**

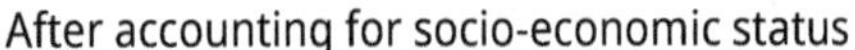

After accounting for socio-economic status

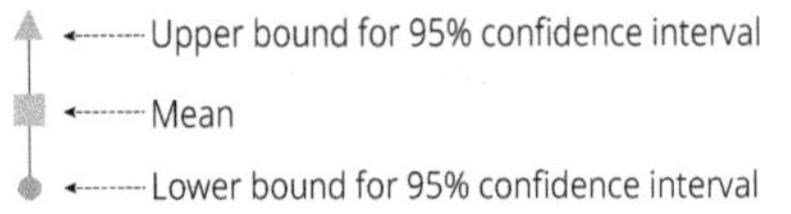

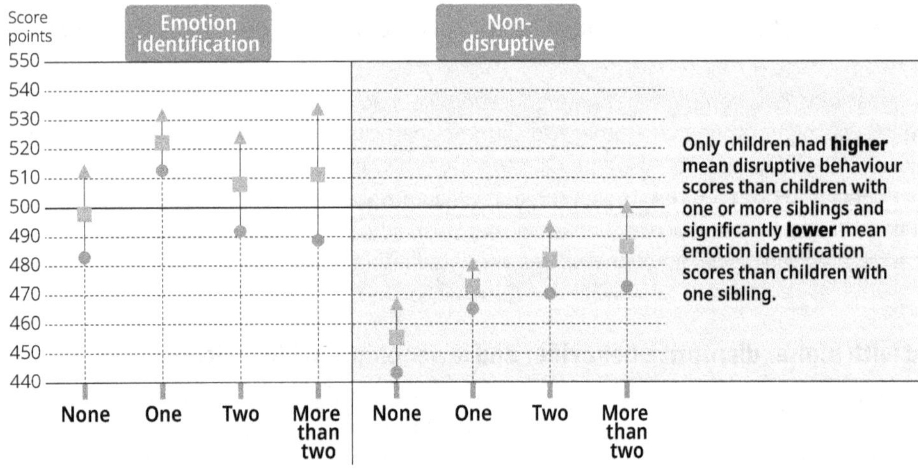

StatLink https://doi.org/10.1787/888934107256

HOME LEARNING ENVIRONMENT AND EARLY SOCIAL-EMOTIONAL SKILLS

The number of books children have access to at home is positively related to their social-emotional skills

In Estonia, 13% of children lived in households with 10 children's books or fewer, 23% in homes with 11-25 books, 32% in homes with 26-50 books, 21% in homes with 51-100 books and 10% in homes with more than 100 children's books. Children in Estonia had, on average, a lower number of children's books than children in the United States and England (the most frequent category in both the United States and England was more than 100). Children in homes with more books had, on average, higher social-emotional outcomes in the direct assessment of emotion identification and emotion attribution. This association remained significant after controlling for socio-economic status (Figure 5.12).

The indirect assessment yielded similar findings. Educators reported significantly higher prosocial behaviour and less disruptive behaviour in children from homes with more than 100 children's books, in comparison with households that had between 26 and 50 books, after accounting for socio-economic status. The positive association of having a higher number of books at home did not significantly differ by gender, after accounting for socio-economic status.

Figure 5.12 **Social-emotional scores by number of children's books in the home, Estonia**

After accounting for socio-economic status

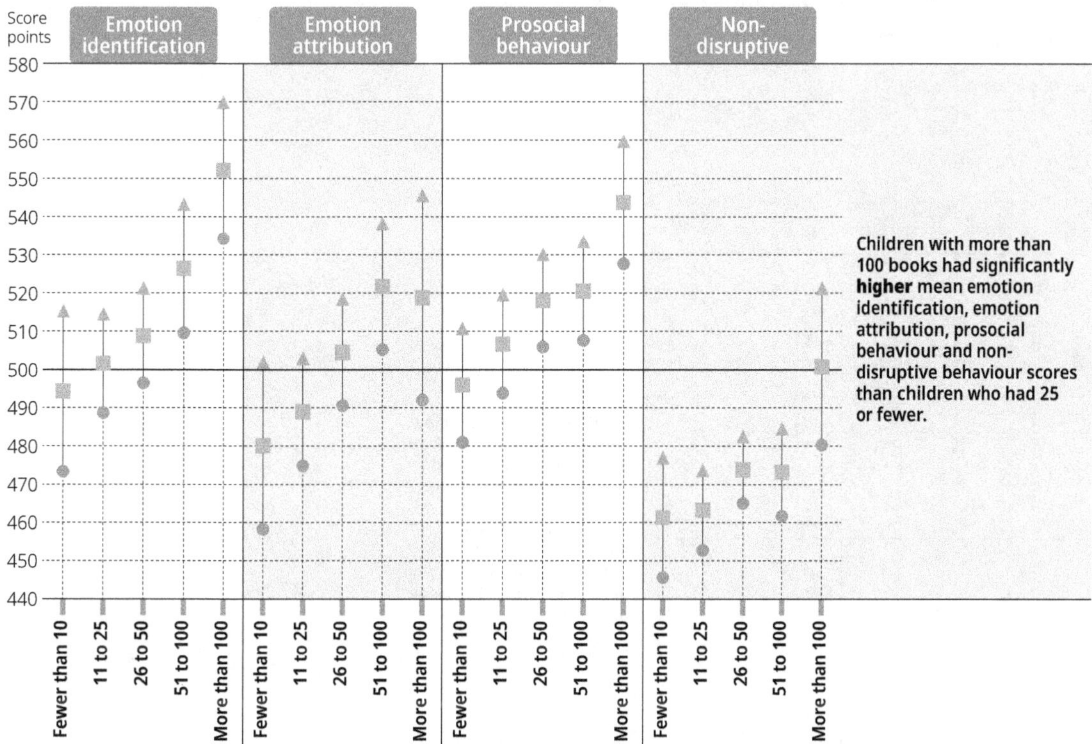

StatLink https://doi.org/10.1787/888934107275

Role-playing and having back-and-forth conversations with parents is associated with social-emotional skills, but doing it every day is not always better.

In Estonia, 6% of children never role-played with their parents (defined as imaginative or pretend play such as playing the role of a chef or shopkeeper), 28% did so less than once a week, 37% did so one or two days a week, 21% did so between three and four days a week, and 9% did so between five and seven days a week. The percentage of children in Estonia who role-played with their parents between three and seven days a week (30%) was lower than in the other two countries participating in the study (around 60% in the United States and 50% in England).

Children who role-played with their parents once or twice a week were better able to recognise emotions and were rated by their educators as having more trust than children who did so between five and seven days a week. (Figure 5.13). However, children who did these activities between five and seven days a week were less disruptive. These results remained significant after controlling for socio-economic status. The results did not significantly differ by gender, after accounting for socio-economic status. While these results were not significant for emergent literacy or numeracy, there was a positive association between children who role-played one or two days a week and scores in working memory compared to children who never role-played, after accounting for socio-economic status.

Role-playing with parents also showed differences in children's social-emotional scores in the other two countries, but the frequency was differently associated with the outcomes. In England, children who did role-play with their parents one or two days a week had significantly higher emotion attribution than children who did not. In the United States, children who did role-play with their parents between 5 and 7 days a week had significantly higher mean emotion identification, emotion attribution, and prosocial behaviour scores than children who did it less than once a week.

In Estonia, fewer than 1% of parents reported that they never had back-and-forth conversations with their children about how they feel, 5% did so less than once a week, 17% one or two days a week, 29% three or four days a week, and 48% between five and seven days a week. These percentages were similar to England and United States. Children who had back-and-forth conversations with their parents between five and seven days a week were less disruptive, according to their educators, than those who did so between three and four days a week, after accounting for socio-economic status. Children in England and the United States who regularly have back-and-forth conversations about how they feel also had higher mean social-emotional scores.

Figure 5.13 **Social-emotional scores by frequency of role-play with parents, Estonia**

After accounting for socio-economic status

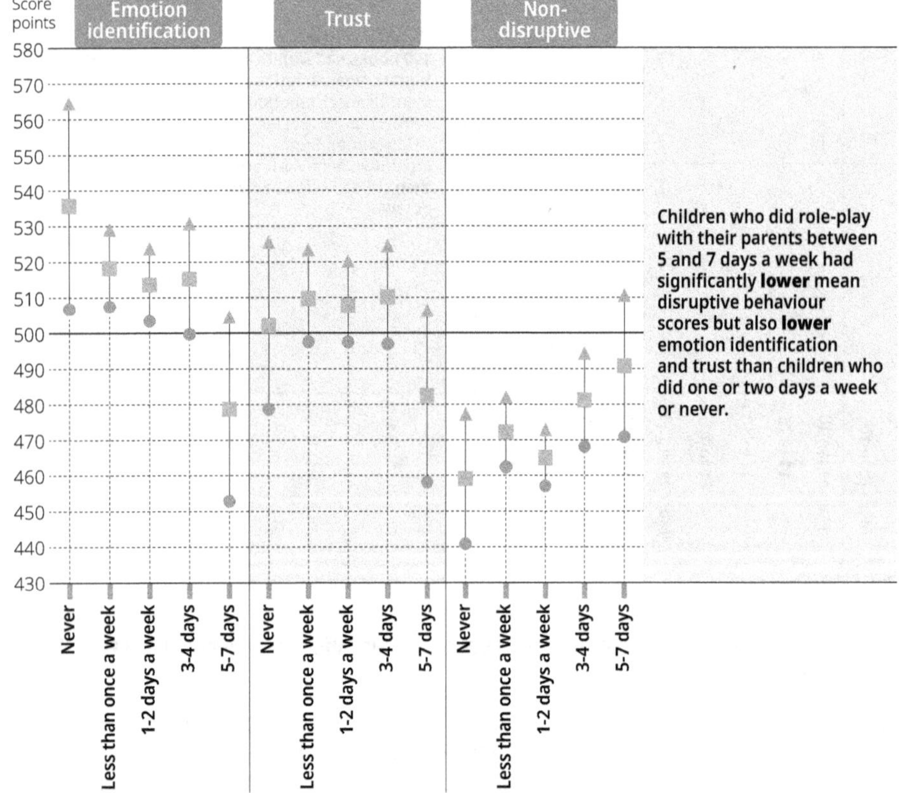

StatLink https://doi.org/10.1787/888934107294

Children whose parents read to them regularly have higher mean emotion identification, prosocial behaviour and trust scores.

In Estonia, 17% of parents read from a book to their child less than once a week, 24% did so one or two days a week, 22% three or four days a week, and 38% between five and seven days a week. The percentage of parents who read from a book to their child between five and seven days a week was lower than in the United States (43%) and England (59%). Children whose parents read to them between five and seven days a week had significantly higher mean trust scores than those whose parents read to them only one or two days a week. At the same time, children whose parents read to them less than one day a week had significantly lower mean emotion identification and prosocial behaviour scores than those whose parents read to them 3 or 4 days a week or between 5 to 7 days a week respectively, after controlling for socio-economic status (Figure 5.14). This association did not significantly differ by gender, after accounting for socio-economic status.

Figure 5.14 **Social-emotional scores by frequency of being read to by parents, Estonia**

After accounting for socio-economic status

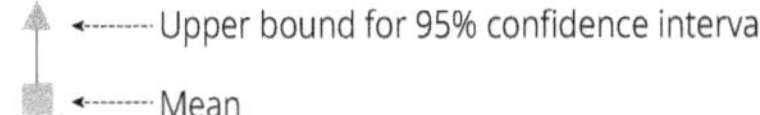

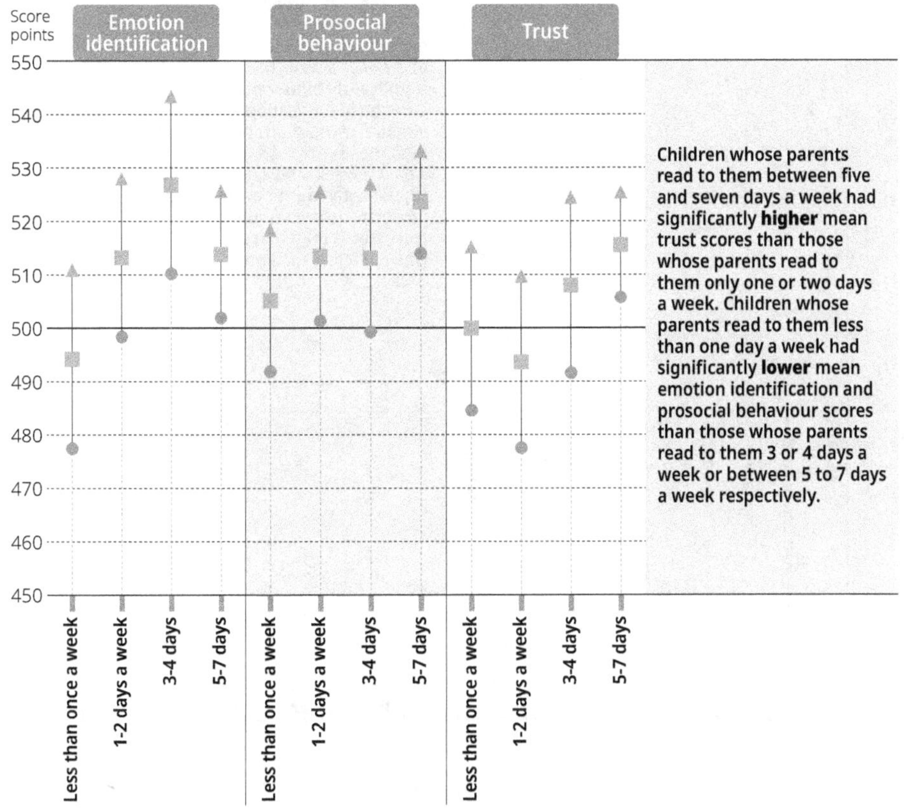

StatLink https://doi.org/10.1787/888934107313

Children who regularly attended activities outside of the home are more empathetic and have stronger prosocial behaviours and trust than those who attended once a week or less

In Estonia, 22% of parents never took their child to special activities outside of the home, 14% did so less than once a week, 40% one or two days a week, 20% three or four days a week, and 5% between five and seven days a week. Examples of special activities include sports clubs, dance, swimming lessons or language lessons. The percentage of parents who took their child to activities outside of the home between one and two days a week was 36% in the United States and 47% in England. Children who attended special activities outside of the home between 5 and 7 days a week had higher mean empathy scores than those who did so one or two days a week, and were also rated as having stronger prosocial behaviour and trust by their educators than those who went one or two days a week or less, after accounting for socio-economic status (Figure 5.15). The positive relationship between going to special activities outside of the home one or two days a week and social-emotional scores did not significantly differ by gender.

Figure 5.15 **Social-emotional scores by engagement in special or paid activities outside the home, Estonia**

After accounting for socio-economic status

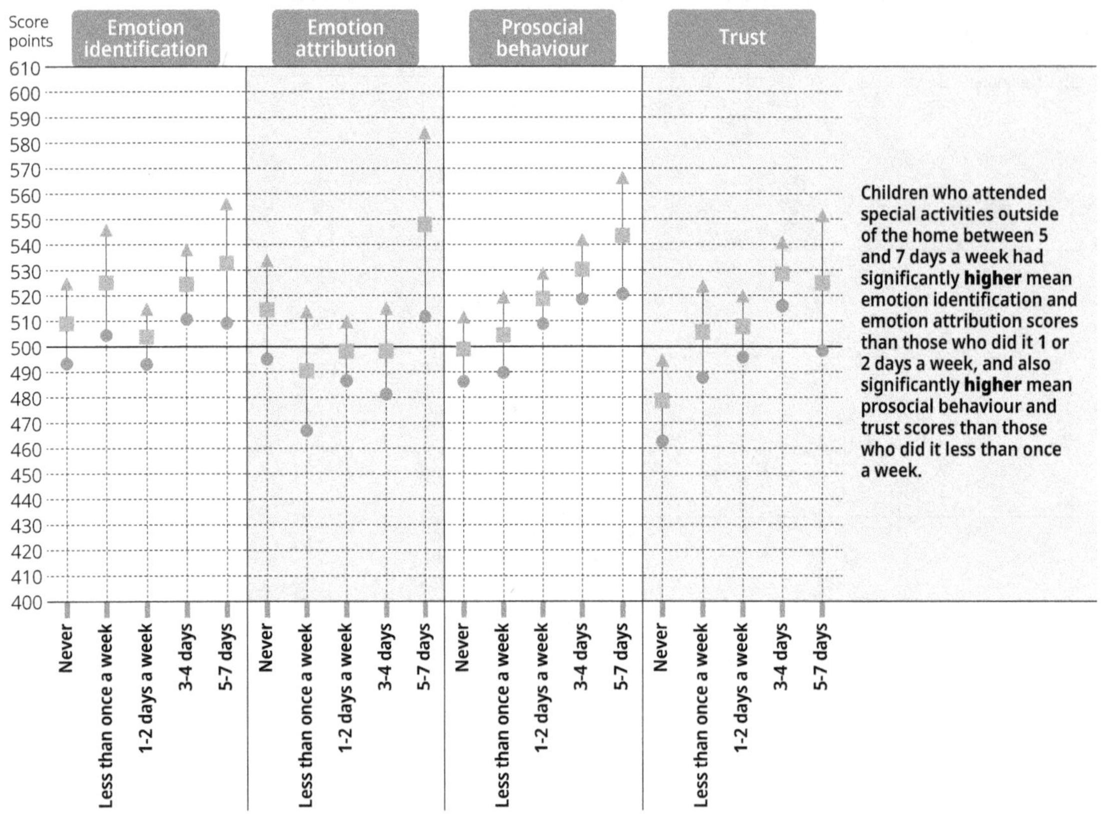

StatLink https://doi.org/10.1787/888934107332

According to educators, children whose parents were very involved in their child's ECEC centre have better social-emotional scores

In Estonia, 80% of parents had a moderate to strong involvement in activities taking place in their child's ECEC centre, which was higher than in the other two countries participating in the study (69% in England and 65% in the United States). Examples of activities include fetes, concerts/plays, parent's evenings and parental workshops. Figure 5.16 shows the social-emotional learning outcomes of children whose parents had a strong involvement and those whose parents did not. According to educators, children whose parents had a strong involvement had better social-emotional learning outcomes, after accounting for socio-economic status. However, these differences were not statistically significant for the children's direct assessment. The positive relationship between parental involvement and children's social-emotional scores did not significantly differ by gender.

Every day use of digital devices is associated with lower prosocial behaviour and trust scores than less frequent use

In Estonia, 9% of children never or hardly ever used a desktop or laptop computer, tablet device or smartphone, 13% used them at least once a month, 39% used them at least once a week, and 39% used them every day. The percentage of children who used digital devices every day was similar in England, but around 10% lower than in the United States. Children who used digital devices every day had significantly lower mean prosocial behaviour and trust scores than children who use them at least once a week. There were no statistically significant differences in prosocial behaviour between children who used digital devices every day and those who never used devices. However, children who used digital devices every day had significantly lower levels of trust than those who used them once a month or never used them. There were no differences in the effects of digital device use between boys and girls.

Figure 5.16 **Social-emotional scores by parental involvement in preschool activities, Estonia**

Score-point differences between children whose parents are moderately or strongly involved in preschool activities and those who are slightly or not involved, before and after accounting for socio-economic status.

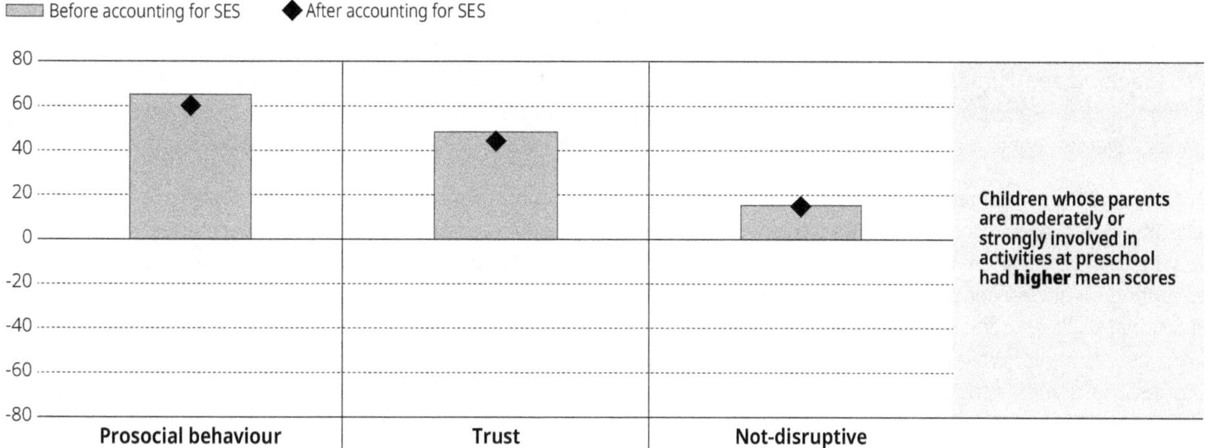

Note: All the differences in this figure are statistically significant.

StatLink https://doi.org/10.1787/888934107351

Parents in IELS were asked whether they, or other carers, did educational activities with their children on a digital device (e.g. computer, laptop or smartphone). In Estonia, around 31% of children never or hardly ever did educational activities with their parents on a digital device, 36% did so less than once a week or never, 20% did so one or two days a week, 8% did so between three and four days a week, and 4% did so between five and seven days a week. The percentage of children who did educational activities with their parents on a digital device was lower than in the other two countries participating in the study (the most frequent occurrence in England and the United States was one or two days a week, while in Estonia it was less than once a week). The results did not show a robust association between children who did educational activities on a digital device and those who did not, after controlling for socio-economic status.

Figure 5.17 **Social-emotional scores by use of digital devices, Estonia**

After accounting for socio-economic status

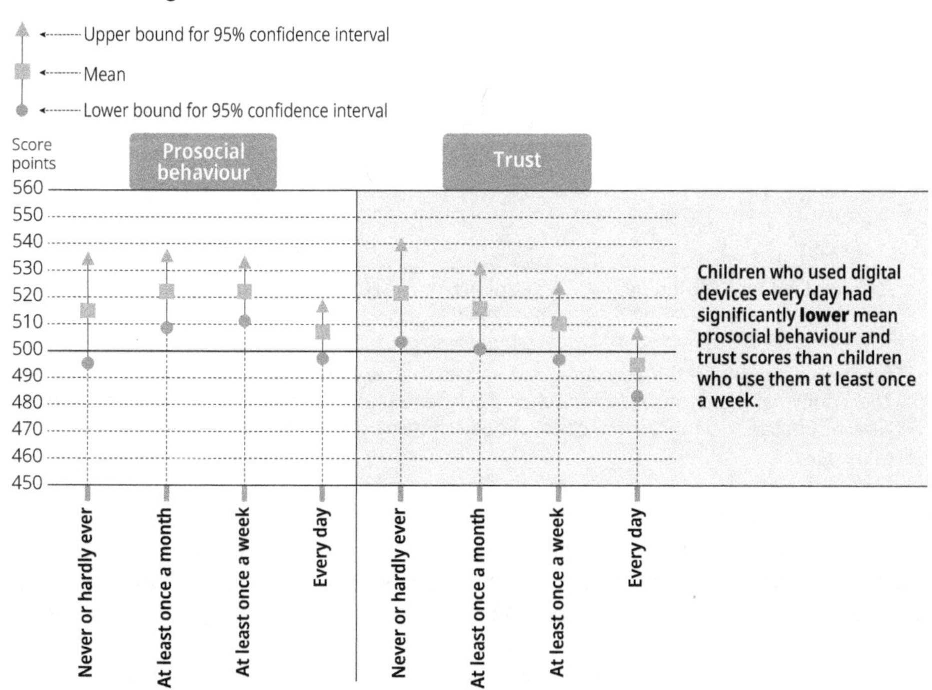

StatLink https://doi.org/10.1787/888934107370

RELATIONSHIP BETWEEN SOCIAL-EMOTIONAL SCORES AND OUTCOMES IN OTHER LEARNING DOMAINS

Children's social-emotional skills are associated with emergent literacy and numeracy, after accounting for socio-economic status

Many studies have shown that social-emotional skills are significant predictors of students' academic performance in areas such as mathematics and reading, after accounting for socio-economic status (Suárez-Álvarez, Fernández-Alonso and Muñiz, 2014[32]; Chamorro-Premuzic and Furnham, 2008[33]). Although previous research has typically assessed students attending primary, secondary and higher education, recent evidence from neuroscience suggests emotion and cognition are interrelated during early infancy development (Bush, Luu and Posner, 2000[2]; Davidson et al., 2002[3]; Posner and Rothbart, 2000[4]).

Figure 5.18 shows the percentage of variation in emergent literacy and numeracy scores explained by social-emotional scores, after accounting for socio-economic status. The first bar presents the percentage of variation in numeracy explained by educators' indirect assessments of children's social-emotional skills (prosocial behaviour, trust and non-disruptive behaviour), after accounting for socio-economic background. The second bar shows the association with the direct assessment of children's social-emotional skills (emotion identification and emotion attribution). The third bar shows the combined effect of the direct and the indirect assessments. While the domains in the second bar were measured using the same assessment method – tablet-based stories and games – the first bar used educator assessments as an independent method. Therefore, the percentages in the first and third bars serve as a proxy of the minimum and maximum variation associated with social-emotional skills, regardless of the assessment method.

The data shows that social-emotional scores were predictive of emergent literacy and numeracy scores in Estonia. Children's social-emotional scores, together with socio-economic status, explained between 10% and 31% of the variation in emergent literacy scores, and between 5% and 27% of emergent literacy scores, after accounting for socio-economic status. Similarly, children's social-emotional scores explained between 6% and 26% of the variation in emergent numeracy scores, after accounting for socio-economic status.

Figure 5.18 **Percentage of the variation in emergent literacy and numeracy scores explained by social-emotional skills and socio-economic status, Estonia**

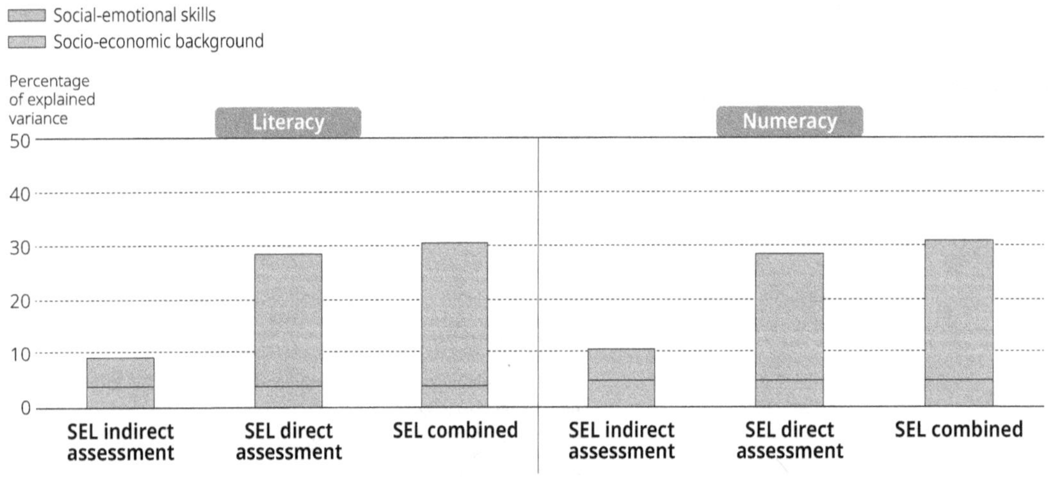

Note: SEL = social-emotional learning. The orange bar shows the percentage of variation in each IELS outcome explained by socio-economic status. The green bars show the additional variance explained when social-emotional skills (indirectly assessed, directly assessed or combined direct and indirect) are introduced to a regression model already containing socio-economic status.

StatLink https://doi.org/10.1787/888934107389

Figure 5.19 shows the percentage of variation in mental flexibility, inhibition and working memory scores (self-regulation skills) explained by social-emotional scores, after accounting for socio-economic status. The bars represent the different measures of social-emotional skills based on educator reports, direct assessments or the combined effect of both. Children's social-emotional scores, together with socio-economic status, explained between 7% and 14% of the variation in working memory scores in Estonia, and between 4% and 11% of emergent working memory scores, after accounting for socio-economic status. Despite sharing the same assessment method, the association between inhibition and empathy skills is weaker. Importantly, educator reports also support the relationship between emotion and cognition in the indirect assessment of social-emotional skills through an independent method. Indeed, educators' indirect assessment explains a significant amount of variation in self-regulation scores after accounting for socio-economic status.

In short, children with higher prosocial behaviour, trust and non-disruptive behaviour, as rated by their educators, had significantly higher emergent literacy, numeracy, and self-regulation scores. At the same time, the direct assessment showed that children who were more empathetic had significantly higher scores in these domains as well.

Figure 5.19 **Percentage of the variation in self-regulation scores explained by social-emotional skills and socio-economic status, Estonia**

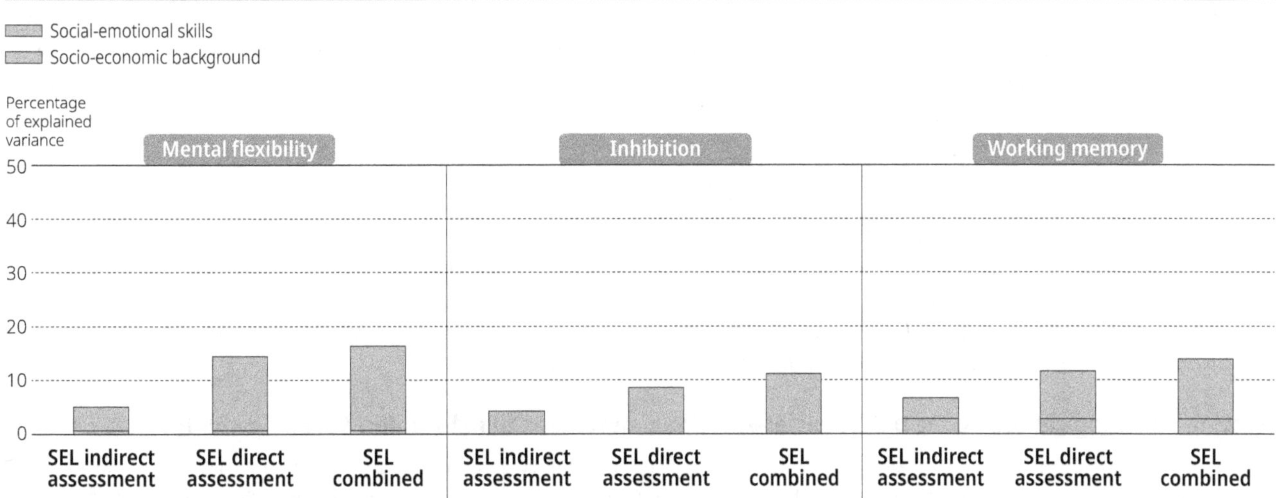

Note: SEL = social-emotional learning. The orange bar shows the percentage of variation in each IELS outcome explained by socio-economic status. The green bars show the additional variance explained when social-emotional skills (indirectly assessed, directly assessed or combined direct and indirect) are introduced to a regression model already containing socio-economic status.

StatLink https://doi.org/10.1787/888934107408

SUMMARY AND CONCLUSIONS

The average five-year-old child in Estonia exhibit social-emotional skills at the same or higher levels than their counterparts in England and the United States

When presented with a range of stories and situations, children in Estonia were better able to identify the feelings of the characters than children in England and the United States. Children in Estonia had significantly higher mean emotion identification scores than children in England and the United States.

Children's ability to recognise emotions is a precursor of the ability to feel empathy towards others, and the emotion attribution scores in IELS reflect children's ability to recognise their own and other's emotions. The results show that children in Estonia scored similarly to children in England and the United States in emotion attribution.

According to educators, children in Estonia had significantly higher mean prosocial behaviour than children in the United States and England. However, educators in Estonia rated children significantly more disruptive than children in the United States and England.

Parents in Estonia were more likely to rate children's empathy skills as more developed than educators (e.g. whether the child is considerate, helpful, caring). Similar findings are observed in England and the United States. This might indicate differences between children's empathy development in early childhood education and care (ECEC) settings and at home, as well as different expectations of parents and educators. On the other hand, parents in Estonia rated children's emotional control as less developed than educators. This finding, however, differs from what is observed in England and the United States, where both parents and educators rated children's emotional control similarly.

Children's social-emotional skills are related to their emergent literacy, numeracy and self-regulation skills

Children's social-emotional scores through direct and indirect assessments were excellent predictors of scores in other aspects of the assessment, even after accounting for socio-economic status. In Estonia, children's social-emotional scores accounted for between 5% and 27% of their emergent literacy scores (compared to between 13% and 33% in England and the United States), between 6% and 26% of their numeracy scores (compared to between 12% and 28% in England and between 7% and 22% in the United States), and between 4% and 11% of their working memory scores (compared to between 7% and 18% in England and between 5% and 22% in the United States), after accounting for socio-economic status.

The development of early skills are interrelated. Cognitive skills are a necessary, but not sufficient, condition to foster early social-emotional learning. For example, children need a minimum level of literacy skills to interact well socially; have rich interactions with peers, friends, and parents; and, ultimately, to open the door to social-emotional learning. However, having high levels of literacy does not always imply high social-emotional skills, and vice versa.

The differences in early social-emotional skills by socio-economic background in Estonia are narrower than in England

Socio-economic background had a significant relationship with children's social-emotional development in Estonia in emotion identification, prosocial behaviour and trust. However, unlike England, this association was not significant in emotion attribution and disruptive behaviour. The United States showed similar results except in emotion attribution, where the association with the socio-economic background was significant.

Socio-economic background was associated with the frequency with which children engaged with different activities. Parents from a higher socio-economic background were more likely to read to their child from a book, take their child to special activities outside of the home, have frequent back-and-forth conversations with their child, and provide a higher number of children's books than parents from a lower socio-economic background. These home learning activities are associated with higher scores in social-emotional skills. As in England and the United States, educators in Estonia reported increased parental involvement in the child's preschool by parents from higher socio-economic backgrounds.

Russian-speaking children have better social-emotional outcomes than Estonian-speaking children

Russian-speaking represent 21% of all children in Estonia. Russian-speaking children had significantly higher outcomes than Estonian-speaking children in emotion identification and emotion attribution, and were rated by their educators as having better prosocial behaviour and trust, after controlling for socio-economic status. As Russian-speaking children generally came from lower socio-economic backgrounds, their scores were even higher after controlling for socio-economic status. According to educators, however, Russian-speaking children were as disruptive as Estonian-speaking children.

While girls typically had better social-emotional scores than boys, the gender gap in Estonia was more prominent than in the United States and England. Furthermore, Russian-speaking children showed more prominent gender differences than Estonian-speaking children.

Differences between Russian-speaking and Estonian-speaking children may relate to different family-based expectations and experiences, although there appeared to be few differences in the activities both groups of parents undertook with their children. Parents of Russian-speaking children in Estonia were as likely to do role-play with their parents, read to their children from a book, and have similar numbers of books at home as parents of Estonian-speaking children. Parents of Russian-speaking children showed a similar level of involvement in the child's centre as Estonian-speaking children. However, Russian-speaking children were more likely than Estonian-speaking children to use electronic devices as well as go to special activities outside of the home. Nonetheless, Estonian-speaking children were more likely to have back-and-forth conversations with their parents than Russian-speaking children.

Home and family learning environments have a positive relationship with children's social-emotional scores

After accounting for socio-economic background, the home and family learning environment were a powerful predictor of children's social-emotional scores. The following factors were positively related to children's social-emotional scores in Estonia: mother's tertiary education, having at least one sibling, a high number of children's books at home, parents who regularly read to their child, going regularly to special activities outside of the home, and parental involvement in the preschool the child attends.

Parents of boys in Estonia were as likely to have back-and-forth conversations with them, read to them from a book, and provide a similar number of books at home as parents of girls. Also, parents of girls showed a similar level of involvement in the child's centre to parents of boys, according to educators. However, girls in Estonia were more likely than boys to do role-play activities with their parents as well as go to special activities outside of the home.

Children who had experienced social, emotional or behavioural difficulties before the age of five have lower social-emotional skills at age five

Parents in IELS provided information on whether their child had a low birth weight or premature birth, learning difficulties and social, emotional or behavioural difficulties. Additionally, the child's ECEC centre provided information on whether the child was classified as having special educational needs. The data showed that social, emotional or behavioural difficulties were more highly associated with lower social-emotional outcomes than low birth weight, learning difficulties, or special educational needs – except in the case of trust and empathy skills, where learning difficulties were more highly associated. Disruptive behaviour was particularly associated with social, emotional or behavioural difficulties, as might be expected. When analysed alone, children with a low birth weight had lower emotion identification skills than children born weighing over 2.5 kg. However, these differences disappeared when controlling for children's learning and social, emotional or behavioural difficulties.

References

Abrahams, L. et al. (2019), "Social-emotional skill assessment in children and adolescents: Advances and challenges in personality, clinical, and educational contexts", *Psychological Assessment*, Vol. 31/4, pp. 460-473, http://dx.doi.org/10.1037/pas0000591. [25]

Baldwin, D. and **L. Moses** (1996), "The ontogeny of social information gathering", *Child Development*, Vol. 67/5, p. 1915, http://dx.doi.org/10.2307/1131601. [31]

Baumrind, D. (1968), *Manual for the Preschool Behavior Q-Sort*, University of California. Institute of Human Development. [20]

Bowlby, J. (1983), *Attachment and Loss, Volume 1: Attachment, Second Edition*, Basic Books, New York, https://www.abebe.org.br/files/John-Bowlby-Attachment-Second-Edition-Attachment-and-Loss-Series-Vol-1-1983.pdf (accessed on 31 July 2019). [30]

Buchanan, A., E. Flouri and **J. Brinke** (2002), "Emotional and behavioural problems in childhood and distress in adult life: Risk and protective factors", *Australian & New Zealand Journal of Psychiatry*, Vol. 36/4, pp. 521-527, https://doi.org/10.1046/j.1440-1614.2002.01048.x. [17]

Bush, G., P. Luu and **M. Posner** (2000), "Cognitive and emotional influences in anterior cingulate cortex", *Trends in Cognitive Sciences*, Vol. 4/6, pp. 215-222, https://doi.org/10.1016/s1364-6613(00)01483-2 (accessed on 30 July 2019). [2]

Caprara, G. et al. (2000), "Prosocial foundations of children's academic achievement", *Psychological Science*, Vol. 11/4, pp. 302-306, http://dx.doi.org/10.1111/1467-9280.00260. [9]

CASEL (2015), *2015 CASEL Guide: Effective Social and Emotional Learning Programs: Middle and High School Edition*, Collaborative for Academic, Social, and Emotional Learning, http://secondaryguide.casel.org/casel-secondary-guide.pdf (accessed on 14 November 2019). [22]

Chamorro-Premuzic, T. and **A. Furnham** (2008), "Personality, intelligence and approaches to learning as predictors of academic performance", *Personality and Individual Differences*, Vol. 44/7, pp. 1596-1603, http://dx.doi.org/10.1016/j.paid.2008.01.003. [33]

Ciarrochi, J., P. Heaven and **S. Supavadeeprasit** (2008), "The link between emotion identification skills and socio-emotional functioning in early adolescence: A 1-year longitudinal study", *Journal of Adolescence*, Vol. 31/5, pp. 565-582, http://dx.doi.org/10.1016/j.adolescence.2007.10.004. [13]

Daniel, E. et al. (2014), "Developmental relations between sympathy, moral emotion attributions, moral reasoning, and social justice values from childhood to early adolescence", *Journal of Adolescence*, Vol. 37/7, pp. 1201-1214, http://dx.doi.org/10.1016/j.adolescence.2014.08.009. [15]

Davidson, R. et al. (2002), "Neural and behavioral substrates of mood and mood regulation", *Biological Psychiatry*, Vol. 52/6, pp. 478-502, https://doi.org/10.1016/s0006-3223(02)01458-0 (accessed on 30 July 2019). [3]

De Fruyt, F. and **B. Wille** (2015), "Employability in the 21st century: Complex (interactive) problem solving and other essential skills", *Industrial and Organizational Psychology*, Vol. 8/2, pp. 276-281, http://dx.doi.org/10.1017/iop.2015.33. [24]

Duncan, G. et al. (2007), "School Readiness and Later Achievement", *Psychological Association*, Vol. 43/6, pp. 1428-1446, http://dx.doi.org/10.1037/[0012-1649.43.6.1428].supp. [10]

Flèche, S., W. Lekfuangfu and **A. Clark** (2019), "The long-lasting effects of family and childhood on adult wellbeing: Evidence from British cohort data", *Journal of Economic Behavior & Organization*, http://dx.doi.org/10.1016/J.JEBO.2018.09.018. [16]

Fontaine, N. et al. (2011), "Predictors and outcomes of joint trajectories of callous–unemotional traits and conduct problems in childhood", *Journal of Abnormal Psychology*, Vol. 120/3, pp. 730-742, http://dx.doi.org/10.1037/a0022620. [14]

Garber, J. and **K. Dodge** (1991), *The Development of Emotion Regulation and Dysregulation*, Cambridge University Press. [5]

Garner, P. and **B. Waajid** (2008), "The associations of emotion knowledge and teacher–child relationships to preschool children's school-related developmental competence", *Journal of Applied Developmental Psychology*, Vol. 29/2, pp. 89-100, http://dx.doi.org/10.1016/j.appdev.2007.12.001. [12]

Hinnant, J. and **M. O'Brien** (2007), "Cognitive and emotional control and perspective taking and their relations to empathy in 5-year-old children", *The Journal of Genetic Psychology*, Vol. 168/3, pp. 301-322, http://dx.doi.org/10.3200/gntp.168.3.301-322. [29]

Hogan, A., K. Scott and **C. Bauer** (1992), "The Adaptive Social Behavior Inventory (Asbi): A new assessment of social competence in high-risk three-year-olds", *Journal of Psychoeducational Assessment*, Vol. 10/3, pp. 230-239, http://dx.doi.org/10.1177/073428299201000303. [19]

Kankaraš, M. and **J. Suarez-Alvarez** (2019), "Assessment framework of the OECD Study on Social and Emotional Skills", *OECD Education Working Papers*, No. 207, OECD Publishing, Paris, https://dx.doi.org/10.1787/5007adef-en. [26]

Leerkes, E. et al. (2008), "Emotion and cognition processes in preschool children", *Merrill-Palmer Quarterly*, Vol. 54/1, pp. 102-124, http://dx.doi.org/10.1353/mpq.2008.0009. [7]

Posner, M. and **M. Rothbart** (2000), "Developing mechanisms of self-regulation", *Development and Psychopathology*, Vol. 12/3, pp. 427-41, https://doi.org/10.1017/s0954579400003096 (accessed on 30 July 2019). [4]

Rhoades, B. et al. (2011), "Examining the link between preschool social–emotional competence and first grade academic achievement: The role of attention skills", *Early Childhood Research Quarterly*, Vol. 26/2, pp. 182-191, http://dx.doi.org/10.1016/j.ecresq.2010.07.003. [11]

Roberts, W., J. Strayer and **S. Denham** (2014), "Empathy, anger, guilt: Emotions and prosocial behaviour", *Canadian Journal of Behavioural Science / Revue canadienne des sciences du comportement*, Vol. 46/4, pp. 465-474, http://dx.doi.org/10.1037/a0035057. [21]

Rutter, M., J. Kim-Cohen and **B. Maughan** (2006), "Continuities and discontinuities in psychopathology between childhood and adult life", *Journal of Child Psychology and Psychiatry*, Vol. 47/3-4, pp. 276-295, http://dx.doi.org/10.1111/j.1469-7610.2006.01614.x. [18]

Schoon, I. et al. (2015), "The impact of early life skills on later outcomes", http://discovery.ucl.ac.uk/10051902/1/Schoon_2015%20The%20Impact%20of%20Early%20Life%20Skills%20on%20Later%20Outcomes_%20Sept%20fin2015.pdf (accessed on 31 July 2019). [8]

Schroder, H. et al. (2017), "Neural evidence for enhanced attention to mistakes among school-aged children with a growth mindset", *Developmental Cognitive Neuroscience*, Vol. 24, pp. 42-50, http://dx.doi.org/10.1016/J.DCN.2017.01.004. [6]

Strayer, J. (1993), "Children's Concordant Emotions and Cognitions in Response to Observed Emotions", *Child Development*, Vol. 64/1, pp. 188-201, http://dx.doi.org/10.1111/j.1467-8624.1993.tb02903.x. [28]

Strayer, J. (1987), "Affective and cognitive perspectives on empathy", in Eisenberg, N. and J. Strayer (eds.), *Empathy and its Development*, Cambridge University Press, New York, NY, US. [27]

Suárez-Álvarez, J., R. Fernández-Alonso and **J. Muñiz** (2014), "Self-concept, motivation, expectations, and socioeconomic level as predictors of academic performance in mathematics", *Learning and Individual Differences*, Vol. 30, pp. 118-123, http://dx.doi.org/10.1016/J.LINDIF.2013.10.019. [32]

Thompson, R. (2001), "Development in the first years of life", *The Future of Children*, Vol. 11/1, pp. 20-33, http://dx.doi.org/10.2307/1602807 (accessed on 31 July 2019). [1]

Wessberg, R. et al. (2015), "Social and emotional learning: Past, present, and future", in Durlak, J. et al. (eds.), *Handbook of Social and Emotional Learning: Research and Practice*, Guilford Press. [23]

Note

1. The index of socioeconomic status in IELS comprises household income, parents' educational attainment and parent occupation.

Summary and conclusions

This chapter summarises the main findings for Estonia and discusses them in relation to themes such as gender, socio-economic status, and home learning environment.

The first five years of a child's life can be a period of great opportunity, and great vulnerability. The brain's ability to change in response to experiences reaches its highest levels during this time (Knudsen, 2004[1]), which means that children learn at a faster rate than at any other time in their lives, building the foundations for their future cognitive and social-emotional skills development. Building advanced cognitive and social-emotional skills is far more difficult and less effective at later ages without a strong early foundation (Center on the Developing Child, 2016[2]). The International Early Learning and Child Well-being Study (IELS) provides robust and comparable information to participating countries on children's early learning in a range of domains and in relation to a host of individual and contextual factors. This chapter summarises the main findings from IELS in Estonia.

Children in Estonia have strong self-regulation and social-emotional skills and sound literacy and numeracy skills

The average five-year old child in Estonia showed comparatively stronger early self-regulation and social-emotional skills than their counterparts in England and the United States. At the same time, children in Estonia were at or close to the overall averages for emergent literacy and numeracy skills. Children in Estonia scored significantly higher than children in England and the United States in emotion identification and prosocial behaviour. They also scored significantly higher than children in the United States in emergent literacy, numeracy, working memory and mental flexibility, and significantly higher than children in England on inhibition. However, children in Estonia scored significantly lower than children in the United States and England in non-disruptive behaviour and lower than children in England in emergent numeracy.

IELS data showed that children's early learning relies on the interrelated development of cognitive and social-emotional skills. While the percentage of explained variance by the socio-economic status index showed variation across countries, the predictive value of social-emotional skills was relatively stable. In Estonia, children's social-emotional scores accounted for between 5% and 27% of their emergent literacy scores (compared to 13-33% in England and the United States), between 6% and 26% of their numeracy scores (compared to 12-28% in England and 7-22% in the United States), and between 4% and 11% of their working memory scores (compared to 7-18% in England and 5-22% in the United States), after controlling for socio-economic status. IELS data suggest that cognitive skills are a necessary but not sufficient condition to foster early social-emotional learning. For example, children need a minimum level of literacy skills to be able to adequately navigate socially; have rich interactions with peers, friends, and parents; and ultimately, to open the door to social-emotional learning. However, having high levels of literacy does not always ensure having high social-emotional skills, and vice versa.

Conclusion 1: Five-year-olds in Estonia demonstrated balanced strengths across cognitive, self-regulation and social-emotional skills.

Differences between children based on socio-economic background are smaller in Estonia than in England or the United States

The combination of household income, parental occupation and parental educational completion – which together create the socio-economic index applied in this study – were associated with higher literacy, numeracy, working memory, mental flexibility emotion identification, prosocial behaviour and trust. However, relationships between early learning skills and socio-economic background were comparatively smaller in Estonia than in England or the United States. Additionally, the association between socio-economic background and early learning skills was not significant in inhibition, emotion attribution and disruptive behaviour. These results are consistent with findings from PISA (OECD, 2019[3]).

In Estonia, 53% of mothers of five-year-old children had completed tertiary education (i.e. bachelor's degree or master's degree, professional degree or doctorate), which is higher than in the other two countries participating in the study (40% in England and 39% in the United States). Children whose mothers had completed tertiary education in Estonia had better cognitive and social-emotional outcomes than those whose mothers had not. A higher proportion of parents in Estonia were described as being strongly or moderately involved in their children's education than in England or the United States.

Conclusion 2: At age five, gaps in scores for cognitive and social-emotional domains between children from low and high socio-economic backgrounds were already present in Estonia, but were comparatively smaller than in England and the United States.

Early learning among Russian-speaking children, especially girls, is stronger than among Estonian-speaking children, despite coming from lower socio-economic backgrounds

Preschool institutions in Estonia are divided into Estonian, Russian and mixed centres based on the language of instruction. The vast majority of Estonian-speaking and Russian-speaking preschools institutions are public institutions. Russian-speaking five-year-olds represented 21% of the children in Estonia. Despite coming from lower socio-economic backgrounds, Russian-speaking children had significantly higher outcomes than Estonian-speaking children in emergent literacy, numeracy, working memory, emotion identification, emotion attribution, prosocial behaviour and trust, after controlling for socio-economic status. These differences were more prominent after accounting for socio-economic status than before.

In Estonia, there was an overall gender gap in favour of girls in emergent literacy, self-regulation skills and social-emotional skills, but there was no equivalent gender gap for emergent numeracy skills. This result was in line with the patterns observed in England and the United States. However, in Estonia, Russian-speaking children showed more prominent gender differences than Estonian-speaking children. Russian-speaking boys had similar scores to Estonian-speaking boys and girls in literacy, numeracy, working memory, mental flexibility, inhibition, emotion identification, prosocial behaviour and trust, after accounting for socio-economic status. Russian-speaking boys had similar scores to Estonian girls in emotion attribution, but higher than Estonian-speaking boys. Russian-speaking boys had similar scores as Estonian-speaking boys in non-disruptive behaviour, but lower than Estonian-speaking girls.

In Estonia, the assessment language did not necessarily match the language of instruction. Of the 21% of Russian-speaking children in the study, approximately 13% attended a preschool where the language of instruction was Russian, and 8% attended an Estonian or immersion language preschool. It is important to note that children could have attended a different setting prior to the age 5. Nonetheless, the differences by children's language also hold when comparing language of instruction in favour of Russian preschools after accounting for socioeconomic background. On the other hand, Russian speaking-children attending Estonian or immersion language preschools did not significantly differ from Russian speaking-children attending Russian preschools in any of the study's early learning outcomes after controlling for socio-economic status.

The results in IELS were generally aligned with existing evidence that showed that girls whose language of instruction was Russian had better outcomes in sixth grade (i.e. 11 or 12-year-old), followed by girls who studied in Estonian, Russian-speaking boys, and Estonian-speaking boys (Leino et al., 2006[4]). However, data from 15-years old students in PISA showed a performance gap between schools with different languages of instruction. Estonia's first PISA assessment in 2006 showed that the average science, reading and mathematics scores of students in Russian-language schools were significantly lower than those of students in Estonian-language schools. The gap with Estonian-medium schools was still approximately one school year in PISA 2015. In PISA 2018, the performance gap between schools with different languages of instruction remained. An in-depth analysis also showed that Russian-speaking children at Estonian-language schools scored better than their Russian-language school counterparts (Windzio, 2013[5]; Lindemann and Saar, 2012[6]).

Conclusion 3: Russian-speaking girls had a comparatively stronger start than other children in Estonia, as assessed in IELS.

Children with a home language other than the assessment language have poorer early literacy and self-regulation skills in the assessment language

In Estonia, around 6% of children lived in homes where at least one parent mostly spoke a language other than the assessment language at home, which is lower than in the other two countries participating in the study (16% in England and 20% in the United States). Children with a home language other than the assessment languages of Estonian or Russian had similar emergent numeracy and social-emotional skills to other children, but poorer early literacy and self-regulation skills.

Conclusion 4: At age five, children with a home language other than the assessment language had significantly lower literacy and self-regulation skills, indicating additional support may be needed for these children.

Parents' activities with their children matter for children's learning

Findings from IELS showed that parents' activities make a significant difference for their children's learning, regardless of their socio-economic background. For example, children whose parents were more involved in the centre their child attended had higher outcomes across cognitive and social-emotional domains than children whose parents were less involved, after accounting for socio-economic status.

In addition, the number of children's book at home and the frequency with which children were read to by their parents were significantly related to cognitive and social-emotional outcomes. Similarly, regularly taking the child to special activities outside of the home (such as sport, dance lessons, scouts) was significantly associated with both cognitive and social-emotional skills.

Some activities parents do at home were more strongly associated with some skills than others. For example, regularly role-playing with children was positively associated with children's lower disruptive behaviour but less so with emergent literacy and numeracy or self-regulation skills.

In Estonia, there were positive associations between the use of digital devices and self-regulation but negative associations with trust scores. However, scores in emergent literacy and prosocial behaviour were higher for children who used devices at least once a week rather than every day, supporting an approach towards moderate rather than frequent use. Similarly, the results in the United States showed that moderate use of digital devices is associated with higher emergent literacy, mental flexibility, and emotion identification scores. In England, moderate use of digital devices is associated with higher emergent literacy, working memory, and trust scores. The challenge, therefore, remains in how to take advantage of technology, while minimising the risks (Burns and Gottschalk, 2019[7]).

Conclusion 5: Parental involvement and activities were significantly associated with children's early learning scores in IELS, regardless of their socio-economic background.

Conclusion 6: IELS findings suggested that a variety of activities within and outside the home best support children's early learning.

Parents and educators are not fully aligned when evaluating children's early development

Parents and educators are important sources of information about children's early learning. In IELS, parents and educators were asked to evaluate their children's development in a number of cognitive and social-emotional areas. Across countries participating in IELS, parents gave more positive ratings of their children's early learning than educators. Overall, the data showed that parent and educator ratings were not fully aligned.

Children's parents were substantially more likely to describe them as developed above in a wide range of cognitive and social-emotional domains than their educators were. This may reflect educators' greater experience with children in the target age group, leading to them having a more accurate understanding of the average development of five-year-olds. Alternatively, it may reflect differences in how children display early skills in the school environment and how they do so at home, with the people who know them best.

Conclusion 7: Continued communication between the home and the preschool about children's progress is likely to be beneficial for all parties.

References

Burns, T. and **F. Gottschalk** (eds.) (2019), *Educating 21st Century Children: Emotional Well-being in the Digital Age*, Educational Research and Innovation, OECD Publishing, Paris, https://dx.doi.org/10.1787/b7f33425-en. [7]

Center on the Developing Child (2016), *From Best Practices to Breakthrough Impacts*, Harvard University, http://www.developingchild.harvard.edu (accessed on 30 July 2019). [2]

Knudsen, E. (2004), "Sensitive Periods in the Development of the Brain and Behavior", *Journal of Cognitive Neuroscience*, Vol. 16/8, pp. 1412-1425, http://dx.doi.org/10.1162/0898929042304796. [1]

Leino, M. et al. (2006), *New Identity of Russian Speaking Children in Estonian Society*, https://www.socwork.net/sws/article/view/184/572 (accessed on 8 December 2019). [4]

Lindemann, K. and **E. Saar** (2012), "Ethnic inequalities in education: second-generation Russians in Estonia", *Ethnic and Racial Studies*, Vol. 35/11, pp. 1974-1998, http://dx.doi.org/10.1080/01419870.2011.611890. [6]

OECD (2019), *PISA 2018 Results (Volume I): What Students Know and Can Do*, PISA, OECD Publishing, Paris, https://dx.doi.org/10.1787/5f07c754-en. [3]

Windzio, M. (ed.) (2013), *Integration and Inequality in Educational Institutions*, Springer Netherlands, Dordrecht, http://dx.doi.org/10.1007/978-94-007-6119-3. [5]

ANNEX A

Technical note

This technical note provides additional background information on technical aspects relating to the International Early Learning the Child Well-being Study (IELS). It sets out the rationale for the types of assessment used in the study, response rates and other factors influencing the robustness, reliability and comparability of the data. More information on the conceptual and technical aspects of the study can be found in the Assessment Framework and Technical Standards for the study.

Assessment methods

The study used two types of assessment: direct assessment of children's skills through developmentally-appropriate, interactive stories and games delivered on a tablet device and indirect assessment through reports on children's skills from parents and educators. The key benefit of direct assessment is that it provides countries with a common basis for comparing children's early learning. Through careful development, testing and analysis[1], any cultural or other biases are minimised so that countries can have confidence that the results are comparable across countries. Furthermore, delivery of the assessment through a tablet device enhances the reliability of the results through the avoidance of transcription and coding errors.

The indirect assessment provides benefits in triangulating the results from the direct assessment and in providing a fuller picture of children's development and skills. Parents have knowledge of their child over time and in a range of settings, whereas teachers have a comparative group of children at the same age on which to base their assessments. Thus, gaining information from parents as well as from teachers provides greater breadth and depth on children's early learning and development while the direct assessment provides a stronger basis for comparability across countries.

Participation rates

A critical factor influencing the reliability of the results from any survey is the response rates, particularly for any form of direct assessment. The quality standard for child participation rates for IELS was set at 75%, meaning this level of participation rate provides confidence that the sample is representative of children at that age in that country. Each participating country exceeded this standard. Teacher response rates were also very high, 90% or higher in each country. While parent response rates were somewhat lower, these were still higher than is generally expected.

Table A.1 **Response rates for IELS, by informant and country**

Participation rates	England (%)	Estonia (%)	United States (%)
Child	94.9	84.1	92.7
Parent	67.5	86.0	71.2
Educator	89.7	94.1	96.4

Note: The participation rates are weighted and based on participating centre/schools and children.

Quality assurance

Standards for administration and assessment procedures, to achieve standardised implementation procedures, were set out in comprehensive manuals, applicable to each participating country. Precise instructions were provided for centre and school co-ordinators and scripts were provided to study administrators, in addition to the provision of mandatory training.

National and International Quality Assurance Monitors (IQAMs) were appointed to attest that the implementation in each country complied with the standards for the study. These Quality Monitors were independent and observed the administration of the assessments in each participating country in order to attest that the required standards were met. Across all quality assurance activities, the observations showed that all three participating countries generally followed the standardized procedures as outlined in the IELS Technical Standards.

Note

1. The types of analysis used for this study included differential item functioning by gender, country, and language, item-level analysis, latent trait-level analysis, and convergent and predictive validity analysis.

www.ingramcontent.com/pod-product-compliance
Lightning Source LLC
LaVergne TN
LVHW081412110826
845149LV00010B/1713

* 9 7 8 9 2 6 4 3 8 4 6 0 6 *